Frontier Struggles

THE CENTER FOR THE HISTORY OF PSYCHOLOGY SERIES

The Center for the History of Psychology Series
David B. Baker, Editor

David B. Baker and Ludy T. Benjamin Jr., *From Séance to Science: A History of the Profession of Psychology in America*

C. James Goodwin and Lizette Royer, Editors, *Walter Miles and His 1920 Grand Tour of European Physiology and Psychology Laboratories*

Ludy T. Benjamin Jr. and Lizette Royer Barton, Editors, *Roots in the Great Plains: The Applied Psychology of Harry Hollingworth, Volume 1*

Ludy T. Benjamin Jr. and Lizette Royer Barton, Editors, *From Coca-Cola to Chewing Gum: The Applied Psychology of Harry Hollingworth, Volume 2*

Richard I. Evans, *Conversations with Carl Jung and Reactions from Ernest Jones,* edited by Jodi Kearns

James Schlett, *Frontier Struggles: Rollo May and the Little Band of Psychologists Who Saved Humanism*

Frontier Struggles

Rollo May and the Little Band of Psychologists Who Saved Humanism

James Schlett

The University of Akron Press
Akron, Ohio

Copyright © 2021 by The University of Akron Press
All rights reserved • First Edition 2021 • Manufactured in the United States of America.
All inquiries and permission requests should be addressed to the publisher,
The University of Akron Press, Akron, Ohio 44325-1703.

ISBN: 978-1-62922-130-4 (paper)
ISBN: 978-1-62922-131-1 (ePDF)
ISBN: 978-1-62922-132-8 (ePub)

A catalog record for this title is available from the Library of Congress.

∞ The paper used in this publication meets the minimum requirements of ansi/niso z39.48–1992 (Permanence of Paper).

Cover illustration: Nadia Alnashar
Cover design by Amy Freels.

Frontier Struggles was typeset in Minion by Beth Pratt and printed on sixty-pound natural and bound by Bookmasters of Ashland, Ohio.

Produced in conjunction with the University of Akron Affordable Learning Initiative.
More information is available at
www.uakron.edu/affordablelearning/.

For Dan Jones:
From home to our frontiers, friends.
Always.

When a human being resists his whole age and stops it at the gate to demand an accounting, this must have influence.
—*Friedrich Nietzsche*

Contents

Preface	ix
Abbreviations	xiii
Introduction: The Call	1

Part 1: Origins

1. The Country Is Ailing	15
2. A Tremendous Army of Maladjusted Persons	30
3. Hanging Up a Shingle	42

Part 2: Tensions

4. Insurgency	57
5. Dead Ends and Revivals	70
6. Warning Shots	82

Part 3: Battles

7. Defeat	97
8. Threats	110
9. Blitz	123
10. The Calm before the Storm	136
11. The Last Stand	147
12. Victory	159
Conclusion: Frontiers	174
List of Psychology Laws, 1945–77	185
Original Manuscripts Key	187
Notes	189
Bibliography	213

Preface

The call was always for courage: the courage "to meet the anxiety which arises as one achieves freedom," the courage it takes "not only to assert oneself but to give one's self," the courage needed at every step "as one moves from the familiar surroundings over frontiers into the unfamiliar."[1]

It was a call across the decades, one that had come to me when I had most needed to hear it. I was nineteen years old when I first read Rollo May's *Man's Search for Himself*. I had randomly found a reprint of his 1953 book in a bookstore. I had recently survived a brain tumor and had needed to hear about courage perhaps as much as May had needed it the years running up to the book's publication. May had written *Man's Search for Himself* after years of fighting tuberculosis. Of the years he had spent in a sanatorium in the 1940s, May says, "I saw that no one can directly and successfully combat his destiny, but each of us, by virtue of the small margin of freedom that prevails even in the sanitorium bed, can choose his attitude toward that destiny. Shall it be servile abdication or some form of courage?"[2]

I knew that question, and I cannot begin to tell how indebted I am to May for rousing in me the "courageous acceptance of the 'finite'" through my long recovery. I read and reread his books. So, in 2015, when I finished writing my first book, *A Not Too Greatly Changed Eden: The Story of the Philosophers' Camp in the Adirondacks*, after five years of labor, the first book I chose to read for leisure was May's *Psychology and the Human Dilemma*. I got no more than two pages into it when I found what I knew would be my next book. Almost in passing, May mentions how in the early and mid-1950s his "little band of psychologists who were therapists in New York State was engaged in a battle in the state legislature against the overwhelming power of the American Medical Association." He continues: "Each legislative session we would be faced with the introduction of a bill to make psychotherapy a medical specialty. We were faced with immediate extinction and had to fight for our professional lives." May notes how he had been at the "center of the warfare" while leading both the Joint Council of New York State Psychologists on Legislation and the New York State Psychological Association. "Surprisingly, we psychologists won each battle. Ultimately we won the war—for the nation as well as New York State."[3]

I had read this book several times already, but for whatever reason these passages finally stood out. Having worked in the senate in Albany and written about New York history, I was surprised that I had never heard about this "war." When I tried to learn more about it, I was at a near loss. Roderick D. Buchanan's essay on "Legislative Warriors" provided an overview of psychologists' and psychiatrists' mid-twentieth-century "chronic tug-of-war over psychotherapy" and briefly mentioned the "tortuous legislative struggle" in New York. The same was true for Gerald N. Grob's *From Asylum to Community* and John D. Hogan's "A History of the New York State Psychological Association." Shortly before his death in 1994, May had again mentioned these "dangerous years" in the forward to *History of Psychotherapy*. However, I could find no complete account of the battles fought by his "little band of psychologists" and the impact it had on the profession's development in New York and beyond.[4]

From the little I could learn, it was clear that this crisis over the control of psychotherapy was as political as it was existential. More was at stake than just a profession or public policy. After all, psychologists were not the first to battle with the physicians over the legal right to practice. In the early 1950s, osteopaths and chiropractors, among others, were fighting organized medicine over licensing. While those professionals treat various parts of the human body, psychologists treat what makes us human: the mind. The medical profession's attempt to claim authority over the mind threatened to statutorily reduce emotions and mental conditions to biology and accelerate the mechanization of human beings as well as their dehumanization. Many psychologists then, as today, did not object to that biological approach because it made psychology a pure science. But May was not one of them. May, a pioneer of existentialism in America, was notorious for embracing scientifically fuzzy concepts, such as the "self," and he reproached those who dismissed them as unscientific. He said, "It is a defensive and dogmatic science—and therefore not a true science—which uses a particular scientific method as a Procrustean bed and rejects all forms of human experience which don't fit."[5]

Today, such opinions have relegated May to psychology's frontiers. He is a fringe figure. He is psychology's antihero. Rather than fit the profession's concept of itself, he stood outside it—on the frontier—and inspired psychologists to accept their limitations and develop the powers they never knew they had. Facing the nation's most powerful lobby —organized medicine—May showed New York's psychologists were stronger. Rather than seek a return to "old values," May throughout his career, as his biographer Robert H. Abzug notes, "instead sought to promote individual and social regeneration through the courageous embrace of personal freedom and responsibility not only for oneself but also for the community at large." That was what he did for the psychology community in the 1950s, and *Frontier Struggles* is the story of what he called the "greatest courage." In *Man's Search for Himself*, which was published at the peak of the legislative battles, in 1953, he said, "The hardest step of all, requiring the greatest courage, is to deny those under whose expectations one has lived the right to make the laws. And this is the most frightening step. It means accepting responsibility for one's standards and judgements, even though one knows how limited and imperfect they are. . . . It is the courage to be and trust one's self despite the fact that one is finite; it means acting, loving, thinking, creating, even though one knows he does not have the final answers, and may well be wrong."[6]

Wanting to know more about what May had described as the profession of psychology's "frontier struggles," I set out for answers. I found many in the special collections of fifteen institutions in the United States and Europe, but chiefly in the Rollo May Papers in the Davidson Library at the University of California, Santa Barbara, and the Molly Harrower Papers and Raymond Katzell Papers in the Drs. Nicholas and Dorothy Cummings Center for the History of Psychology at the University of Akron. To piece together this in-the-trenches account of these legislative battles, I used more than 150 original manuscripts, including letters, meeting minutes, and memoranda. There are instances in this book when I have relied on personal accounts detailed in these original manuscripts and other primary sources, coupled with warranted speculation, to set a scene. An example of this practice is seen in the phone call May receives in the introduction and his first encounter with Lawrence Frank in chapter 1.

At the risk of sounding like a Luddite, I will quote Nietzsche, who said, "Science rushes headlong, without selectivity, without 'taste,' at whatever is knowable, in the blind desire to know all at any cost." While New York psychologists' political victories in the 1950s gave humanistic psychology a legislative framework in which it could thrive in subsequent decades, science continued its march forward. With the publication of the *Diagnostic and Statistical Manual*'s third edition (*DSM-III*) in 1980—just three years after Missouri became the fiftieth state to enact a law regulating the profession of psychology—the American Psychiatric Association (APA) achieved through internal action the dominance it had once sought at state houses. Psychodynamic terminology and concepts were removed from the *DSM-III*. With one fell swoop, twenty million people within two decades ended up under the depressive disorder category as a result of a loss of the differentiating factors between normal depression and depression without cause. The "making of man over in the image of the machine" had all but come. Much of what New York's psychologists fought for is as forgotten today as the battles themselves. But May and his little band had stopped medicine at the gate and demanded an accounting. This must have influence.[7]

***

I would like to thank the New York State Library's Reference Services staff for all their assistance in locating primary sources and answering my many questions. For the timely fielding of numerous inquiries and requests for reproductions, thanks also go to Lizette Royer Barton at the Center for the History of Psychology and the Special Collections staff at the Davidson Library. Dan Jones and Stacey Stump have been as reliable research assistants as they have been trustworthy friends, whose thoughts on this book and so much more I will always treasure. Thank you. Lastly, I must thank my parents, John and Pat Schlett, who have taught me the most about courage through the examples they set, and my daughter, Rory, who keeps leading me on to new frontiers to discover new powers, new joys. I love you all.

Abbreviations

ACP	Association of Consulting Psychologists
AMA	American Medical Association
APA	American Psychiatric Association
APsychA	American Psychological Association
GAP	Group for the Advancement of Psychiatry
JAMA	*Journal of the American Medical Association*
MNYAAP	Metropolitan New York Association for Applied Psychology
NPC	National Physicians Committee for the Extension of Medical Service
NYPS	New York Psychoanalytic Society
NYSAAP	New York State Association for Applied Psychologists
NYSCP	New York Society for Clinical Psychologists
NYSMS	Medical Society of the State of New York
NYSPA	New York State Psychological Association
VA	U.S. Veterans Administration
WAWI	William Alanston White Institute
YMCA	Young Men's Christian Association

Introduction: The Call

When the phone rang, he did not want to answer it.

It was winter in New York City. The third of March, 1953. Rollo Reese May was in his office on 411 West 114th Street, near Morningside Park. He was a forty-three-year-old midwesterner who had spent the last half of his life in the city. A pastor turned psychologist. A Neo-Freudian. At home he had a wife, son, and twin daughters. This was supposed to be a quiet time of year for him. Instead, he was working night and day and forced to cancel his regular counseling sessions with clients so he could carry out his duties as the chair of the Joint Council of New York State Psychologists on Legislation.[1]

Although there was a New York State Psychological Association (NYSPA), it was hardly an organization representative of psychologists statewide. Instead, May's Joint Council stood as that unifying body, with delegates from more than two dozen psychology groups statewide serving on it. NYSPA officials had formed the Joint Council less than three years earlier with the goal of passing legislation for psychologist certification or licensing in the state legislature. The Joint Council was what May called the "field headquarters" that dealt with "the front-line problems of psychology." That night, all of New York State—where one in five of the nation's psychologists lived—was the front line, and May feared it would be overrun by the enemy.[2]

Soon May would have to take the subway or taxi to Midtown to deliver a speech to about nine hundred psychologists. It would be one of the largest gatherings of psychologists ever in the nation. The upcoming event weighed on him. He knew he would have to announce either that legislators

150 miles north in the state capitol in Albany were set on "outlawing" the profession of psychology or that the psychologists in the room could go about their business of helping New Yorkers grappling with anxiety or the emotional, marital, or vocational issues that were troubling them.[3]

When the phone rang, May knew the caller would be Arthur W. Combs, a Syracuse University psychology professor who worked part-time as the Joint Council's lobbyist in Albany. To the Joint Council's surprise, the Medical Society of the State of New York (NYSMS) had convinced a Republican senator and assemblyman to sponsor bills to amend the state's Medical Practice Act. The amendment proposed to specify that the "practice of medicine" include the diagnosis or treatment not only of "any human disease, pain, injury, deformity, physical condition" but also of any "mental condition." New York's Medical Practice Act, much like those in many other states, specifically addressed physical conditions, but the law was vague on whether mental conditions fell within the scope of medical practice. Even in states where mental conditions were included in physician licensing laws, the term was rarely defined.

This lack of clarity in the Medical Practice Act of New York, as well as in the acts of many other states, meant anyone could call himself or herself a psychologist and offer or attempt to treat the melancholic, anxious, or neurotic, regardless of whether the individual was trained in psychology or in plumbing. New York regulators could do nothing about these "psychologists," whether they were legitimate practitioners or quacks, so long as they did not engage in any "laying of the hands" or hypnotism. In fact, surveys of telephone directories in Manhattan and Los Angeles indicated a third or more of the people offering psychological services either were unaffiliated with any legitimate psychological organization or lacked any recognized qualifications.[4]

Since the mid-1930s, New York psychologists had been attempting to engage the state in regulating psychologists and curbing the activities of these charlatans. World War II, however, halted that work. When the war ended, that effort started again with greater purpose as the Veterans Administration (VA) propped up the profession of psychology to help it address the waves of veterans returning home with shell shock and other combat-related mental conditions. Civilians, too, were struggling in what the poet W. H. Auden had called "The Age of Anxiety." Psychologists, however, were not alone in wanting to expand their reach among both veterans and civilians.

Psychiatrists, too, were moving beyond their traditional roles in mental hospitals and into what Stanley Cobb, the founder of biological psychiatry, had dubbed the profession's "borderlands." His 1943 book *Borderlands of Psychiatry* had presented a blueprint for how psychiatrists could employ a nosologically system to free themselves of the mind-body dichotomy that had marginalized their role in the community, often stopping at the asylum. In those borderlands were millions of Americans who suffered from psychoneurosis, stammering, alcoholism, epilepsy, and other problems believed to be neurological in nature. This push into the borderlands also coincided with the introduction of "miracle" drugs into the U.S. market, starting with the major tranquilizer, chlorpromazine (Thorazine), in 1954 and the minor tranquilizer, meprobamate (Miltown), a year later. It was, *The New York Times* declared, a "new era of psychiatry."[5]

In the postwar years, psychologists and psychiatrists found themselves intensely competing in the same consumer market. The latter adamantly opposed the former's attempt to statutorily secure the right to independently practice through certification or licensing laws. In the eight years since Connecticut had become the first state to pass a psychologist certification law in 1945, only four other states had passed laws to regulate the profession by 1953. New York had come close to joining them in 1951, but that effort had provoked the wrath of the APA and the NYSMS, the largest state affiliate of the nation's most powerful lobby: the American Medical Association (AMA). On that winter night two years later, May felt pressing on him the "vast power" of the AMA. It was a power that had been "garnered from the role of 'god' which the public, out of its need, had projected upon the physicians" and which legislators "had unthinkingly accepted."[6]

Finally, May picked up the phone. Indeed, it was Combs, who was all too familiar with the uncertainty in the voice he likely heard on the other end of the line. Combs, too, had fallen victim to a sneak attack from the medical profession. He had served as the Joint Council's chair in 1951, when the group had succeeded in convincing the legislature to pass a hybrid certification-licensing law. However, that legislative victory had been short-lived because weeks later Governor Thomas E. Dewey had vetoed the bill under intense pressure from an eleventh-hour opposition campaign mounted by the NYSMS and the APA. Either shortly before or after May's call from Combs, the American Psychological Association (APsychA) had passed a resolution opposing the proposed Medical Practice Act amendment. However, this national group had neither criticized physicians for their role in advancing the restrictive legislation nor challenged the biological premise underlying their claims of exclusivity for the diagnosis and treatment of mental conditions. For more than a decade, the APsychA had shied away from confrontations with its overly aggressive medical counterpart over professional boundaries and rights to practice. Even as the NYSMS and APA moved to turn New York into a battleground state, the APsychA's executive secretary, Fillmore H. Sanford, maintained that it was "undesirable" to "wage a public fight."[7]

But a public fight, May knew, was psychology's best chance of survival. And the fight would start that evening at the New Yorker Hotel in Midtown, where, along with the hundreds of psychologists, reporters from several major newspapers were waiting to hear May's update on the crisis. May saw New York as the pivotal battleground state in a "nationwide movement among reactionary groups in the psychological and psychiatric hierarchies to prevent the work of other professionals in helping people with emotional and personality difficulties." If organized medicine succeeded in establishing control over such work, that "would set the clock back one hundred years." For psychology to develop a more a humanistic approach that could fill the void that more traditional methods in psychology and psychiatry could not address, resistance was imperative. "What our society needs for its survival is not new drugs or methods for curing physical ailments, important as these are," May said at the New Yorker. "What is needed, rather, is that people be helped to learn to live together harmoniously. If we simply continue emphasizing that man is a physical machine, we produce only more effective soldiers and our civilization will indeed be threatened."[8]

The threat was real, Combs told May over the phone, but immediate action by the legislature was not anticipated. New York's psychologists, however, were far from being out of what May later called the "dangerous years." This period of interprofessional "warfare" had flared in 1949 with the initial introduction in Albany of an antipsychology Medical Practice Act amendment, and it was followed by similar restrictive legislation in 1953 and 1954. From that point on, a cold war persisted between the professions, even after New York became the tenth state to pass a law regulating psychologists in 1956. The "battle of the professions" served as a unifying force for psychology, giving academic, clinical, industrial, and consulting psychologists a common enemy and a common goal to which they could aspire. Through these battles, NYSPA emerged as a true statewide organization, but more importantly, its members also drafted the blueprints that other states could follow when developing their own laws for the regulation of psychology. One blueprint was the proceedings of the Conference on Psychotherapy and Counseling. May had organized the conference in 1954 with the help of the influential social scientist Lawrence K. Frank, and the proceedings were published in November 1955. The other was an APsychA guidance for state affiliates on the types of legislation they should pursue. This report was drafted by an APsychA committee chaired by May's successor as Joint Council chair, the New York City social psychologist Stuart W. Cook, and published in November 1955. Armed with these reports, psychologists passed more than twice as many laws regulating psychology in the ten years after the enactment of New York's law than they had the ten years before.[9]

In the late 1970s, May could declare, "We won for the war—for the nation as well as New York State." But it was a war that the Joint Council's members had largely fought alone—with little to no support from psychology's biggest names, such as the conflict-averse Carl Rogers, then at the University of Chicago, or the APsychA. It was a war that also put emerging clinical and humanistic approaches to the ultimate test—not in the laboratory or counseling room but in the political realm. Throughout the early 1950s, the Joint Council was chaired by a series of psychologists who each championed a different approach. The war exposed the strengths and weaknesses of these approaches, as reflected in the personalities and leadership of the people who pioneered them. Combs was the nonconfrontational Rogerian who co-developed an American phenomenology, which he claimed was akin to Rogers's nondirective therapy in that they both were client-centered. Client-centered therapists, May later observed, had a tendency to "not (or could not) deal with the angry, hostile, negative...feelings of the clients," and they consequently did not create an environment in which "*trust and doubt, conflicts and dependence* [can] *come out and can be understood and assimilated.*" Even Rogers questioned whether some client-centered therapists "simply [did] 'not believe in' the importance of negative feelings?" When it came to Combs's leadership of the Joint Council, the answer to this question was seen in his unresponsiveness to and efforts to avoid both intra-organizational disputes and organized medicine's hostility. Combs did manage to unite the state's psychologists for a licensing bill by not engaging the NYSMS and thereby avoiding its input that would fracture the Joint Council's superficial unity. The result was one of the profession of psychology's greatest legislative defeats, which came when this effort was overcome by the medical profession's power manifested in Dewey's veto.[10]

Molly Harrower briefly served as the Joint Council's chair after Combs. She was the clinical psychologist who viewed most psychiatrists as allies, but without her battery of Rorschach and other tests that could provide insights into their personalities and motivations, she wildly misread the overarching political dynamics and warnings that other members of the Joint Council more readily detected. Then there was May and his existentialism, which strayed from Rogers's client-centered approach in that it did not shy away from confrontation or hostility. In his groundbreaking 1950 book *The Meaning of Anxiety*, which was based on his doctoral thesis, May had said, "A person is subjectively prepared to confront unavoidable anxiety constructively when he is convinced (consciously or unconsciously) that the values to be gained in moving ahead are greater than those to be gained by escape." With clearer vision and more eloquence than any of his predecessors on the Joint Council and at NYSPA, May helped New York's psychologists see "the values to be gained." He prepared them for the unavoidable anxiety from confronting "the overwhelming power" of organized medicine year after year. And then there was the sense of social justice that fueled May's successor at both the Joint Council and NYSPA, Cook, whose research on the impacts of racism influenced the US Supreme Court's 1954 decision in *Brown v. Board of Education*.[11]

Not all physicians and psychiatrists opposed psychologists' right to practice psychotherapy and legislative efforts. May identified "reactionary hierarchies" within the medical profession as the Joint Council's political "adversaries." While they often held minority viewpoints within the APA, AMA, and NYSMS, these reactionary hierarchies tended to hold leadership positions with outsized influence. They included Daniel Blain, the APA's medical director; Samuel Parker, the New York City Department of Hospitals' psychiatry director; Iago Galdston, the secretary of New York Academy of Medicine's Medical Information Bureau; and Morris Herman, the secretary of the New York Society for Clinical Psychiatrists. Underlying their opposition were the theories of psychiatrists such as Massachusetts General Hospital's Stanley Cobb, who viewed much of America's noninstitutionalized population as the "borderlands"

Introduction: The Call

into which psychiatry should advance, and the Viennese psychiatrist and psychoanalyst Paul Schilder, whose "eclecticism" acknowledged that the mind and body both uniquely influenced perception but it was the latter, as in biology, that governed the whole.[12]

In this book I follow the buildup to, breakout of, and aftermath of the legislative battles that secured psychology's independence from medicine in America. These battles also laid the legal foundation for the emergence of the humanistic approaches to the human dilemma in the years after the pivotal victories in New York. While books and essays on the history of American psychology briefly mention the battle of the professions—with particular focus on events in New York—*Frontier Struggles* is the first in-the-trenches account that treats the topic not as a footnote but as a saga that was influential in its own right. This book provides the first behind-the-scenes look at the political maneuvers, espionage, infighting, and inspirational fortitude that enabled New York's psychologists to open the door to the legal recognition of their practice in New York and beyond. This book examines the circumstances that created an environment where charlatans could thrive and where the medical lobby could leverage them to almost cripple its newest competitor: the psychologist. From the alliances psychologists formed with leading physicians and psychiatrists, to the strategies the Joint Council deployed to sway legislators and the general public in its favor, *Frontier Struggles* follows the crisis that, in May's words, marked "the change of psychology as a profession in this state from its adolescence to its manhood."

* * *

The war had actually erupted a quarter of a century earlier in Austria, where Sigmund Freud himself joined the fray. It all started in 1924, when Freud had been too busy to analyze Newton Murphy, an American physician. That prompted Freud to refer Murphy to Theodor Reik, a thirty-six-year-old Viennese nonmedical analyst. Reik was one of Freud's earliest students, and the master had even dissuaded this pupil from attending medical school. Murphy came to Reik with a visiting card from Freud reading "obsessional neurosis, full psychoanalytic treatment." During the analysis, Murphy became delusional, with fears of men pursuing him. The physician later complained about Reik's practice to the American consulate, which referred the matter to a Viennese court. Murphy pressed legal charges against Reik for violating Vienna's antiquackery law, which prohibited the treatment of patients by nonmedical practitioners. While Reik later denied he ever stood trial, a May 25, 1927 *New York Times* dispatch detailing the previous day's court proceedings suggest otherwise. At the proceeding, Freud's longtime opponent, Julius Wagner von Jauregg, supported the complainant, maintaining that psychoanalysis was dangerous in the hands of nonmedically trained men. Compared to Austria, other countries to which psychoanalysis had spread, such as Germany, the United Kingdom, and the United States, were far more lenient toward lay analysis, with little to no legislation regulating the practice.[13]

When Freud had made his debut in America, with a lecture at Clark University in 1909, he had been relieved to learn many of the men in attendance were not doctors. He told his audience to "not fear that a medical education is necessary to follow what I shall have to say. We shall now accompany the doctors a little way, but soon we shall take leave of them." He differentiated organic brain diseases from the memory of traumatic experiences that results in hysteria. He said, "Against the serious brain diseases medical skill is in most cases powerless." Four years later, in his introduction to *The Psychoanalytic Method*, by the Swiss lay analyst Oskar Pfister, Freud admitted that "the practice of psychoanalysis calls much less for medical training than for psychological instruction and a free human outlook." He added, "The only guarantee of the harmless application of the analytic procedure must depend on the personality of the analyst." By March 1926, as Reik awaited trial, Freud confided to Paul Federn, the vice president of the Vienna Psychoanalytic Society, that "the battle for lay analysis must be fought out at some time or other. Better now than later. As long as I live, I shall do everything in my power to prevent psychoanalysis from being swallowed up by medicine."[14]

Freud made his views public with the short work *The Question of Lay Analysis*. In this 1926 book, Freud stressed that "*no one should practice analysis who has not acquired the right to do so by a particular training. Whether such a person is a doctor or not seems to me immaterial.*" While Freud did believe that the training of a psychoanalyst should include an introduction to biology, with an emphasis on "the science of sexual life" and "familiarity with the symptomatology of psychiatry," he saw "the great mass of what is taught in medical schools [as] of no use to him." More important than "a knowledge of the anatomy of the tarsal bones" and "the constitution of carbohydrates" were "branches of knowledge which are remote from medicine and which the doctor does not come across in his practice." These branches of knowledge included the history of civilization, mythology, the psychology behind religion, and the science of literature. Medical knowledge would not further the lay analyst's efforts "to understand a neurosis and cure it nor does it contribute to a sharpening of those intellectual capabilities on which his occupation makes the greatest demands."[15]

Reik's case ended with the charges against him being dismissed, but the debate over lay analysis was far from over. Later in 1927, the *International Journal of Psycho-Analysis* published a symposium on lay analysis featuring twenty-four psychoanalysts and two psychoanalytical societies. Freud believed *The Question of Lay Analysis* had not played a role in the outcome of the case against Reik; in fact, he said the book had "accomplished nothing at all" because "everyone continues firmly to hold the opinion which he previously advocated." In his epilogue to the symposium, Freud noted that his American colleagues—the majority of whom were based in New York—had "most summarily rejected lay analysis." Their "resistance," he said, was "entirely due to practical considerations," namely those stemming from the "mischief" and "many abuses" committed by lay analysts who consequently had injured patients and the reputation of analysis. To him, it was "understandable that in their indignation they should dissociate themselves widely from these unscrupulous and mischievous persons and should wish to exclude the laity from any participation in analysis." However, Freud believed practical considerations alone should not decide the question of lay analysis, and he viewed the Americans' resolution against it as a form of "repression." Policies against lay analysis—whether adopted by the government of Austria or the one the New York Psychoanalytical Society (NYPS) passed in 1926—could not "hinder the work of lay analysts." Rather than wage a futile fight against them, he asked, "Would it not be more expedient to take into account the fact of their existence, providing them with opportunities for training, which in turn would give the medical community influence over them and of their admission to co-operation, so that it would be to their interest to raise their moral and intellectual standard?"[16]

Freud's proposal, however, was too radical for Americans, and decades passed before the American Psychoanalytic Association agreed to provide psychoanalytic training to nonphysicians. In many regards, the positions that had been outlined in the symposium by New York's psychoanalysts, and others in Europe who later fled to the state before World War II, stood as the battle lines that went uncrossed for decades in the case of lay analysis. By the 1950s, it was clear that the AMA and APA wanted to ensure those lines extended beyond psychoanalysis to any form of treatment of mental conditions, most importantly psychotherapy.

For example, in the symposium, Abraham A. Brill, the Austrian-born psychiatrist who had founded in 1911 both the NYPS and American Psychoanalytic Society had said Freud's requirement for lay analysts to defer patients to a physician when in doubt would reduce them to "second-raters." Smith E. Jelliffe, also of New York, who had founded the first English-language psychoanalysis journal in 1913, called the *Psychoanalytic Review*, had maintained "lay analysts have no business to enter in, even if medical analysts are still grossly inadequate." In Vienna, Paul Schilder, who would later train and inspire a generation of psychiatrists in Brooklyn, said, "Lay analysis for the sick (even neurotics are sick) should remain a rare exception and occur only under the responsibility of a consultant or physician. The layman's position here is simply that of a physician's assistant." In Berlin, Karen Horney, a founding member of the Berlin Psychoanalytic Institute, argued that "we must give medicine preference" because it was medical training that was "most desirable as a preliminary to analytic training."[17]

Coincidentally, it was Horney's opposition to lay analysis at the American Institute for Psychoanalysis, which she helped establish in New York City in 1941, that shortly afterward led to the founding of the William Alanson White Institute (WAWI), also in the city. It was at the WAWI that May not only received his psychoanalytic education but also joined the faculty. From there he quickly climbed the ranks of the New York psychology community, and he helped finish the fight that Freud had started: to save psychotherapy from being "swallowed up by medicine." Although Freud had not believed the question of lay analysis should be determined by "the local conditions in America," he had held out the hope that in that country mankind could prepare a "corrective" to the "intolerable pressure imposed on us" by civilization. He predicted that "once more an American may hit on the idea of spending a little money to get the 'social workers' of his country trained analytically and to turn

Introduction: The Call

them into a band of helpers for combating the neuroses of civilization. Aha! a new kind of Salvation Army."[18]

* * *

Indeed. After World War II such a Salvation Army of clinical, consulting, vocational, social, and pastoral psychologists had been mobilized, not by one American but largely by the American government. In the two decades after symposium on lay analysis, the APsychA's membership grew sevenfold to 4,174 by 1947. New York had 913 of those psychologists—a fifth of the APsychA's membership and more than double any other state. The effectiveness of this army against the neuroses of civilization, however, would have been limited had it not been for May and his band of helpers in New York. This band was led by students of Freud's dissident pupils: May had studied under Erich Fromm and Alfred Adler, and his close ally on the Joint Council, Harry Bone, under Otto Rank. Even more, the band was aided by Freud's own nephew: Edward L. Bernays, the public relations pioneer and renowned "father of spin." He helped New York's psychologists win what May called the "fight for our professional lives."[19]

The battles of the professions are covered in these pages in three parts. The first part (chapters 1–3) follows the rise of the psychologists who would lead the Joint Council during the war years and the psychological approaches they represented as well as the proliferation of quacks and the postwar environment that precipitated the need for professional regulation. The second part (chapters 4–6) follows the events immediately leading up to the formation of the Joint Council and psychology's early skirmishes with medicine. The third part (chapters 7–12) covers the battle years from Dewey's veto in 1951 to the enactment of New York's licensing bill in 1956. The conclusion covers the subsequent spread of certification and licensing laws across the country and the state of the profession of psychology up until May's death in 1994.

A list of abbreviations for frequently referenced organizations can be found above. It is important to note that because the American Psychological Association and American Psychiatric Association use the abbreviation APA, in this book the former is abbreviated as APsychA and the latter as APA.

Part 1
Origins

Chapter 1
The Country Is Ailing

The war was far from over. For Rollo May it had not even begun, yet he had already had more than one brush with death. It was 1944: the summer of the invasion of Normandy. Each day brought a new military offensive presented in boldface headlines on the front pages of the New York newspapers: "U.S. on the Offensive in France," one day; "Japan Bombed Again by U.S.," another; and then, "Allies Pierce Enemy Lines—All Out Caen Offensive," the next. Breaking up the monotony of bombing headlines were those about the New York Yankees and the mounting presidential campaigns, with Franklin D. Roosevelt announcing his fourth-term bid against New York's Republican governor, Thomas E. Dewey. More and more, the Allies were a projection of strength, but then May noticed an article at the bottom of the front page of the *New York Times*. It covered the testimony that the Senate Subcommittee on Wartime Health and Education had heard the previous day in Washington, revealing, the *Times* said, the "grave condition of the country's health."[1]

In his preliminary statements, the subcommittee's chair had announced that an investigation of Selective Service records had found a third of all US draftees, roughly four million men through June 1, had been deemed ineligible for military service. A quarter of them had been unfit because of mental conditions. Selective Service director general Lewis B. Hershey had warned, "I know of nothing that represents so much potential danger as the accelerated growth of mental disease, which is [relieving] so many people from the duties of citizenship." The Selective Service's medical director, Colonel Leonard Rowntree, had lamented about "soft and flabby"

American youth and how Americans could "no longer regard [themselves] as a sturdy, healthy nation; the country is ailing."[2]

Rowntree's testimony struck May on many levels. At thirty-five, May could no longer pass as a youth. He was far from being soft and flabby, but he was one of those ailing Americans unfit for duty. Just two years earlier, May had had the complexion of a skeleton as his life was commandeered by "the captain of the death of men": tuberculosis. By the time of May's diagnosis in 1942, the disease had eaten half his lung, brought his weight down to 130 pounds, and left him coughing uncontrollably. That diagnosis had come one year into his transition from being a New Jersey pastor to a psychology graduate student enrolled at Columbia University's Teachers College in New York. All his projects and relationships had suddenly "lost their value." What had followed were several months spent in an Adirondack sanatorium in Trudeau, New York.[3]

At that time, tuberculosis patients had largely been expected to play a passive role in their recovery. The Trudeau Sanatorium's medical director, Fred H. Heise, believed the treatment of pulmonary tuberculosis was "based fundamentally on complete or partial rest of the mind and body," a health-promoting atmosphere with "an ample supply of so-called 'fresh air,'" and a proper diet. For months, lying in bed, staring at the ceiling, and waiting for his monthly X-ray, May had not known whether he would live or die. "I lived quite consciously in a state of constant anxiety which I would characterize like a horse running wild," he later recalled. By the fall of 1943 he had been admitted to another sanatorium not far from Northwestern University, where he had taught a summer psychology course. This stay in a sanatorium was shorter than the preceding one, and May returned to New York.[4]

"Who's to blame?" Rowntree asked at the congressional hearing. The colonel could not blame American youth—they were victims of society. "I should say our modern civilization or society, the Federal and State governments, the communities, the parents, the churches, the doctors and the dentists, all are involved in a condition which can only be remedied by concerted efforts."[5]

So far as mental health issues were concerned, the answer to Rowntree's question of who was to blame varied from profession to profession. One of May's advisers, Paul Tillich, a philosophical theology professor at Union Theological Seminary, blamed "the breakdown of the religious tradition" and the "meaninglessness of modern technological civilization." Erich Fromm, one of Sigmund Freud's dissident disciples who had mentored May, blamed individual isolation and a powerlessness that drove a mass "escape from freedom" toward totalitarianism. For the New York social scientist Lawrence K. Frank, the blame lay with the sickness of a society whose traditional culture had disintegrated and its ideas, conceptions, and beliefs "upon which our social and individual lives were organized" had decayed. That rendered individual therapy for mental illness or punishment for criminal behavior of no value "beyond mere alleviation of our symptoms."[6]

Meanwhile, more medical men, such as Freud, who had died three weeks after the start of World War II, blamed biological urges, namely the libido and death instinct, as the sources of civilization's discontent. Lawrence Kubie, a New York neurologist, psychiatrist, and psychoanalyst, did not believe people were any more neurotic than they had always been; instead, "in this age of increased life expectancy, growing population density, and unlimited destructive power, we can no longer tolerate the destructive forces which the world once could accept with relative impunity." Similarly, the pioneering psychiatrist Austen F. Riggs believed nervousness was the result of the maladjustments to the rapidly and enormously changing modern environment, in which "the great wealth of opportunity is fraught with the danger of a greatly increased temptation of unwisdom." Iago Galdston, the secretary of the New York Academy of Medicine's Medical Information Bureau, believed the psychogenic factors in abnormal behavior advanced by Sigmund Freud, Alfred Adler, and Carl Jung were overshadowing the simpler and contributing physical factors: "The simple energy factor in all functions of the nervous system is neglected. To use a crude simile, we look for trouble in the ignition system when in reality the gas tank is empty."[7]

Who was to blame? How Rowntree's question was answered—and more importantly by whom—would largely influence the framework of those "concerted efforts" in the coming postwar years. Reading the *Times*'s article, May saw in Rowntree's statements something that validated his decision to return to New York in 1941 and enroll in the Teachers College's new clinical psychology doctoral program. That decision had come just three years after he had received his divinity degree from Union Theological Seminary. In the intervening years he had served as a pastor of the First Congregational Church in Verona, New Jersey. He was a gifted counselor, heavily influenced by the individualistic psychology of another one of Freud's dissident disciples, Adler. After graduating from Oberlin College in 1930, May spent three years in Greece teaching at Anatolia College. For two of those summers he attended seminars in Vienna given by a chain-smoking Adler, who two decades earlier had broken from Freud. Adler had argued that the need for superiority and its resultant "inferiority complex"—not sexual libido—was the main thrust behind personality. Those summer seminars inspired May to pursue a religion fused with psychology, though he was torn between pursuing that career path and his love for art. Prior to returning to the United States from Vienna in 1933, May served as the secretary of the International School of Art. He seriously considered becoming an artist until his teacher, the Venetian Joseph Binder, talked him out of it. May entered Union Theological Seminary that year, but the pastorate would leave May disappointed. During his two years in Verona, he found the weddings over which he presided depressing and the funeral services coming closest to "some reality." He later quipped that at the latter "at least someone had genuine feelings."[8]

By the summer of 1944 May was trying to get his dissertation back on track. The Allies' advances in Europe and the Pacific, coupled with the subcommittee's reported findings and testimony, added weight and urgency to his work. He could already see that "psychological disorientation on a wide scale" would arise in the war's aftermath. In the *Teachers College Record*, he noted Rowntree's call for "concerted efforts" and warned, "Conditions will become worse before they become better, because our age, so successful in the handling of physical problems, is still woefully inadequate and almost hopelessly untrained in dealing with the broader psychological difficulties." One illustration of such success in handling physical problems was an announcement by the War Shipping Administration's medical director, Daniel Blain, just one month before the subcommittee's hearing. Blain had revealed the discovery of a "miracle drug," ergotamine tartrate, which purportedly cured shell shock's physical effects in two hours.[9]

However, May believed psychiatry was too much of a defensive measure, one that, with its "medical background and outlook," was geared toward dealing with people after long durations of emotional or psychological tension had caused the body to break down. Even more, May's sanatorium experiences had made him wary of medicine's doctor-knows-best approach, which usurped patients of their sense of responsibility in their

Joseph Breitenbach. Rollo May, 1967. Image courtesy of Frank Mt. Pleasant Library of Special Collections & Archives, Leatherby Libraries at Chapman University

recovery. He saw promise in the nondirective approach to counseling that Carl Rogers had advanced in his *Counseling and Psychotherapy*, published two years earlier, in that it "intended to increase the client's autonomy and sense of responsibility." Attributing his recovery to the acceptance of his anxiety and "the sheer exertion of [his] will," May had come "to believe less in the doctor and medicine than in [his] own strength to face each day as a new battleground." And when he looked at the profession into which he was entering, he saw more battlefields on the horizon. In the *Teachers College Record*, he sounded the rallying cry: "This general problem of psychological health cannot be solved by psychiatry. . . . The real hope for the future must lie in dealing with persons before they break in psychosis. This means that we must be able to help people in a state of psychological tension and confusion to face their problems, solve them creatively, and move ahead in constructive living." Such crusading was characteristic of May. His role as an editor of a radical student magazine had abruptly ended his studies at Michigan State College. Whether he was expelled or asked to leave is not clear, but May had rebounded by meeting with the dean of Oberlin and being admitted after an hour's discussion even though he had made no formal application.[10]

Who was to blame? The question consumed May as much as it did Rowntree. For May, however, the question was not whom to blame but what. The what was anxiety. It was a condition for which May had gotten "plenty of firsthand data" while lying in a sanatorium bed and something he had spent years researching for his dissertation. Except by the summer of 1944, his dissertation hit a wall. May's adviser, Tillich, insisted May "know *everything* about anxiety. Everything ever written, thought, every research up to this day." Overwhelmed with learning everything about anxiety, and struggling with certain psychosomatic aspects of it, May was "floundering in the material."[11]

One day that summer, May ventured downtown to Greenwich Village. He walked up to a brownstone and knocked on the door. A fifty-four-year-old Lawrence Frank opened the door to a six-foot-tall midwesterner with a square jaw and brown eyes. It is not clear whether this was a scheduled meeting or an unannounced visit. Either way, Frank welcomed May into his home, even though he had no obligation to help the student. Frank was not a professor at the Teachers College, or anywhere else.[12]

By the time of May's visit, Frank's reputation as a pioneer of developmental child psychology had been cemented, with his studies on the subject in the 1920s and 1930s serving as a foundation and his subsequent work at New York City–based research centers building on top of that. In 1923, the Laura Spelman Rockefeller Memorial had commissioned Frank to design and promote a child development program that spread parenting best practices through popular media outlets, university extension programs, and other groups. He further advanced parent education efforts by creating *Parents' Magazine* and the journal *Child Study* and through organizations such as the Child Study Association of America. His foundation-sponsored experience deepened in 1931 when he became an officer of the Rockefeller-backed General Education Board, and from 1933 to 1936 he headed its child growth and development program. From 1936 to 1942, he served as an executive of the Josiah Macy Jr. Foundation, where he oversaw the dispersion of substantial funds.[13]

Prior to Frank's involvement in the Macy Foundation, the organization had been dedicated to medical research and education. However, under the influence of Frank—who lacked an MD or PhD—its scope broadened to include human growth, development, and social functioning. One major project Frank had helped launch while at the Macy Foundation was the Sarah Lawrence Nursery School, whose research team and collaborators, such as Benjamin Spock, conducted extensive studies on child personality development. America's involvement in World War II and the election of a new president of the Macy Foundation had ended Frank's access to huge funds, but he remained influential in the field, even at smaller organizations, such as the Caroline Zachry Institute of Human Development. He was serving as the vice president of this organization off Washington Square when May visited him.[14]

Frank led this "stray student down from Columbia," as May later described himself, to a large table before the front windows. Frank's wife was in the background packing for her and her husband's vacation, probably in Holderness, New Hampshire, where they had a cottage. At the table, May brought Frank up to speed on his dissertation work. By that time, May had already spent an extensive amount of time building case studies for his dissertation. That summer May was conducting psychological assessments for the Court of Family Relations of young women at a city shelter and in crises stemming from premarital pregnancies.[15]

May had only uttered a few sentences when Frank grasped his problem and succinctly laid out the framework for May's approach to the problem of anxiety. Frank reviewed the psychosomatic approach; research by the Hungarian American psychologist and pioneer of psychosomatic medicine, Franz Alexander; and several other topics. May left Frank's house with a handful of reprints. While riding the subway uptown, May marveled at how Frank's mind had been able to organize his problem in such an orderly way—a concept the social scientist had called "organized complexity." The student had a "new inspiration" for his dissertation, which would reveal how anxiety lurked behind nearly all the political, economic, business, professional, and domestic crises griping modern humankind.[16]

It would not be the last time Frank would rescue May as he endeavored to change the landscape of American psychology.

* * *

Anxiety was literally almost everywhere in New York that summer. In a Midtown East apartment that July, a thirty-seven-year-old W. H. Auden started drafting his longest and last book-length poem, *The Age of Anxiety*. The poem, which would not be published until 1947, is a dialogue between four strangers who meet in a New York City bar and are as different as their loss of self-worth and loneliness are alike, according to May. Pressured to conform to cultural trends, or whatever "the wheel wills," Auden's characters are marked by an alienation and helplessness that underlies the anxiety giving this age its name. May noted they must yield to "the rise and fall / In pay and prices" and are reduced in the labor force to a "market-made . . . commodity." A month after starting work on this poem, Auden, who had recently read the new English translation of Søren Kierkegaard's *Either/Or*, declared in the *New Republic*, "The basic human problem is man's anxiety in time." When New York's Governor Dewey accepted the Republican nomination for president at the Republican National Convention that June, he said, "True, we now pass through dark and troubled times. Scarcely a home escapes the touch of dread anxiety and grief."[17]

That year saw publication of the first English translation of another one of Kierkegaard's works: *The Concept of Dread*, translated by Walter Lowrie, who had interpreted the Dutch *angst* as "dread." May later brought to Lowrie's attention the fact that the German *angst* had been what Freud and Kurt Goldstein had used for "anxiety." Lowrie later conceded and granted May permission to use this alternative translation in his dissertation when quoting from *The Concept of Dread*. When May read the book, he was "powerfully struck" by how it described what he and his fellow tuberculosis patients had been experiencing. In his nearly decade-long struggle with tuberculosis, May could "immediately experience" Kierkegaard's theory of anxiety that pitted being against nonbeing. In contrast, Freud's evolving theories of anxiety had seemed more distant to May. In 1916, Freud had described anxiety as the byproduct of repressed libido, but ten years later he had revised this theory to reverse the order of causation. Anxiety, in Freud's second theory, is phylogenetically inherited and serves as a "danger signal" that triggers the ego to impose repressive impulses that in turn create symptoms. Freud, with his technical genius, May concluded, "*knew about* anxiety," whereas Kierkegaard, with his ontological genius, "*knew* anxiety." Unlike fear, which "refer[s] to something definite," anxiety, Kierkegaard said, relates to "something which is nothing," namely freedom. He saw freedom as an abyss of possibilities that afflicts those who gaze into it with "dizziness" and leaves them "grasping at finiteness." This "dizziness of freedom" impairs the individual's ability to pursue a possibility and bring it into reality.[18]

The publication of *The Concept of Dread* and Auden's work on *The Age of Anxiety* illustrated how, May believed, the nation was in the midst of a shift from an "age of covert anxiety" to an "age of overt anxiety." This transition, May pointed out, was evident in the "Middletown" studies by Robert and Helen Lynd, a husband-and-wife team of sociologists who, for eighteen months ending in 1925, had conducted a field study on contemporary

American culture in a midwestern city. They had called the city, Muncie, Indiana, Middletown for its "middle-of-the-road quality."[19]

Insecurities and anxieties were infrequently mentioned in the Lynds' 1929 book, *Middletown*, though they had observed the "drowning of incipient social problems under a public mood of everything being 'fine and dandy.'" They also noted the increased isolation of working-class men and rapid "cohesion and conformity" among business-class men. When the Lynds returned to Muncie in 1935, they had found a city reeling more psychologically than economically from the Depression, which had started six years earlier. Since the last study had ended, Muncie's population had grown by more than 30 percent to forty-seven thousand. Amid an influx of unfamiliar people, who brought with them different manners and concepts of modern art, freer sex, and the "bachelor girl," the community experienced a "heightening of insecurity" that fueled a "greater insistence upon conformity and a sharpening of latent issues." Muncie's residents struggled with what the Lynds called a "confusion of the ideal (its values)." Echoing Kierkegaard's "dizziness of freedom," the Lynds noted a "growing awareness of the complexity of the choices" applicable to "every department of living" and how these overwhelming options tended to make Muncie's residents "huddle back defensively away from innovation." Residents gravitated "toward being 'like other people,' 'playing safe,' 'being regular,' 'voting the good-fellow ticket straight.'"[20]

The rift between "the power-dominance-aggression values of the business world and the affectional-loveable-human values of family" had widened to intolerable degrees. On top of this was Muncie's "chaos of conflicting patterns," where the traditional culture required men to get a job and be the family's breadwinner but the Depression had blocked for many the path of gainful employment. This narrowed the moneymaking role for many men and pushed marriage out of reach and postponed children, consequently upending the traditional cultural requirements of women. These conflicting patterns, the Lynds said, were not "wholly condemned, but no one of them [was] clearly approved and free from confusion."[21]

Few were spared this confusion, whether they were in Muncie or New York City, and it was only the beginning. Such a vast social upheaval had decades earlier swept through Europe and Russia, priming them for the existential and related phenomenology movements that thrived there in the first half of the twentieth century. Existentialism had deeply taken root in Tillich's Germany as well as France, Holland, and Switzerland, but it had failed to penetrate Britain, where the religious tradition had remained strong. As geopolitical and economic forces added pressure to that tradition in places such as Muncie and New York, they were likewise being primed for existentialism and phenomenology, though an Americanized version of the latter took hold first, in upstate New York.[22]

* * *

With roots going back to 1910, the phenomenological approach generally sought to help the patient understand his or her subjective experiences—and consequently rebuild his or her inner world. This type of observation was achievable through what the movement's founder, the German philosopher Edmund G. A. Husserl, had called "psychological-phenomenological reduction." This operation of mind required the observer to refrain from making value judgments about phenomena, essentially putting "the world between brackets." Four decades later, Donald Snygg, the chair of Oswego State Normal School's psychology department in upstate New York, had called for a "phenomenological system of psychology." However, rather than being influenced by Husserlian phenomenology, Snygg's approach grew out of German Gestalt psychology.[23]

Snygg's 1941 paper on "The Need for a Phenomenological System of Psychology" had left a marked impression on Arthur W. Combs, who had been working on his doctorate in clinical psychology under Rogers at Ohio State. Combs was "astounded" by Snygg's phenomenology and found that where psychology "had seemed so confusing and inconsistent," it "now fell nearly into an orderly, systematic whole." After completing his coursework in 1943, Combs accepted a faculty position at Syracuse University, not far from Snygg in Oswego. In 1945, Combs received his PhD, and the two began collaborating on a "perceptual theory as an explanation for relationships between human experience and behavior," culminating four years later in *Individual Behavior: A New Frame of Reference for Psychology*.[24]

Despite his leanings toward phenomenology, Combs remained an ardent follower and practitioner of the signature counseling method of his mentor, Rogers: nondirective therapy. In fact, Combs believed the phenomenological approach to behavior that he and Snygg were refining, also known as perceptual psychology, was nondirective therapy in that they were both "client-centered." Both, Combs said, were "concerned always with the way things appear to [the] client." This emphasis on the meaning of events from the client's perspective grew out of Combs's rejection of the theories of behaviorism that held stimuli dictated behavior. Instead, he said, "It is not the event but the meaning of the event which is important in the individual's behavior." That made this technique the "recognition and, acceptance of personal meaning."[25] Rogers, meanwhile, was slow to embrace phenomenology, but he believed if behavior was determined by the perceptual field, then the "primary object of study for psychologists would be the person and his world as viewed by the person himself."[26]

Anxiety was actually what had led Combs to Rogers and put him on the path to phenomenology. After receiving his bachelor's degree in science from Ohio State in 1935, Combs taught high school science while also working at the same institution toward a master's degree in school counseling. He received his master's degree in 1941, a year after Rogers joined Ohio State's faculty. In addition to serving as Combs's mentor as Combs worked toward his doctorate in clinical psychology, Rogers also counseled the student, who had been struggling with increasing anxieties.[27]

Over the course of five or six sessions, Rogers's nondirective therapy helped Combs "explore the relationships of [his] childhood home" and "made it possible for [him] to cut loose from [his] neurotic expectations of [his] parents." That allowed him "to pursue fulfillment elsewhere" and "paved the way for further growth of [him]self." By the time he received his PhD in 1945, Combs was already growing into a leader in the emerging field of perceptual psychology, and he would quickly rise within the ranks of New York's psychology professional circles.[28]

* * *

As World War II entered its last year, greater attention turned toward demobilization—a process that would greatly affect New York. By then more than 1.2 million New Yorkers had been enlisted in the armed forces, and nearly a quarter million of them had already returned to the state. By the war's end New York would contribute more people to the war effort than any other state. In January 1945, Governor Dewey, who had lost the previous November's presidential election to Franklin D. Roosevelt, laid

Stanley Cobb, *Borderlands of Psychiatry*, 1943. Cobb, the founder of biological psychiatry, said, "The problem of psychiatry in the United States in 1943" was that it did not focus on the 6 million Americans who were neither committed to a mental hospital nor could legally be committed to one. They lived in what Cobb called the "borderlands of psychiatry." BORDERLANDS OF PSYCHIATRY by Stanley Cobb, Cambridge, Mass.: Harvard University Press, Copyright © 1943 by the President and Fellows of Harvard College. Copyright renewed © 1970 by Stanley Cobb.

out a series of initiatives geared toward assisting veterans in transitioning to civilian life. One of these initiatives was illustrative of the differing roles the state envisioned psychologists and psychiatrists would play in the demobilization effort. Dewey proposed creating a general counseling service that would incorporate directive psychological techniques to help reestablish veterans in their communities. He also proposed a veterans' psychiatric consulting service under which state psychiatric facilities "should be extended and placed at the disposal of veterans" and more psychiatrists would be trained to meet demand.[29]

By 1945 there were only approximately four thousand psychiatrists nationwide. Even though it was widely acknowledged that psychiatrists could not alone meet the demands of demobilization, they were keen on expanding their reach into what Massachusetts General Hospital's chief psychiatrist, Stanley Cobb, called the "borderlands of psychiatry." In his 1943 book by that name, Cobb said these borderlands consisted of the vast segment of the population that lived outside of psychiatry's traditional market of an estimated six hundred thousand hospital inmates and an additional three to five million people who were in the community but met legal requirements for institutionalization. In the borderlands there were an estimated six million free and unsupervised individuals suffering from psychoneurosis, stammering, alcoholism, epilepsy, and other neurological problems.[30]

While acknowledging the largest of these borderlands—psychoneuroses—was the most difficult to define and measure, Cobb believed the Cartesian "mind-body" dichotomy that had placed much of this segment out of psychiatry's reach was an "artifact"; all that differentiated psychology from physiology was "complexity." He urged his colleagues: "Cast out as unavailing the discussion as to whether this or that disease is physical or mental, psychotic or neurotic and simply make a list of the disorders, diseases and syndromes we see in the clinic." Nearly a decade before the publication of the first *Diagnostic and Statistical Manual of Mental Disorders*, Cobb made a shortlist of those disorders, diseases, and syndromes. They included common maladjustments to interpersonal relations, or "neuroses," such as nervousness, anxiety attacks, hysteric reactions, depressive reactions, and obsessive and compulsion reactions. He believed their main etiology "was probably in the psychological sphere" and they seldom led to institutionalization, yet there was "little sense in dividing this group off and putting it in opposition to all the other psychiatric reactions, most of which [were] lumped under the term 'psychosis.'"[31]

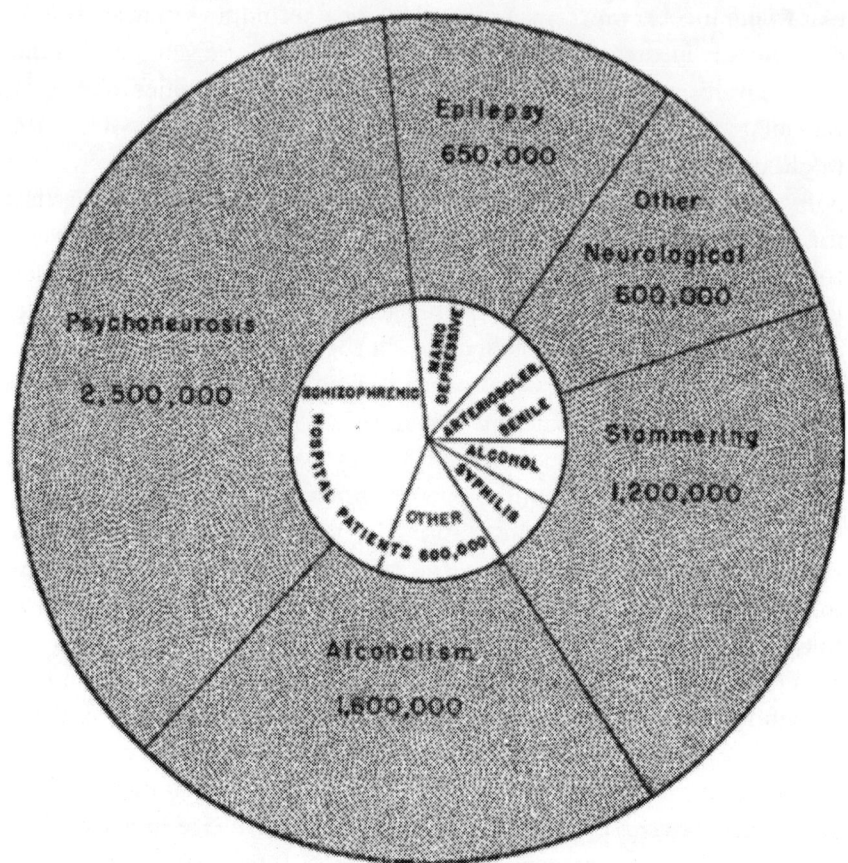

Stanley Cobb, *Borderlands of Psychiatry*, 1943. Within psychiatry's borderlands, Cobb estimated there were 2.5 million people suffering from psychoneuroses, 1.6 million suffering from alcoholism, 1.2 million from stammering, 650,000 from epilepsy, and 600,000 from other neurological disorders. BORDERLANDS OF PSYCHIATRY by Stanley Cobb, Cambridge, Mass.: Harvard University Press, Copyright © 1943 by the President and Fellows of Harvard College. Copyright renewed © 1970 by Stanley Cobb.

In many ways, Cobbs's proposal to jettison the mind-body problem was already being implemented in American psychology. Experimental psychologists had been more than willing to dissolve the borders that separated psychology from the established sciences. An APsychA survey of more than a hundred articles published in the top fourteen psychology journals between 1888 and 1938 had found a marked decline in literature on the mind-body problem. During the same period, reverse trends were seen with papers employing statistical aids and using animal subjects. In his presidential address to the APsychA at its 1939 annual meeting in Berkeley, California, outgoing president Gordon W. Allport pointed out that whereas "earlier literature solutions to the [mind-body] problem were boldly offered in monistic or dualistic terms; today the fashion is to deny the existence of the body-mind problem." Allport had criticized his colleagues for placing too much emphasis on behavioristic studies of animals while the mind-body problem had remained unsolved and understanding of higher mental processes, such as human speech, had remained marginal. The result had been a "schism" between pure and applied psychologists and an "appreciably unhistorical" modern psychology. He found it hypocritical how the purist "generally repudiates a dualism of mind and body, [yet] he welcomes the equally stultifying dualism of laboratory and life."[32]

To illustrate the behaviorists' overconfidence, Allport recalled how one had challenged him to name "a single psychological problem not referable to rats for its solution." Allport had been as shocked by the proposition as he had been for the challenger's ignorance of "the historic problems of the aesthetic, humorous, religious, and cultural behavior of men," among other things. He warned that this belief that psychology "has no essential relation to life, and that human events lie entirely beyond our control ... undermines the very civilization that has endowed psychology with its freedom, in return charging it with the contribution of useful knowledge." He pleaded that "we avoid authoritarianism, that we keep psychology from becoming a cult from which original and daring inquiry is ruled out by the application of one-sided tests of method; that we come to evaluate our science rather by its success in enhancing—above the levels achieved by common sense—our powers of *predicting, understanding,* and *controlling* human action."[33]

Chapter 2
A Tremendous Army of Maladjusted Persons

Before the war ended, the letters kept coming. They came from drug addicts, suicidal students, and shoplifters. There was the man who had started to hear voices; the twenty-four-year-old woman who had been talked out of using birth control by a marriage counselor who routinely performed abortions; and there was the melancholic twenty-eight-year-old woman who had cracked after having been persuaded to publicly disclose her troubles to her class. There was the man who had wanted help with his bad habits but demanded to see no one other than a hypnotist. There was also the woman who had been living with an alcoholic whom she expected to marry after his incarceration. The thought of living with a drunkard was appalling, but not more so than living alone. She asked for advice. "Please answer by return mail."[1]

The one thing they all had in common was a listing under the "psychology" section of the Chicago telephone directory promoting "The Advisory Service, for professional consultation in the personal, emotional, and educational problems of normal people." The letters all went to a social worker, Lee R. Steiner, who had received her master's degree in social work from Smith College in 1929. She had later worked as a medical social worker at that school's affiliated Institute for Child Guidance in New York. She also had been a staff member at the Institute for Juvenile Research at the University of Illinois at Chicago and the University of Chicago. In 1933, the Illinois Society for Mental Hygiene tasked her with studying "psychology quackery." She pursued this task with the vigor of an investigative journalist.

After growing frustrated with her interviews of "consultants," their misrepresentations of their educational backgrounds, and their bragging about client satisfaction, she decided to broaden the scope of the study beyond practitioners. She also sought to study those seeking help from "dubious sources" and paying heavy fees for their services. That prompted Steiner—with permission from her colleagues—to list the fake advisory service in the telephone directory.[2]

Two years into her study, Steiner moved to New York City, where she mailed approximately 250 letters to listed "consultants" and asked whether they helped people with their personal problems, what methods they employed, and what their fees were. The responses, again, poured in. Only this time, rather than receiving woeful letters, she was inundated with consultants' marketing materials and course catalogs. She waited two years before responding to any of the consultants, and she would spend the next decade investigating various forms of psychological quackery, including what she called the "gremlins in the inkpot" (newspaper advice columnists); the "misery at the microphone" (radio show advisers); vocational guidance counselors' "fabricated systems"; and "entrepreneurs for cupid" (matchmakers).

Steiner's investigations culminated in her book *Where Do People Take Their Troubles?* Published in 1945, this book cast light on "the freedom given to pseudo-psychologists" while also underscoring the pressing need to protect the profession of psychology and the general public from this quackery. "'Psychological consultation' is anybody's stamping ground," Steiner said. "Anyone can call himself a 'psychologist' and charge a fee for giving advice to people regarding their personal problems." Throughout the twelve-year period of Steiner's study, no state had regulated psychology, outside of a few with laws relating to school psychologists or court examiners in commitment cases. Aside from those measures, all New York had was a state attorney general's opinion stating that only licensed physicians or surgeons could practice hypnosis or claim to treat mental diseases. However, because people suffering from mental diseases commonly denied anything was wrong with them, Steiner said this ruling was "practically without teeth." Even more, New York psychologists had not even been required to pay business taxes. Together, Steiner said, this lack of regulation had created an environment where "the sky was the limit" and where pseudopsychologists were "answerable to no one."[3]

One of the only avenues people with problems had for finding legitimate applied psychologists was by asking them whether they were members of the APsychA or contacting the New York City–based Psychological Corporation. However, these organizations had long played—and would continue to play—a passive role in the fight against quack psychology. In fact, by 1927, the APsychA's twelve-year effort to control the profession of psychology through organizational certification had, as Samuel W. Fernberger noted, ended in "more or less total failure." That unsuccessful effort had started in 1915 with the APsychA passing a resolution declaring, "This Association discourages the use of mental tests for practical psychological diagnosis by individuals psychologically unqualified for this work." Four years later the APsychA voted to create a committee "to consider methods of procedure for certifying Consulting Psychologists." Preliminary certification procedures were created in 1921, only to be largely ignored by the association's membership. In 1925 the Committee on Certification of Consulting Psychologists developed detailed qualifications for consulting psychologists, only to have its report on this matter be, as Fernberger said, "pigeon-holed" by the APsychA council. The council had refused to publish the report or adopt it for instruction and guidance.[4]

A year later the Committee on Certification began coming to terms with the futility of its mission, noting in another report that the APsychA's scientific leanings had placed it "at a partial disadvantage in the maintenance of professional standards." The committee doubted the APsychA could "be counted for effective opposition to the energy and resources which would be mustered by a colleague charged with misconduct and his professional life to fight for." In response to this report, the APsychA council moved to create a Committee on Certification Policy, which in 1927 declared the certification of consulting psychologists was an impractical endeavor that should be abandoned. A motion to this effect passed, ending the APsychA's attempts to self-regulate the profession of psychology.[5]

* * *

Medicine, however, was far from immune to quacks within its own ranks. In fact, the AMA had been warring against quacks since its inception in 1847. One of quacks' most vocal and formidable adversaries was

Morris Fishbein, a Chicago physician who in 1924 became the editor of the *Journal of the American Medical Association* (*JAMA*). He went on to hold that position for a quarter century, and over that period the journal's exposés of quacks made him a defendant in thirty lawsuits, none of which he lost. He was viewed as the "official mouthpiece of medical science" whose "delight to expose charlatans" was renowned. Although he did not view psychoanalysis as an established science, Fishbein held Freud in high esteem for attracting "greater attention to the process of the human mind to stimulate acceptance . . . that the study of objective changes in the human body is not sufficient for mental aberrations." In fact, his 1925 book, *The Medical Follies*, was mute on the topic of quack psychology. However, Fishbein's *The New Medical Follies*, published two years later, devoted an entire chapter challenging the "cultist movement" of psychoanalysis and the "invasion of the field by psychoanalytic amateurs."[6]

Fishbein's attack—and to an extent the AMA's—on lay analysts had followed two major victories that the medical profession had won the previous year in both America and Europe. In May 1926, New York governor Alfred Smith's signed a bill amending the state's Medical Practice Act, which had been specifically designed to drive out quack doctors. The law's provisions included a requirement for physicians to annually register with the secretary of state so a list of duly licensed practitioners could be maintained. It also regulated use of the title "doctor," established prohibitions against false and deceptive advertising, and empowered the state attorney general to prosecute quacks. Around that time, Austrian authorities also prosecuted one of Freud's nonmedical pupils, Theodor Reik, for his violation of Austria's antiquackery law. This action in a Viennese court had prompted not only Freud's book on *The Question of Lay Analysis* but also the symposium on the topic published in the *International Journal of Psycho-Analysis*. Although the charges against Reik were dismissed, the symposium expounded the position of psychoanalysts in New York. In his concluding remarks on the symposium, Freud observed how "the bluntest rejection of lay analysis has been by our American colleagues."[7]

In the early 1930s, it had been the medical profession that took the lead in waging the legislative fight against quack psychologists. The medical profession's effort to control the practice of psychology, at least in New York, began after the dead, bruised body of a twenty-five-year-old woman named Starr Faithfull had been found on a deserted Long Island beach in June 1931. In Albany, New York, William L. Love, the state senate's only physician member, believed Faithfull had been a "victim of psychanalysis" and called for a legislative investigation into "pseudo psychiatrists and bootlegging psychologists." He said such quacks had been preying on "neurotic or erotic" women and over the past two years the state had seen a wave of false mental "cures." Indicative of how accepted pseudopsychologists had become in the community, the newspaper for Love's senate district in Brooklyn chastised his proposal. "A State investigation of the practices of those who are finding a way to prosperity by using what little science knows of a field where faith and suggestion mean everything would be an amusing farce," said a *Brooklyn Daily Eagle* editorial. "If psychiatrists know little, the legislators know nothing about a sort of healing which is older than Galen or Hippocrates." Love responded to this criticism, saying, "Evidently you have no conception of the harm these untrained pseudo-psychiatrists are doing. Some of them have hung out signs without qualification whatever, and they are not checked up by the State."[8]

Faithfull had been a beautiful young woman with a tragically sensational background, starting with her sexual abuse as a child by a relative who went on to become the mayor of Boston. Due to this childhood trauma, when older, according to her stepfather, she had "led a very erotic, exotic life, with much drink and many love affairs." Her death sparked a tabloid frenzy, with the coroner determining the cause of death as drowning but the Nassau County district attorney pursuing murder charges. Despite an international criminal investigation that extended to Scotland Yard and multiple suspects and grand jury hearings, the case remains unsolved.[9]

Love's belief that Faithfull had been a victim of psychoanalysis appears to have stemmed from the fact that her family had pushed her to see several "alienists," who had recommended changes of scenery and exercise. These alienists, however, had never been reported to be suspects in her death. In March 1932 Love introduced legislation that would amend the state's Mental Hygiene Law to make it a misdemeanor to practice psychology without being properly certified or to impersonate a qualified psychologist. These offenses would have been punishable by a fine of $500 to $1,000 or up to six months' imprisonment. The bill also featured an exemption for clergy, noting its provisions would "not be construed to abridge the free practice of any religious belief."[10]

Love's bill represented one of the earliest attempts—if not the first in New York—to legislatively counter the rise of pseudopsychologists. However, the bill's reach was extremely limited in its application to qualified psychologists, who under state law were authorized to sit on commissions that examined the competency of persons suspected of being mentally defective. Even with this narrow scope, the *Brooklyn Daily Eagle* criticized the legislation, saying that until psychology became more scientific, it was "just as well for legislators to leave it alone," and the legislature did just that. Although Love had years earlier been eyed as a prospective candidate for the US Senate or state lieutenant governorship, he introduced this bill shortly after his era of political influence had entered its twilight. Earlier that year, Love had crossed his party's leadership by becoming the only Democrat in the senate to vote for the continuation of an investigation by a joint legislative committee into corruption in New York City's courts and police departments. As punishment, party leaders supported a primary opponent who had defeated Love in September, prompting him to run and lose as a Republican in the general election. Neither his successor in the senate nor any other legislators attempted to champion his fight against quack psychologists.[11]

Filling Love's role as a crusader against psychological quacks was New York State deputy attorney general Sol Ullman. In early 1934, he prosecuted the first case against a lay analyst for practicing psychoanalysis without a license, in violation of the state's Medical Practice Act. The lay analyst was May Benzenberg Mayer. She was fifty-three years old and was described as a "cult leader" and founder of the Pojodaj House, an Upper East Side school where psychology and psychoanalysis were taught. Ullman prosecuted the case on behalf of the State Board of Medical Examiners after Mayer had subjected a Brooklyn woman with a paralyzed left leg to a "dream course" and later claimed this victim could not be cured because she was not "philosophically ready." This victim had also loaned Mayer $5,300 to cover the school's second mortgage but was only repaid $2,800. Over six years, the victim had also paid $3,185.65 for Mayer's lessons, lectures, and treatments. Despite these financial damages, the state's interest in this case was squarely on the issue of the legality of medical practice. In spring 1934, Mayer was convicted of practicing psychoanalysis without a license and sentenced to pay a $500 fine and serve a one-year suspended jail term. Mayer's lawyer threatened an appeal on the grounds that psychoanalytic treatment did not fall within the meaning of the practice of medicine under the Medical Practice Act. Ullman welcomed the prospect of such an appeal, saying the Office of the Attorney General was interested in learning the opinion on this matter of the state's highest court, the New York Court of Appeals.[12]

In 1916, that court had ruled that the Medical Practice Act was broad enough to permit Christian Science practitioners to offer prayer to secure "the overthrow of moral, mental and physical disease." However, for such practitioners to qualify under this exception, "the religious tenants of a church must be practiced in good faith." By the time of Mayer's conviction, it still was not clear whether the court would permit such unlicensed healing of mental disease outside the context of religious practice, as was the case of psychotherapy and psychoanalysis.[13]

* * *

It was a few years after the Mayer decision that applied psychologists launched their own lobbying efforts to better control their profession, only to have those efforts frustrated by the medical profession. In January 1937, the Association of Consulting Psychologists (ACP), then in the process of combining with the APsychA's Clinical Division and reorganizing into the American Association of Applied Psychology, announced a plan to lobby the New York legislature for a bill that would curb the "illicit trade" of quacks and control the use of the term "certified psychologist." In announcing the legislative plan in New York City, Percival Symonds, an education professor at Columbia's Teachers College and a former ACP president, said, "As a professional group, psychologists are unable to protect their name and reputation against unscrupulous persons. . . . Usually they do not infringe on the laws relating to the practice of medicine and cannot be prosecuted under any law in the State. Psychologists feel they need to protect their own group against unqualified and untrained individuals." The bill, as the ACP envisioned it, would provide for the creation of a board of examiners that would have three or more members who would be tasked with vetting consulting psychologist applicants. The minimum requirements for certification included a doctor of philosophy or education from an accredited college with a psychology major and three years of experience as a junior or assistant psychologist.[14]

The bill, Symonds said, was a form of "permissive licensing" that would "not limit the applications of psychology to those who meet certain qualifications, but will guarantee that those who are registered as licensed psychologists can be counted upon by the public as having the training and competency which the state requires." Symonds acknowledged that psychologists had been "struggling for a clearer definition of our own position and our relations with others with whom we work." He warned there would be "overlap and conflict with the work of other professions," particularly psychiatrists, guidance counselors, and social workers. Yet he attempted to limit his profession's trespasses first by saying, "The applications of psychology to those suffering from mental disorders are probably rightfully reserved for those whose training fit them successfully to meet such problems, namely, those who have had training which a medical course gives." In light of these considerations, the preliminary ACP legislation defined the practice of psychology as "the application of the principles and techniques of the science of psychology to the measurement, evaluation, explanation, interpretation, motivation, guidance, or redirection of human behavior."[15]

Symonds claimed the ACP's proposed legislation had been endorsed by the New York City superintendent of schools and New York University's dean. However, the proposal had lacked support from state lawmakers. Even after going through nine to ten revisions, the bill was never introduced in the assembly or senate. The ACP bill's failure to gain support in the legislature likely had much to do with opposition to it from the New York Academy of Medicine's Committee on Public Health Relations. That committee had "expressed itself in sympathy with the efforts to formulate qualifications of competency in applied psychology, but discouraged the legislation." Alternatively, the committee had recommended the "simpler and more efficient method" of certification, pointing out that "although physicians are licensed, the certification of specialists by the several national boards has not been made any easier thereby." Even New York psychiatrists had to follow this recommended course of action, and that same year New York governor Alfred E. Smith signed into law their own certification bill.[16]

Psychologists, however, pushed forward with their licensing efforts. In 1939, *The Journal of Consulting Psychology* featured a report from the American Association of Applied Psychology and its Committee on Legislation featuring language for a Model "Certified Psychologist" Act. However, this description downplayed the fact that the bill had components of licensing legislation. It did include a certification component, under which it prohibited uncertified and unlicensed individuals from designating themselves as or their occupations by words such as "'psychologist,' 'psychometrist,' 'psychoanalyst,' 'psychopathist,' 'psychotherapist,' 'psychotherapeutist.'" or any other phrases suggesting a practice in psychology. Steuart Henderson Britt, a psychology professor at George Washington University, had been appointed to chair the Committee on Legislation, probably because he not only held a PhD in psychology from Yale University but also was a lawyer admitted to the Missouri and New York bars and the US Supreme Court. For the bill, Britt consulted with eight psychologists, with four of them being from New York (Douglas H. Fryer, Ethel L. Cornell, Elaine F. Kinder, and Symonds), two from Pennsylvania (Robert G. Bernreuter and Charles A. Ford), one from New Jersey (James Q. Holsopple), and one from Indiana (Harriet E. O'Shea).[17]

With Symonds and Fryer both being former ACP presidents, it was unlikely Britt was unaware of the medical profession's opposition to providing a definition for the "practice of psychology." In fact, Britt's definition for this practice strongly resembled the ACP's from 1937. The only differences were that Britt's definition referred to the "application of the principles and techniques of psychology"—as opposed to the "science of psychology." It also substituted the "redirection" of human behavior with its "re-training or re-education." Meanwhile, the medical profession pushed back. In 1939, the medical lobby swiftly got a bill passed in New Jersey that inserted mental conditions into the definition of the terms "physician" and "surgeon," threatening to grant medical doctors exclusivity over such conditions. However, "mental conditions" was a broad and undefined term, and it was expected among New Jersey psychologists that it would take a court decision to clarify how adversely the law would limit the scope of their work. That same year the Ohio Association of Applied Psychologists fought legislation that would have defined psychologists, whose statutory roles in the state had largely been limited to certain court proceedings, as people "entitled to practice medicine."[18]

To no avail, legislation for the licensure and registration of psychologists was introduced in Pennsylvania in 1937, for a "certified consulting psychologist" in Illinois in 1939, and for licensed "consulting psychologists" in Kansas in 1940. By 1941, more legislative activity was expected in several states, but the effort to pass certification or licensing legislation in New

York had been all but aborted. In his introductory remarks to the *Journal of Consulting Psychology*'s spring 1941 issue, which had featured a "Symposium on Certification and Licensing," Fryer, the chair of the Committee on Legislation for the New York State Association of Applied Psychologists (NYSAAP), stated that the psychologists in the state supporting "self-certification" vastly outnumbered those favoring state certification. Fryer said New York psychologists had been "jolted partially into this point of view" by administrative concerns over an insufficient number of certificates that would be issued. There had also been the threat that "a profession with legal support for the claim of its field as the solution of all human problems [i.e., medicine] would fight the certification of psychologists to the last ditch." He also noted "considerable confusion as to what is gained in legal certification," but there was also confusion within the committee as to what was needed for a valid certification bill.[19]

The NYSAAP's reluctance to confront the medical profession or provoke its hostility did not help the cause of passing a minimal measure to protect the public and psychology's name through certification legislation. With no way forward on either front, the NYSAAP started preparing the policies and procedures for self-certification. However, as Carney Landis of the Psychiatric Hospital and Institute in New York City had pointed out, "This type of certification means little or nothing to the general public. It does not necessarily imply legal responsibility either of or for the individual or the group. No state organization would have any police power in the real sense of the term. Such a certification has little prestige value and less economic value." Landis argued that state associations should not begin lobbying for licensing legislation until they all had agreed on standards, competence, responsibility, and other concerns. Over the next five years, he said, state and national committees should vigorously work toward establishing those standards so temporary "certificates of specialized psychological competence" could be issued. That would lay the groundwork for a five-year licensing legislation campaign in state houses beginning in 1946.[20]

Defeated in New York, Fryer believed the prospects for legal certification looked better "west of the Alleghenies where the problems of certification are fresher." A nationwide survey of legislative activity by Britt found that there was a recognized need for certification or licensing in nineteen states (plus the District of Columbia), with three-quarters of them west of the Alleghenies. Meanwhile, psychologists were at odds over the desirability of such legislation in three more states: New Jersey, New York, and Ohio. Out of these twenty-two states, actions for certification seemed imminent in only Illinois and Kansas. Even Britt acknowledged "there may be little or no need for immediate steps toward legislation in the majority of states."[21]

* * *

The United States' entrance into World War II made New York psychologists' decision to halt their lobbying effort more a matter of necessity than choice. Shortly after the *Journal of Consulting Psychology* had published its symposium on certification and licensing, Britt had been appointed chair of the Emergency Committee's Subcommittee on Listing Personnel. He had assembled a list of twenty-three hundred qualified psychologists for uniformed service by July 1941. Just before the bombing of Pearl Harbor, he urged the Emergency Committee to expand its national personnel office. That prompted the formation of the Office of Psychological Personnel, of which he was named director in February 1942. Mobilization became the profession's primary concern, and certification and licensing would not be treated as a major topic in the *Journal of Consulting Psychology* throughout the war.[22]

In 1944, members of the Connecticut Valley Association of Psychologists and the Connecticut State Psychological Society had begun planning for certification legislation. Over a sixteen-month period, they mounted a lobbying campaign that culminated in the Connecticut Certified Psychologists Act, which Governor Raymond E. Baldwin signed into law on July 19, 1945. The act created a three-person board of examiners tasked with certifying psychologists who were at least twenty-one years old, had received a doctor of philosophy in psychology or a doctorate degree in education from an educational institution registered with the state, had at least one year of experience practicing psychology, and had passed an examination given by the board. The act prohibited the use of the title "certified psychologist" by anyone not so certified by the board. Any false representation as such was punishable by a fine of $500, but such conduct was deemed a violation and not a misdemeanor.[23]

The time for state legislatures to "tidy up a bit," as Steiner called it, had come. However, psychologists' legislative success in Connecticut largely stemmed from their decisions to bypass all intra- and interprofessional controversies. According to Karl F. Heiser, a member of the Connecticut

Society's Council of Directors and one of the three appointees to the new board of examiners, the bill limited certification to basic training and general ability instead of establishing standards for clinical and industrial psychology. He attributed this limited scope to the "lack of professional agreement on duties, necessary training and standards of such specialists." Rejecting Britt's model act, Heiser said, "The status of psychology does not justify a strict definition of psychological practice, competence or training."[24]

The bill was sponsored by Representative Edwin O. Smith, a six-term Republican from Mansfield. It resembled legislation that had been introduced in Kansas six years earlier in both bills sought to distinguish certified individuals from others without restrictions on practice, similar to certified public accountant acts. In fact, during the bill's public hearing in mid-March, Smith had to assure a legislative committee that "this case [was] not a licensing act to prevent those of this profession from practicing" and it would not "draw a line around any group to exclude competition." During the public hearing, the legislative committee was especially concerned about the bill impeding medical doctors from practicing psychology. The Connecticut Society's president, Walter L. Miles, assured the legislators this concern was unfounded because the bill included a provision that authorized the board of examiners to waive the requirement for a doctor of philosophy in psychology. "This bill is not in any way aimed against medical men," Miles said. This unwillingness to hold medical doctors to similar standards as psychologists came as both professions were becoming acutely aware of the former's shortcomings in practicing psychology. For example, studies by the Omaha neuropsychiatrist Abram E. Bennett had revealed how psychiatric patients were grossly misdiagnosed with organic diseases that resulted in unnecessary surgeries. Bennett warned, "The result is a tremendous army of maladjusted persons going from doctor to doctor and receiving illogical medical and surgical therapies that only aggravate their personality problems."[25]

Less than a month after the July 1945 enactment of the Connecticut Certified Psychologists Act, the United States dropped an atomic bomb on Nagasaki, prompting Japan's surrender. In September, the reorganized APsychA was officially inaugurated. The world war ended as psychologists' war with the medical profession was just beginning.

Chapter 3
Hanging Up a Shingle

The war was over, and so was her marriage. Up until that fall of 1945, when she moved to New York City from Madison, Wisconsin, Molly Harrower had lived in what she called "the suburbs of myself." She rented an apartment on the Upper East Side and lived amid the "fantastic crags, that rise / That soar, triumphant, with a Titan's pose." She was thirty-nine years old, jobless, and financially unstable. She had even lost her dogs in her divorce from the neurosurgeon Theodore Erickson, which had been finalized earlier in summer. To her, the future lay ahead "with a big question mark." That, however, only fed her exhilaration, her "sense of rightness of what was happening, and an eagerness to accept the challenge of a totally unstructured life." It was under these conditions that Harrower famously declared in a poem, "Life, you will lose a lover when I die." That was the year she launched one of the nation's first private psychodiagnostic practices out of her home office at 118 East Seventieth Street.[1]

Up until her venture of "hanging up a shingle," Harrower had financially supported herself with research grants. To her surprise, the shift from research to private practice was simple. Within a few days of opening her practice, she started seeing a steady stream of patients referred to her by overwhelmed psychoanalysts and psychoanalysis-oriented psychiatrists. Initially, her core battery of tests included the Rorschach, Wechsler-Bellevue, and figure drawing, to which she later added several others. She employed these tests to measure patients' IQ (Wechsler-Bellevue), productivity (Rorschach), relation to reality (Wechsler-Bellevue, Rorschach, drawings), unusual thought content (Rorschach, most unpleasant concept), constructive fantasy (Rorschach), drive (Rorschach, most unpleasant concept), emotional tone (Rorschach, Szondi), and social attitude (thematic apperception test). Not wanting to divide her "living" and "working" lives, she saw her patients in her home office, allowing her to shuttle "back and forth, both literally and figuratively, without noticing the transition." She spent approximately three hours with each patient, and usually within the next three days she would send the referent a report with her summary of test findings, which also covered anxiety and an overall examination of personality.[2]

Private practice proved to be far more lucrative than she had imagined, its income dwarfing the monthly $150 research grant stipends on which she had lived for the past eight years. By the summer after she hung her shingle, she had found for herself a cottage on Long Island's north shore, initially furnished with only a card table, crates, couch, and "primitive appurtenances." For the next thirty-four summers, she would return to this idyllic spot with "swimming in the deep ocean at my door." Even though the divorce had been "shattering," whether in the city or on the shore, Harrower was thriving. She was independent and reaping the benefits of clinical psychology's elevated status, which she had helped raise during the war by pioneering Rorschach testing for U.S. and Canadian military personnel. Her practice—and the independence it provided—was wholly dependent on the medical profession.[3]

In New York, Harrower managed to build a thriving private practice and avoid the obstacles posed by sexism by tapping her "top military brass" contacts and accepting referrals from her former military colleagues. They turned to her for the psychodiagnostic evaluations that they had utilized during the war. Her tests helped their overwhelmed psychiatric practices become more manageable. By the end of her first year in the city, she was elected to the National Committee for Mental Hygiene. It was Harrower's first foray into public policy, and it almost consumed her thriving practice. Since 1919, the psychiatry-centered National Committee had also had an international arm, and Harrower was offered the new executive officer position as coordinator of the Preparatory Commission for the inaugural conference of the World Federation for Mental Health, scheduled for 1948 in London. Not wanting to put on hold for two years her "fast-developing four-way program of consulting, diagnosis, therapy, and research," Harrower withdrew her acceptance of this position a few days after giving it. This retraction, however, did not stop her rise as an emerging leader among New York City psychologists. She was later appointed vice-chair of the International Committee in Midtown and chair of the World Federation of Mental Health's Technical Advisory Committee.[4]

* * *

Harrower became involved in the mental health movement as the national dialogue shifted from fighting the war to fighting mental illness. Just as military leaders had heavily leaned on multidisciplinary research to win the war, those involved in the mental health movement did the same on this other front. It was a time, Harrower later recalled, when "psychologists had formed realistic working relationships with psychiatrists despite the legal battle over therapeutic 'turf' that was soon to develop."[5]

When President Harry S. Truman signed the National Mental Health Act on July 3, 1946, psychiatry became the federally appointed vanguard of the fight on mental illness. The act's purpose was "the improvement of the mental health of people of the United States through the conducting of researches, investigations, experiments, and demonstrations relating to the cause, diagnosis, and treatment of psychiatric disorders." Its focus on "psychiatric disorders" guaranteed psychiatry a leading role in this federal campaign for mental health and limited psychology's role in it. In September 1944, during a House subcommittee hearing on the act's predecessor bill, the National Neuropsychiatric Institute Act, the surgeon general of the US Public Health Service, Thomas Parran, had recommended changing the bill's title to the National Psychiatric Institute Act or National Mental Health Act. He had said the term "neuropsychiatric" could be too limiting by excluding psychiatric conditions caused by imbalances in the endocrine system or defects in the cardiovascular system. The term also excluded mental illnesses and mental maladjustments that seemed to be "purely psychic," and he cautioned that the term "may mask our ignorance of the basic biochemistry of the human organism." This scope, however, was too broad for Congress, which narrowly defined "psychiatric disorders" in the National Mental Health Act. These psychiatric disorders included "diseases of the nervous system which affect mental health," as had been recommended by the acting administrator of the Federal Security Agency, Watson B. Miller.[6]

The National Mental Health Act approved funding for developing a National Institute of Mental Health; maintaining state and local public health services; training mental health professionals such as psychiatrists, nurses, social workers, and clinical psychologists; and supporting research projects recommended to the surgeon general by the National Advisory Mental Health Council, which was also created under the law. With the law's enactment, psychiatry made a full advance into what Stanley Cobb three years earlier had called the profession's "borderlands."[7]

Meanwhile, psychologists had to walk the fine line of justifying their role in this initiative without ceding too much to psychiatry as it advanced into the borderlands. In his first appearance before a congressional committee, the APsychA's new secretary, Donald G. Marquis, stressed how the psychologist was a "member of a team of scientists and professional workers" who were "concerned with the problem of psychiatric disorders," particularly in the "devising and administration of measures for the prevention, the diagnosis, and the treatment of such disorders." Echoing Colonel Rowntree's call for "concerted efforts" a year earlier before another congressional committee, Marquis said the problems of psychiatric disorders were "so great as to demand the coordinated and concerted attack of all the sciences and professions." However, Captain Francis Braceland, the neuropsychiatric branch chief of the Navy's Bureau of Medicine and Surgery, went so far as to call the general medical practitioner—not the psychologist—"the first line of psychiatric defense." He held out prophylactic measures as key to "tomorrow's psychiatry," which on top of its traditional mission of "care for disease" would be concerned with "large-scale prevention."[8]

While physicians were reluctant to even acknowledge psychology when testifying on the National Neuropsychiatric Institute Act in 1944, the overwhelming demands on the medical profession's ranks after Japan's surrender made such a stance untenable. Those demands were most pressing at the VA, which by 1945 had been admitting thirty-six hundred veterans with neuropsychiatric diseases each month. Within two years that rate would increase to fifty-four hundred. Around 60 percent of VA hospital beds were devoted to neuropsychiatry, but only 2 percent of its doctors were trained in psychiatry. There were only approximately five thousand civilian and military psychiatrists in the United States, and demand projections called for two to four times that amount.[9]

It was a grim situation, and the responsibility for its improvement fell on Daniel Blain, the War Shipping Administration's medical director. Blain had run a successful rest center program for merchant marines suffering from convoy fatigue, a type of war neurosis. This program involved the creation of resort-like rest centers designed to "simulate [a] home-like environment" for merchant marines. Those service members' ratio losses were 400 percent higher than that of all of the armed forces. At the recommendation of the APA's president, Blain was appointed as the director of Neuropsychiatric Services of the VA in October 1945. He was forty-seven years old, and up until 1941, when he had joined the US Public Health Service, he had been affiliated with several private institutions that stood as new alternatives to psychiatry's hospitalization model. These clinics provided mentally disturbed individuals with a therapeutic environmental change in bucolic northeastern settings. Following his graduation from Vanderbilt University Medical School in 1929, he had interned in pathology and medicine at the Peter Bent Brigham Hospital in Boston and did his residency under Stanley Cobb at Boston City Hospital. His subsequent fellowship at the Austen Riggs Center in Stockbridge, Massachusetts, would later serve as an inspiration for the rest center program he developed for the War Shipping Administration and his subsequent VA work.[10]

In western Massachusetts's Berkshires, the Austen Riggs Center's namesake internist had developed a therapy regimen for psychoneuroses that, much like Blain's rest resorts for merchant mariners, had provided a temporary environmental change. Riggs believed nervousness was the result of multifaceted conflicts waged on reflexive, instinctive, intellectual, social, and ethical levels. When people were under the pressure of emotional strain, Riggs believed, nervousness produced symptoms, causing in certain individuals an overreaction or "overmobilization." The environmental change, coupled with a structured routine that included reeducation classes, exercise, rest, and craftsmanship tasks, removed the strains patients would face at home or work.[11]

Following his 1932 fellowship at Austen Riggs, Blain had worked at the Silver Hill, a private hospital in New Canaan, Connecticut, founded by one of Riggs's protégés, and Blythewood Sanitarium, another private institution in Greenwich, Connecticut. In 1938, Blain and his former Austen Riggs colleague John A. P. Millet established the Tratelja Farms Sanitarium, an eight-hundred-fifty-acre estate consisting of two working farms at Diamond Point, near the southwestern shore of Lake George in New York's Adirondacks. The founders' aim had been, according to Millet, "to demonstrate the possibility of providing modern methods of medical and psychiatric treatment at a lower cost than is possible in the usual small private sanitaria and psychotherapeutic centers." At Tratelja, patients had been assigned various outdoor occupations; they had performed gardening or construction and indoor jobs, such as weaving or upholstery. This work conducted by patients had been designed to help reduce operating costs while at the same time offering first-class treatment to low-income patients. Deviating from Riggs's approach in Stockbridge, psychiatrists at the Adirondack sanitarium had subjected patients to psychoanalysis and electroshock therapy. Riggs had been staunchly opposed to Freud, though his approach had likewise prioritized the exploration of each patient's personal experiences by allowing him or her to talk at length about them. Millet described Tratelja Farms as a combination of "something of the insight of Freud, the craftsmanship of Austen Riggs and the freer vision of those who face a changing civilization with the determination to adapt to whatever lies ahead, and to keep their conceptual hypotheses free from prejudice."[12]

Blain had served as Tratelja Farms' associate director until 1942, when he entered the US Public Health Service and was commissioned as a medical officer with the rank of lieutenant commander. By 1945, more than one thousand men had been treated at the rest homes he had established for the War Shipping Administration in conjunction with the United Seamen's Service. When he became the chief of the VA's Neuropsychiatric Division that year, his experience with, and focus on, outpatient care proved vital. The VA projected to have 132,000 nervous cases for hospitalization by 1965, and Blain planned to reduce that number by 25 percent through an expansion of the administration's outpatient clinics. Twenty-nine such clinics were operating under direct contracts with the VA by 1947.[13]

Within its first few days of operation in 1946, for example, the VA's New York City mental hygiene clinic received serval hundred applications from veterans seeking admission, and in later months it was processing up to fifty new patient requests daily. Blain saw clinical psychologists and clinical social workers as crucial to enabling psychiatrists to manage this overwhelming demand. He envisioned there being one clinical psychologist and two clinical social workers for every psychiatrist at a clinic. Together, they enabled psychiatrists to take on five to ten times more patients. Blain singled out clinical psychology's methods as representing "one of the most fruitful elements in preventive psychiatry."[14]

Blain valued clinical psychology mainly because it promised to strengthen psychiatry's claim of exclusivity to the diagnosis and treatment of mental disorders and diseases. At a time when he was preparing the VA for an influx of inexperienced psychiatrists, he believed clinical psychology's improved diagnostics could "supplement experience" and better evaluate therapeutic methods. The multiplying effect clinical psychologists had on psychiatrists' patient loads was also doubly important in view of the radically expanded scope Blain had for his profession. At the National Conference of Social Work in Buffalo in May 1946, he noted how psychiatrists' attention had traditionally focused on the 6 percent who were "sick." However, he declared, "[It is] the 94 per cent who are well who are the most important. Mental health is more important than mental disease." Blain said medical science's "chief reason for existence" was "in changing sick people into healthy people and in keeping the healthy from getting sick." This strategy was even more aggressive than Cobb's proposed advancement into the "borderlands" because it placed the entire US population under psychiatry's jurisdiction.[15]

Well aware of how this national mental health plan hinged on his success at the VA, Blain said at the conference that psychiatry and the medical profession were then "in both an enviable and a dangerous position." He continued: "Faced with the task of stemming a rising tide, they have a glorious opportunity for national service. If, however, they fail to exert leadership and to deal successfully with mental diseases and maladjustment, the prime responsibility will be taken away and will fall into the hands of others."[16]

***

However, those "others," such as consulting and pastoral psychologists, were already lining up to compete with psychiatry, regardless of whether it succeeded in stemming the rising tide at the VA. For example, that year May opened a private psychotherapeutic practice in New York City, even though he was still years away from completing his doctoral thesis. Rogers, also in 1946, published his *Counseling with Returned Servicemen*. In this postwar primer on nondirective counseling, Rogers and one of his Ohio State graduate students, John L. Wallen, warned that returning service members would have to confront problems from which they had been removed, such as parenting children born while they were away, having a wife who went to work during the war, going back to a job, or pursuing more schooling. Whatever the problem was, a nondirective counselor needed to be less focused on "eliminating the manifest problems that the client has stated" and more concerned with providing "an environment in which the client [could] grow to increased self-understanding."[17]

At the same time, Rogers's protégé in Syracuse, Combs, was also using the nondirective approach to counsel returned veterans. Meanwhile, in New York City, the pastoral psychologist Seward Hiltner was positioning the clergy to meet the needs of returning service members. As executive secretary of the Federal Council of Churches' Commission on Religion and Health, Hiltner helped develop a series of pamphlets designed to help the clergy understand returning veterans' attitudes and problems. Hiltner saw the return of so many veterans as posing one of the church's greatest challenges, especially in regard to creating "a thorough understanding of their specific attitudes and problems." Harry Bone, who was then teaching a course with Hiltner on pastoral psychology at Union Theological Seminary, contributed to the Federal Council of Churches' first pamphlet. Bone emphasized how important it was for ministers to "listen uncritically and to remember that they [could not] solve the problem of the serviceman, only help him to help himself."[18]

Bone was a close friend of and mentor to May. Their relationship appears to have started in the mid- to late 1930s through their involvement in New York City's Young Men's Christian Association (YMCA) or student Christian lecture circuits. Bone was a native of Topeka, Kansas. Prior to receiving his doctorate in psychology from the Sorbonne in Paris, he had briefly attended Union Theological Seminary and emerged as a leader in the executive corps of the YMCA. In 1929, Bone coauthored a book on *The Sex Life of Youth*, though it ignored Freud's theories on the topic. Shortly after that he went to the Sorbonne in Paris to work on a doctorate in psychology. It was around this time that Otto Rank was, as one historian observes, "moving toward a kind of religious psychotherapy." That may explain why Rank accepted the pastoral psychology–oriented Bone under his wing. During the summer of 1934, Bone, then thirty-five years old, helped Rank establish his Psychological Center at the Cité Universitaire. Anaïs Nin went to the center at Rank's request and befriended Bone there. Compared to the "big, loud, overflowing" American artist Hilaire Hiler, who had also been attending classes at the center, Bone, said Nin, was "the cool one, [with] a high brow, laughing eyes, a stiff poise." Nin said that after having lunch with Bone and listening to him talk about Rank, she knew the teacher "more as a human being now than as a man of ideas." By 1935, Bone was practicing as a consulting psychologist in New York and lecturing on the "Psychology of Personality" at the YMCA's central branch on Third Avenue.[19]

It was two years later when May reentered New York City's Christian student community, after years of struggling to financially support his family. During the spring of 1934—only a few months after he had enrolled at Union Theological Seminary—May learned his parents had divorced. That prompted him to leave New York for East Lansing, Michigan, "to take care of what was left of [his] family—[his] mother and younger sister and brother." He got a job as the student YMCA secretary at Michigan State College and the director of men students at a church in East Lansing. By the summer of 1937, he was in the South lecturing student workers of the Methodist Episcopal Church on "Counseling and Personality Adjustment." By that fall he was back in New York, serving as the director of students' Christian activity at New York University.[20]

At some point, May met Bone, who wrote the introduction to the young pastor's 1939 book, *The Art of Counseling*, which was based on his lectures in North Carolina and Arkansas during the summers of 1937 and 1938. May acknowledged Bone's "indispensable aid" in its preparation. Even though May left the pulpit two years after this book's publication, he and Bone remained close, with Rank being a major influence on both of them. In fact, next to Paul Tillich, Rank played one of the greatest roles in shaping May's early theories for opposing the application of a purely scientific approach to human understanding. For example, in *The Art of Counseling*, May seized Rank's criticism of Freud's "natural science psychology," which was "led astray in its theories of ultimate determinism in personality." May added it was "sheer folly" to hold "that the whole of the creative, oftentimes unpredictable, certainly intangible, aspects of human mind can be reduced to cause-and-effect, mechanistic principles." A year later, in his second book, *The Springs of Creative Living*, he noted how Rank's will therapy "emphasizes the present of the patient rather than the past, and the willing of the individual rather than the causological factors."[21]

Bone and May's rapport continued to strengthen as they participated in the New York Psychology Group, which had been formed in 1941. This group consisted of psychologists, psychiatrists, theologians, anthropologists, and others who gathered for quarterly meetings at various members' apartments at which they debated the psychology of faith and love as well as ethics and psychotherapy. Several of its prominent members included Seward Hiltner, Paul Tillich, and Erich Fromm. May's participation in the group, however, ceased with his contraction of tuberculosis in 1942. Rogers attended several meetings during the group's final year, in 1945.[22]

* * *

At the first postwar national meeting of the APsychA's Military Division in Philadelphia in September 1946, Blain elaborated on the scope of duties for VA psychological staff and delivered a sobering outlook for the profession of psychology. Blain described psychology and psychiatry as "brothers" with a history of not "uniting against a common outside threat" and tending not "to protect each other under any circumstances." These brothers did "not see eye-to-eye on many things, but are now sincerely looking for some common basis on which to determine the proper clinical functions of each." Illustrative of psychologists' reluctance to see eye-to-eye with psychiatrists, Blain observed how various presenters at the conference danced around the "moot problem of the proper distribution of functions of psychiatrist and psychologist in relation to the patient." It reminded him of "the way Tom Sawyer and his enemies used to challenge each other—'I dare you to step over that line.'"[23]

Unlike the psychologists, though, Blain did not hesitate in stepping over that line. He acknowledged how during the war, when there had been a shortage of physicians, psychologists had often been "called upon to assume the major responsibility for psychiatric cases and do the best they could." Now that the exigencies of the war were behind them, Blain said it was time for psychologists to operate solely within the scope of their training and that "it is in the realm of therapy that the psychologist is probably least trained and experienced at this stage of the development of the profession." He did not explicitly place diagnosis outside the competencies of psychologists, but he noted that this task demanded "knowledge of the structure and physiology of the organic parts of the body-mind machine." He was especially critical of the practices of the "untrained person" in "alleviating emotional ills," which was more of a correlative than causative effect facilitated by the person's "innate character and interest in other human beings." Drawing what would stand as a line in the sand for the next decade during the battle of the professions, he declared, "I deplore the demand that people who are frequently undeserving because they lack proper background be accorded responsibility in carrying out a complicated technical therapeutic process."[24]

Five days after Blain's May 1946 address to the National Conference of Social Work in Buffalo, he and fourteen other prominent psychiatrists informally gathered in New York City to form the Group for the Advancement of Psychiatry (GAP). Also at GAP's first meeting was Robert Felix, chief of the US Public Health Service's Mental Hygiene Division and an architect of the National Mental Health Act of 1946. According to historian Gerald N. Grob, William Menninger drove the GAP's formation, believing psychiatry needed to play a more active role in influencing cultural and environmental factors beyond the scope of diagnosis and treating mental illnesses. They capped membership at 150, and shortly afterward three members were elected to the Council of Representatives of the APA in unprecedented, contested elections. The GAP emerged as a political force that quickly evoked resentment from association traditionalists, who suspected the social change–oriented advocacy group would steer psychiatry away from its roots in medicine and unjustifiably broaden its scope.[25]

In late 1944, the APA council authorized the association's president to appoint a five-person Special Committee on Reorganization tasked with recommending a candidate for the new full-time position of medical director. Karl Menninger believed it was imperative for American psychiatry to define its purpose and goals, and his special committee favored the appointment of a medical director as a "feasible step" to achieve that end, according to Grob. Meanwhile, the more biology-leaning psychiatrists believed their psychodynamic counterparts were attempting to hijack the association and this proposed medical director could become a dictator. Wanting to quell concerns that this new position would undermine the association's democratic roots, Menninger's special committee, in May

1946, instead recommended the creation of a medical adviser position. In October 1947, the special committee recommended Blain for this position, which the council accepted and the association's president announced the following February. However, with Blain disapproving or the title "medical adviser" as too weak and vague, he was named, as originally proposed, medical director.[26]

Blain's charge included providing "psychiatric advice and information in connection with the administrative office of the Association." His services would be available to members, affiliate societies, the general public, private organizations, and universities. The association described him as providing "authorized consulting and advisory service in the general field of psychiatry." The medical director's office was in Washington, DC. By March 1948, Blain was working there on a part-time basis as he wrapped up his duties with the VA, and he shifted to full-time in the fall. Through the creation of the medical director position and Blain's appointment to it, the APA erected one of the greatest barriers to psychologists' resurging efforts to attain legal recognition of their profession. In him, New York's psychiatrists also gained a powerful new ally.[27]

Part 2

Tensions

Chapter 4
Insurgency

A breakthrough for the professionalization of psychology seemed imminent. That was, until after the emergence of an insurgency in Harrower's living room.

It was the winter of 1948. A bill for the certification of psychologists was advancing rapidly through the senate in Albany. On February 2, 1948, Senator Thomas C. Desmond, a Newburgh Republican in his ninth term, introduced legislation authorizing the New York State Education Department to regulate the use of the title of "certified professional psychologist." It was a title that the bill reserved for a psychologist who was at least twenty-one years old, was of good moral character, was a US citizen or someone who had legally declared the intention of becoming one, was the recipient of a doctor of philosophy in psychology, had at least one year of experience deemed satisfactory by a board of examiners created under the legislation, and had not failed an examination given by that board in the last six months. The introduction of the bill, which was projected to cover one thousand psychologists statewide in education, industry, and clinical work, was widely publicized in newspapers. "Desmond Bill Would Affect Psychologists," read one headline; "New Desmond Bill Would Bar Quack Doctors," read another.[1]

To much less fanfare, Desmond had introduced a similar version of the bill a year earlier. Prior to the introduction of the 1947 bill, no such legislation for the certification of psychologists in general, as opposed to school psychologists, had been introduced in the state. Since the New York

Academy of Medicine's evisceration of the ACP's draft legislation in 1937, efforts to attempt legal certification had largely been abandoned in Albany. In fact, at its annual meeting in Albany in January 1946, the NYSAAP's Committee on Certification had recommended relaunching the association certification program that it had created at the medical profession's recommendation a decade earlier but that had been suspended during the war. The NYSAAP committee acknowledged, "It will be impossible to prevent poorly qualified people from advertising themselves as psychologists until a system of legal certification of psychologists is established." However, the association "felt that it would not be feasible at this time to attempt legal certification, although this is the ultimate goal of the certification program." The NYSAAP adopted this recommendation, and the only difference between the requirements for membership in the association and for certification was the former required a PhD with one year of supervised experience in the application of psychology, whereas the latter required a year of supervised clinical psychology experience plus an additional year of clinical field experience.[2]

The NYSAAP's Committee on Certification had believed "more experience with the problems of certification is necessary before any type of legislation can be sought." However, the introduction of Desmond's bill forced the association, which two months earlier had reorganized into NYSPA, to lobby for the bill. Desmond had been interested in the problems posed by quack psychologists since 1946, one year after the publication of Lee Steiner's *Where Do People Take Their Troubles?*, which was largely based on research she had conducted in New York City. Desmond's interest in this issue also came during the same year that the San Diego City Council had passed an ordinance requiring the licensing of "professions, businesses, trades, lings and occupations" conducted within the city. Despite frequently being referred to as the first psychologist licensing law, it provided only a license in name, because anyone, regardless of educational background or experience, could obtain a legal document identifying the holder as a "psychologist" by paying a twenty-dollar annual fee. Also in 1946, Virginia's governor signed a bill for the certification of clinical psychologists. The Virginia law exemplified clinical psychologists' ability to leverage their close professional relations with members of the politically influential medical community to secure legislation that was favorable to their specialty at the expense of the greater profession.[3]

***

As organized psychology pushed for general legislation, whether certification or licensing, clinical psychologists such as Harrower believed their ties to the medical profession could still lend their specialty an advantage. At the Canadian Psychological Association's annual meeting in April 1947, she noted how "the spectacle of the psychologist knocking for admittance at the pearly gates of the medical world was a novel, if not a startling, sight." With a thriving part-time private practice in New York City that was largely dependent upon psychiatrists, Harrower had no apprehension about approaching the "medical St. Peter."[4]

Holding this opinion, Harrower, either intentionally or unintentionally, started to become a valuable asset in the medical profession's campaign against lay analysts. With Macy Foundation support, Harrower by fall 1947 was collaborating with Lawrence S. Kubie, a psychiatry professor at the Yale University School of Medicine and a practicing psychoanalyst in New York City, on a study about the qualifications of lay analysts in the city. Kubie's interest in this study with Harrower had likely stemmed from his vision for the widespread adoption of programs for a doctorate in medical psychology. He recognized that the twelve to sixteen years it took to train specialists in psychoanalytic psychiatry was too long for the profession to keep up with demand. In the late 1940s he began aggressively advocating for a new curriculum for a doctorate in medical psychology requiring six to eight years of study. He envisioned there being twenty thousand of these nonmedical psychoanalysts whose services would be more educational than therapeutic; they would "educate young people before they are wed in the job of parenthood."[5]

Harrower had no intention of publicly releasing the results of her lay-analyst survey due to its confidential nature. Regardless, few lay analysts responded to the questionnaire she sent, owing, presumably, she said, "to a fear that it would in some way influence their position." This unresponsiveness, which Harrower believed was "in itself an interesting result," was not surprising—not when the president of what was arguably the nation's most anti–lay analysis organization, the NYPS, said her research was "commendable." In fact, Harrower's August 1947 letter to Adolph Stern, the society's president, requesting the names of lay analysts to whom she could send questionnaires, appears to have triggered an investigation within the organization of the legality of lay analysis. One month later, the NYPS's executive secretary requested from the New York Psychiatric Advancement Committee a draft opinion for official use on whether it was necessary to be a physician to practice psychoanalysis.[6]

At the time of this inquiry, thirteen years had passed since the first successful prosecution of a lay analyst for practicing without a license under the state's Medical Practice Act. However, the conviction of May Benzenberg Mayer had never been appealed to the state's highest court, as the prosecuting deputy attorney general had hoped, leaving it a nonprecedential case. Mortimer Edelstein, a lawyer representing the New York Psychiatric Advancement Committee, noted that this case had aligned with the opinion of a Medical Society of the County of New York's Committee on Civic Policy. In 1933, the county society had issued a report declaring that psychoanalysis was a method of "diagnosing and treating nervous and mental diseases and cannot be legally practiced except by licensed physicians." Edelstein did not know if organized medicine's attitude on this matter had changed since then, but, under his reading of the Medical Practice Act, the terms of the definition for practice of medicine did not in themselves answer the society's question. This definition read: "A person practices medicine within the meaning of this article, except as hereinafter stated, who holds himself out as being able to diagnose, treat, operate or prescribe for any human disease, pain, injury, deformity or physical condition, and who shall either offer or undertake, by any means or method, to diagnose, treat, operate or prescribe for and human disease, pain, injury, deformity or physical condition." Edelstein concluded, "It is not possible to predict accurately whether the practice of psychoanalysis by a layman would subject the analyst to legal action for violation of the Medical Practice Act. It is possible."[7]

Edelstein's analysis came a few months after Senator Desmond introduced his certified psychologist legislation, which sidestepped this question of the legality of lay analysis under the Medical Practice Act by not including a definition for the practice of psychology. By February 1948, the senator's bill was being supported by a reorganized NYSAAP that had just become NYSPS as well as the Metropolitan New York Association for Applied Psychology, the Upstate Psychological Association, the Association of School Psychologists, and the Rochester Psychology Society. Missing from the bill's list of supporters were groups representing the medical profession and clinical psychologists. Three weeks after Desmond announced the reintroduction of his bill, several of the state's leading clinical psychologists mobilized an opposition campaign against the legislation. They primarily opposed its failure to exclusively certify clinical psychologists. Even worse than this, in their eyes, was the bill's grandfather clause that proposed to grant a certificate to psychologists with five years of experience even if they lacked a PhD.[8]

Harrower emerged as a leader in clinical psychologists' fight against Desmond's bill. When it was reintroduced, she was already engaged in a similar campaign at the federal level, consulting with a VA branch in New England on the development of a policy for the use of clinical psychologists in psychotherapy. The branch's two top neuropsychiatrists had decided to allow clinical psychologists to perform psychotherapy for training purposes, but more therapeutic activities would not be permitted without joint approval from the APA, GAP, and APsychA. Working with the GAP's Committee on Clinical Psychology was Margaret Brenman, a senior staff clinical psychologist at the Austen Riggs Center; Harrower; and David Shakow, chair of the APsychA's Committee on Training in Clinical Psychology. Herbert I. Harris, the VA branch's chief neuropsychologist, expressed alarm to Harrower upon learning that many Boston-area psychology graduate students were "eager to embark in the private practice of psychology and psychotherapy as soon as they have obtained their doctorates." He said, "We feel that you are as strongly against such activity as we are, since the standing of all clinical psychologists will suffer severely from such attempts at private practice, and the possibility of distressing legal situations may also arise."[9]

Desmond's bill was a prime example of one of those "distressing legal situations," and Harrower rose to challenge it with the support of the fledgling New York Society for Clinical Psychologists (NYSCP). Convinced that Desmond's bill had "all the chances of being passed," more than one hundred clinical psychologists employed by public and private agencies on February 25, 1948, gathered at Bellevue Hospital. There they overwhelmingly decided to organize this group to "meet the problems of the professionally qualified practitioner in psychology." Harrower's living room had served as the "birthplace" of this organization, and it became politically active weeks before this mass meeting at Bellevue. Indicative of this group's close ties to the city's psychiatric community, it used the Kings County Psychiatric Hospital in Brooklyn as its temporary mailing address. The formation of this group was indicative of the growing ranks of clinical psychologists in

New York City and their spread outside of VA clinics and hospitals. By March the NYSCP's membership had swelled to 250 clinical psychologists from the greater New York City area. However, when Desmond reintroduced his bill, clinical psychologists were in the minority. Nationally, they accounted for 16 percent of the APsychA's membership. To amplify their voice within their own profession, the city's clinical psychologists relied on another profession with which they were uniquely allied: psychiatry.[10]

On February 17—fifteen days after Desmond announced his certified psychologist legislation—the NYSCP petitioned Morris Herman, the secretary of the New York Society for Clinical Psychiatrists and the associate director of Bellevue Hospital's Psychiatric Division. Tatiana Juzak, secretary of the NYSCP, said, "We are heartily in favor of the idea of certification but feel that the bill as it now is formulated would enhance rather than alleviate the evils against which it is directed." By not limiting certification to psychologists with clinical experience, the legislation threatened to put emotionally disturbed and mentally sick people in the hands of industrial, vocational, and educational psychologists and guidance counselors. That would "lead only to disaster both for the public and the profession." Juzak requested the New York Society for Clinical Psychiatrists "give Senator Desmond the benefit of [its] counsel." Further, Juzak said the public "would be adequately protected" through strict enforcement of the section of the state's Mental Hygiene Law pertaining to certified psychologists, even though it only addressed the role of psychologists in certain judicial proceedings. If a new certification method were to be pursued, Juzak said her society preferred it be administered by the commissioner of mental hygiene and not of Education Department, as proposed by Desmond. In essence, the NYSCP was advocating for the exact opposite of the type of legislation the APsychA's Planning and Policy Board had recommended less than a year earlier—one based on Virginia's certification law rather than Connecticut's. Juzak stressed the certification of clinical psychologists was "a very serious and important matter and deserves special consideration."[11]

What followed was the rapid mobilization of the New York medical profession's powerful lobbying apparatus. Within days of the NYSCP sending this grievance letter, the New York Psychiatric Advancement Committee and New York Academy of Medicine's Committee on Public Health Relations were collaborating to ensure Desmond's bill did not pass the senate, whose Finance Committee at the time was reviewing it. It was this academy committee that a dozen years earlier had dashed New York psychologists' last effort for legal certification. The Psychiatric Advancement Committee was essentially the political arm of the city's major psychiatric departments at Bellevue and Kings County Hospital, with its executive board consisting of psychiatrists, psychologists, and psychiatric social workers from these hospitals.[12]

Theodore S. Weiss, the Psychiatric Advancement Committee's executive secretary, called the bill "a very bad one," primarily because it required only one year of experience rather than the five years required of qualified psychologists under the Mental Hygiene Law. His preference for that law's standard was likely influenced by his prior experience as the psychiatrist-at-large for New York City's Department of Correction and as a psychiatrist for the Court of General Sessions' psychiatric clinic. He also opposed the proposed administration of the certificates by the Education Department and believed that task should be left to the commissioner of mental hygiene. Weiss wrote to Desmond and urged the senator to make these changes. There are indications Weiss made similar recommendations to the Senate Finance Committee's chair and the commissioner of mental hygiene, and he urged Edward H. L. Corwin, chair of the academy's Public Health Committee, to do the same.[13]

Underlying the medical profession's opposition was the conviction that only clinical psychologists, who were already officially subordinate to psychiatrists in the VA, were capable of adequately "working with emotionally disturbed and mentally sick people." With no consideration of the spread or value of nondirective therapy, Weiss opined to Corwin that rather than "protecting the public," the bill would achieve the opposite by affording "state sanction to those who are not adequately trained in the field of clinical psychology."[14]

Shortly after its formation, the NYSCP created a Committee on Certification and Legislation, headed by Florence Halpern, a master's-level clinical psychologist at Bellevue. She was a native New Yorker, forty-eight years old and entering the stage of her career that would later earn her the reputation as the "grandmother of psychology." She had started working at Bellevue in 1933, initially as an intern and later as a staff psychologist. In 1940, she had published a paper on her use of the Rorschach test to interpret the effects on schizophrenics of insulin-shock therapy, a treatment that put patients into deep comas through induced hypoglycemia.

The Bellevue psychiatrist Joseph Wortis had introduced this treatment to the United States in the mid-1930s, though its use at the hospital ceased in 1942 following the death of a patient. In 1943, Halpern cowrote *The Clinical Application of the Rorschach Test*, which writer Damion Searls calls "the most influential Rorschach book of all," despite being panned by many of her contemporaries. For example, while at the University of Wisconsin, Harrower said the authors' theoretical discussion was "disappointing" and they showed "a fundamental lack of appreciation of the method." Nevertheless, she said the book might "prove of interest and be somewhat of an eye-opener to psychologists and physicians in various fields who have not as yet realized the applicability of the method to their particular sphere of interest." Later in the 1940s, one area of interest in which Halpern became deeply involved was substance abuse. She conducted Rorschach-related research for the New York City mayor Fiorello La Guardia's Committee on Marijuana and the Research Council on the Problems of Alcohol.[15]

Likely in response to the reintroduction of Desmond's bill in February 1948, the Academy of Medicine's Committee on Public Health Relations created its own Subcommittee on Certification of Psychologists. Its chair was Stanhope Bayne-Jones, a retired army brigadier general and the president of the Joint Administration Board of New York Hospital–Cornell Medical Center. Other members included Harrower, S. Bernard Wortis at Bellevue, and Carl Binger, a psychoanalysis-oriented psychiatrist at Cornell University Medical College. The subcommittee held its first meeting at the Academy of Medicine's East Harlem office. Two days later Corwin sent a letter to Desmond detailing his problems with the certification bill. Within a week, the senator decided to "hold up passage of the bill," which had been favorably reported out of the Finance Committee and was on the third reading calendar of the senate. He charged the academy subcommittee with working out "a bill which would be agreeable not only to physicians, but also to the large number of psychologists who are for the bill in its present form." Indicative of how Desmond did not view it as a priority to turn the legislation for certification into one for licensing, he told Corwin, "Regardless of the distinctions that may be needed between the practice of psychiatry and psychology, it seems apparent that the public is in need of protection from the many 'quack psychologists,' who are now permitted to operate."[16]

* * *

The room made Karl Heiser uncomfortable. It was not so much the wood-paneled council room in the New York Academy of Medicine's headquarters that brought the forty-three-year-old psychologist discomfort, but rather the people sitting around its long table. As one of the men responsible for the nation's first certified psychologist law, in Connecticut, Heiser had been appointed by the APsychA to work with state associations interested in certification or licensing legislation. In the three years following the Connecticut law's enactment, Heiser had helped develop health and welfare policies in Austria (occupied by the Allies) and joined the University of Michigan in Ann Arbor, where he taught and evaluated other colleges' doctoral programs.[17]

Heiser slowly realized he had no allies in the academy's stately boardroom. In front of him sat seven people: Harrower and four other members of the Subcommittee on Certification of Psychologists, Corwin's assistant, and Halpern. Heiser watched Harrower closely for clues on where she stood on the questions before the subcommittee, but she wore a poker face. The subcommittee's chair, Bayne-Jones, asked him about the concepts behind the Connecticut certification law, and Heiser, likely in his trademark soothing voice, explained its general objective of establishing professional standards in statute. According to minutes from the meeting, he called the Connecticut law a "starting point from which the profession could work." Although Connecticut psychologists had believed it was too soon to define the profession's various fields, Heiser said a definition for the clinical field was currently possible because of its vast expansion over the past three years. When fields reached this point of becoming "clearly demarcated," Heiser said, psychologists needed to consider laws for licensing rather than certification. When Wortis asked about the law's effectiveness is curbing psychological quacks, Heiser admitted that "little had been done toward that objective." Bayne-Jones recognized that a certification law was only a "first step toward better control of the practice of psychology."[18]

Halpern came armed to the meeting with a statement of proposed standards drafted by the NYSCP. She insisted the bill provide for the certification of clinical psychologists and that it differentiate them from psychologists practicing in other fields. In addition to recommending three years of clinical experience for certification, the NYSCP wanted half of that time to be spent in institutions dealing with the mentally ill. While Halpern said this would have rounded out a minimum level of experience, it also would have ensured that every certified psychologist in the state was accustomed to being subordinated to a physician. Heiser noted that some doctorate programs, such as the University of Michigan's, already placed clinical psychology students at schools, clinics, and mental hospitals for training. Halpern emphasized the last type of training, saying, "Nothing can take the place of hospital experience."[19]

If there was to be a certification bill, however, the subcommittee believed it should define multiple fields of psychology or only clinical psychology. The subcommittee was indifferent to the fact that the inclusion of such definitions would turn it into licensing legislation. The APsychA's Policy and Planning Board had opposed the formulation of such specification in legislation, and Heiser told the subcommittee he personally favored certification. He said, "I am afraid [licensing] would have to include definitions of clinical psychology which I believe would be so edited by the medical society as to preclude anything that might be called psychotherapy unless under or in consultation with a physician." He added it was just as important for psychologists to guard their profession against such "fencing in" as it was for them to obtain certification or licensing. Regardless, Heiser resigned to the will of the subcommittee, saying that "the psychologists want whatever the doctors want and that there could be no bill until the two groups agreed." Not prepared to make a formal recommendation to Desmond, the subcommittee decided to meet again with other New York psychologists involved in the certification effort and planned another meeting. Heiser's feeling of discomfort did not leave him as he left the academy building. He hoped, but was not sure, the meeting "moved us all a bit forward instead of in reverse."[20]

A few days later, after his return to Ann Arbor, Heiser wrote to Harrower to express that sentiment as well as his "discomfort at what seemed really to be our 'testifying' to a comm. of the medical profession which is set up to advise the legislature on legislation for psychologists." He also fumed about the "clinical people's being impelled to take the problems to the people who are now concerned in it." He reiterated that the definitions favored by the subcommittee would more than likely require any practice of therapy conducted by psychologists be done under the supervision of a licensed physician. "Such statutory fencing in at this time would be disastrous—or don't you think so?" Heiser's question, negatively posed, hinted at his doubts about her alliance to the greater psychology profession, and they would soon prove to be not unfounded.[21]

Harrower responded pejoratively to what she called Heiser's "interesting memorandum." She accosted him for taking such a negative view of the academy and its motives. She dismissed his concerns and said, "There does not seem to me to be the slightest desire on the committee to impose anything on psychologists which psychologists do not want." However, she also stated the subcommittee viewed the draft legislation prepared by the NYSCP as being "a starting point of what psychologists themselves want," even though groups representing the majority of the state's psychologists had already endorsed Desmond's bill. She challenged his assertion that the "clinical people took their troubles to the Academy of Medicine," saying Desmond first approached it for feedback on his bill. She added, "[The clinical psychologists,] through me, asked that the Academy take note of their reactions." Further, she chided him for his "appraisal [that] has tended to emphasize a lack of agreement between psychologists and a particular group of medical men which . . . does not exist." She assured him she had never heard her medical colleagues express any interest to "'railroad' anything through." They were actually more "open minded and lenient" on the question of therapy than the GAP, whose meetings she had also attended."[22]

After assuring Heiser that his concerns were unfounded, Harrower declared, "Nothing whatsoever in the training of a psychologist to date enables him to do therapy." This inadequacy made the proposed requirement for psychologists to practice therapy under the supervision of a licensed physician "something that might actually bridge what is otherwise an impossible gap." She said she believed these meetings with psychologists would result in the subcommittee declaring, "We are not ready for legislation." With this letter, Harrower put the leadership of the APsychA and New York's psychological groups on notice that her alliances were with the medical profession. Her defection would be complete when she shared with Corwin her letter to Heiser as well as his memo to her. The seriousness of this action was not lost on Harrower, who confessed to Corwin that she had been "a little in doubt as to whether or not to pass this memorandum on to you." She justified her decision to share it, saying, "I feel I am a member of the committee more than a fellow psychologist of Mr. Heiser."[23]

Harrower's letter to Heiser was dated four days before the next subcommittee meeting. It is not clear as to whether he received it in time to notify the psychologists invited to attend the meeting of her hostility toward the profession in general and her pessimistic outlook for legislation. Stricken with laryngitis, she was unable to attend the June 9 meeting, leaving Bayne-Jones, Corwin, Binger, and Wortis to interrogate George K. Bennett, the president of both NYSPA and the Psychological Corporation, and Douglas H. Fryer, an associate professor of psychology at the New York University College of Arts and Sciences. Fryer was the former ACP president who had also advised Steuart Henderson Britt on the Model "Certified Psychologist" Act in the late 1930s. Bennett, like Britt, was an industrial psychologist who was also a past president of the APsychA's Industrial Division and the current president of the Society for Industrial and Organizational Psychology. Although the subcommittee's legislative review had primarily focused on the regulation of clinical psychologists, Bennett told its members that certification was equally important to educational psychology, which included vocational guidance. This was the field, he said, in which "victimization of the public is most likely to occur." He explained NYSPA's position on certification, saying that through the establishment of a legal minimum standard of training and experience, "self-ordained" psychologists would be thwarted in their efforts to build prestige. Such statutorily defined training was "all that can be asked now."[24]

As Heiser struggled to reach an agreement with the academy in 1948, Kentucky lawmakers introduced a bill for the "certification of clinical psychologists." Its minimum training standards were in line with those in Desmond's bill, requiring a PhD in psychology and one year of experience, but in the field of clinical psychology. To receive a certificate, applicants would also have to pass a written examination in psychology. What set the two apart was the Kentucky bill's inclusion of a definition for the "practice of clinical psychology." It was defined as follows:

> A person practices clinical psychology within the meaning of this Act who (a) renders to individual clients for fees or personal profit, any professional service requiring the application of recognized principles, methods, and procedures of the science and profession of clinical psychology, such as the administration and interpretation of standardized tests of mental abilities and personality characteristics, for the purpose of psychological diagnosis, classification or evaluation; or (b) for fees or personal profit, applies such psychological techniques for purposes of reeducation,

guidance or readjustment. Nothing in this definition shall be construed as permitting the administration or prescribing of drugs or in any way infringing upon the practice of medicine.

The bill was enacted March 25 and went into effect on June 17. Its scope was limited to the offering of services for a fee, as favored by Bennett in New York, but because of its exclusive focus on the specialty of clinical psychology, it was the type of legislation the APsychA and NYSPA were fighting against. Just as psychologists had used terms suggesting therapeutic methods, such as "reeducation" or "readjustment," to covertly extend their practice into therapy, the Kentucky bill used similar language but with the caveat that there must be no "infringing upon the practice of medicine" by any method. Kentucky law defined the "practice of medicine" as "the treatment of any human ailment or infirmity." The Court of Appeals of Kentucky had ruled that this meant "the practice of medicine shall be construed to be the attempt to effect the cure of such ailment by the application of some method without regard to the method used."[25]

As the summer of 1948 ended, sixteen states and the District of Columbia were exploring legislation for the certification or licensing of psychologists. Such statewide legislation had already been enacted in only three states, the last two of which were exclusively for clinical psychologists. Talks over options for certification or licensing legislation were set to resume in New York in the fall.[26]

Chapter 5
Dead Ends and Revivals

In early December 1948, George R. Wendt was getting anxious about a flight he would soon take from Rochester to New York City. Soon, representatives from NYSPA would meet in the city with those from the NYSCP, which, through its ties to the medical lobby, had amassed more political capital than that of the vastly larger and older psychology organization. During the war, Wendt had served on the National Research Council's Committee on Aviation Medicine, and since 1945 he had been the chair of the University of Rochester's Department of Psychology. Earlier that year, he had been appointed co-chair of NYSPA's Committee on Legislation, also referred to as the "Wendt committee." Its members included, among others, Harrower, Institute of Welfare research director Joseph McVicker Hunt, former NYSPA presidents John G. Peatman and Wallace H. Wulfleck, current president George Bennett, and president-elect Combs. The last was the Syracuse University psychologist who was a pupil of Carl Rogers and whose star was rising as he was readying his landmark book on phenomenology with Donald Snygg at Oswego State.[1]

The joint meeting would be held at Florence Halpern's Midtown apartment on December 10. "I suppose that no other meeting of N.Y. State psychologists which has occurred in recent years will be quite so important as this one Friday evening," Wendt said to Harrower. With a fifth of the country's psychologists being located in New York, he added, "Failure to agree on a course of action can delay the development of psychology a great deal. Taking the wrong course of action can be equally or even more damaging."

Wendt's emphasis on the importance of this meeting likely did not resonate with Harrower. She knew the New York Academy of Medicine's Subcommittee on Certification of Psychologists was, unbeknownst to the Rochester psychologist, already taking steps that NYSPA representatives would unequivocally denounce as the "wrong course of action." Harrower had reluctantly joined NYSPA's Committee on Legislation, at the request of Hunt. After the intense deliberations between the professions earlier that year, Harrower said she was "so sick of meetings and professional obligations." She agreed to apply for the Committee on Legislation position because "it would be wise if some kind of coordination occurred between the work of the medical group and the psychologists."[2]

Two weeks earlier, Bayne-Jones had circulated among his academy subcommittee's members, which included Harrower, draft legislation modeled after the Kentucky act that was already in effect in the commonwealth. The subcommittee described the bill as one for the certification of New York clinical psychologists, but its inclusion of a definition for the practice of clinical psychology—nearly identical to the Kentucky law—made it more akin to licensing legislation. Bayne-Jones defended this course of action, saying that the certification of all categories of psychologists was "neither necessary nor feasible" and that "clinical psychology [was] a special field of most appropriate concern to the New York Academy of Medicine."[3]

For several weeks, Harrower kept from Wendt and his fellow committee members the news that the academy was preparing a draft bill with a far narrower scope than they favored. She did not attend the December 10 joint meeting. Rather than cooperating with Wendt, Harrower accosted him, as she had the APsychA's legislative consultant, Heiser, for the way "psychologists resent the 'interference' of the Academy." She even blamed two letters that Wendt had mailed to Binger, of the Committee on Public Health Relations, for spurring the academy's involvement in this legislative matter. She then defended the subcommittee's dismissal of NYSPA's opposition to a narrowly tailored bill for the certification of psychologists in a specific field. She said, "Whether we like it or not, clinical psychology is a highly specialized branch of general psychology. Its closeness to the province of medicine makes it imperative that a smooth working relationship obtains here. The training of clinical psychologists is a matter of real concern for psychiatrists."[4]

On December 20, the academy's Committee on Public Health Relations approved the subcommittee's report for the draft legislation. Poor weather had led to the cancelation of Wendt's flight to New York City, making him miss the meeting. Before the full committee's action, Wendt had invited it to meet with NYSPA's legislative committee and the NYSCP "with a view toward coordination of several proposed or contemplated bills." Bayne-Jones's subcommittee had not yet been discharged, but he declined this offer, saying its members felt that "such work is outside our terms of reference." In late December, the Committee on Public Health Relations forwarded the draft bill to Senator Desmond, who told Bayne-Jones that "thorough study will be given to the draft, and effort will be made to secure agreement to the proposal by the psychologists group, and the commissioners of education and mental hygiene."[5]

Such agreement would prove to be elusive. On January 7, 1949, seventeen representatives from NYSPA, the APsychA, the Conference of State Psychological Associations, the NYSCP, and academia and industry gathered to discuss the academy bill. They reached the unanimous conclusion that it stood "no chance" of passing the legislature because it would "excite the immediate opposition" of psychologists, vocational counselors, personnel workers, and others in state agencies. Wendt dismissed it as "unworkable to us." The psychologists' list of grievances included the fact that the academy bill was for licensing—not certification—and it would "prohibit the normal activities of several thousands of ethical employees in psychology, industry, education, the state departments and other agencies." Further, by focusing on a single field, the bill would "induce the fragmentation of psychology" and "invite evasion of the law" due to the "generality of applications" under the definition of the practice of clinical psychology. The bill's requirement that all psychological rehabilitation be conducted "in conjunction with a qualified physician trained in psychiatry" was especially burdensome given that, in Wendt's estimate, 80 percent of the services rendered by psychologists in clinical psychology were "wholly non-medical in nature."[6]

The threat against their profession that the academy bill represented served as a unifying cause for the patchwork of psychological and related associations in the state. At a January 9 meeting, their representatives agreed on the "key clauses" of a certification bill. Wendt described this development as an "important achievement, since we have searched long to find legislative devices which would meet the immediate need of protecting the public without at the same time ruinously affecting the long-run health of the profession which serves the public." This intraprofessional achievement, however, mattered little without interprofessional agreement. Desmond stressed to Wendt, "It is important that you get together with the New York Academy of Medicine if at all possible, and try to reach an agreement." Wendt implored Harrower to assist in facilitating a meeting between Bayne-Jones, Binger, Corwin, and Wortis from the academy and a handful of New York psychologists. However, Bayne-Jones did "not see how a meeting such as the one proposed could result in agreement on the criticisms." He advised Wendt to draft his own bill and present it to Desmond. Then, during legislative conferences or hearings, legislators would "formulate a more inclusive bill than the one we submitted." What Bayne-Jones likely did not say—and what Wendt presumably knew—was that the medical lobby would exert far more influence in this legislative process than would its counterpart in psychology. Despite her earlier assertions that the academy would not "impose anything on psychologists which psychologists do not want," Harrower found herself apologizing to Wendt over the fact "that we could not all have gotten together and pushed a bill through which was satisfactory to all of us." Nevertheless, she justified the academy's bill, saying it had "contributed in some measure to the clarifying or ideas of the bulk of persons involved.[7]

For New York's psychologists, it was a lesson on the political strength of the medical lobby and evidence of how interprofessional cooperation was a dead end. For New York's psychiatrists and clinical psychologists, the status quo remained, and that was all they needed to retain their leading role in the rapidly expanding mental health field.

* * *

Clinical psychologists' honeymoon with the medical profession did not last long, at least when it came to their partnership in shaping public policy relating to the regulation of psychologists in New York. Fractures in their partnership began to show in January 1949, when one or more representatives from the NYSCP joined those of other psychological and related groups in holding that the state legislature would never pass the academy bill that had been forwarded to Senator Desmond. Whoever represented clinical psychologists at the meeting, however, did not speak for the entire society, as some, including the chair of its Public Relations Committee,

Jerome W. Kosseff, continued to publicly support the academy's bill. Not a year had passed from when the NYSCP played a major role in convincing the academy to mount opposition to Desmond's certification bill, and New York's clinical psychologists were already collaborating in the Wendt-led effort to reach consensus on key clauses for new certification legislation.[8]

Even before the academy's Committee on Public Health Relations approved of the licensing bill, the AMA escalated its attacks on quack psychologists and the inadequacy of the legislative measures enacted to deal with the problem. The November 1948 issue of *Woman's Home Companion* featured "Beware the Mind Meddler," by Morris Fishbein, *JAMA*'s editor. In the article, which also appeared three months later in *Reader's Digest*, Fishbein said there was "an imperative need in this country for the control of a new kind of quack: today's untrained 'psychological expert.'" He emphasized that quacks frequently used the title of "clinical psychologist" and said only legislative measures could "control these psychological witch doctors effectively."[9]

Fishbein, however, panned the three existing state laws and one municipal ordinance that attempted such control as lacking the "adequate standards stipulating who may and who may not dispense psychological advice." Hampering lawmakers' efforts to resolve this problem with licensing bills, such as those contemplated in New York, Connecticut, and Virginia, was a "lack of yardsticks with which to measure competence and incompetence." He blamed the psychological profession for not developing those yardsticks. He called on the APA, APsychA, and National Vocational Guidance Association to cooperate on establishing a board tasked with creating standards and certifying practitioners. Once that was achieved, he believed there would be "little difficulty in getting the forty-eight states to adopt legislation implementing their decisions." Given how the APsychA had wrestled with this issue for years and how its network of state chapters was limited, Fishbein's "little difficulty" comment was a gross overestimation of the association's influence.[10]

Fishbein's article irked clinical psychologists, who dismissed it as an AMA attempt to assert "control in this field [clinical psychology] rather than public health." However, a more forceful rebuke came from New York City psychiatrists. Fishbein's suggestion that a "lack of yardsticks" was hindering licensing legislation for psychologists represented a break from the position New York's medical profession had held for more than a dozen years. Fishbein suggested that licensure was an acceptable path so long as "members of the profession can develop such standards." Taking issue with Fishbein's proposal was Samuel Parker, who was not only the director of psychiatric services at Kings County Hospital but also the director of psychiatry of New York City's Department of Hospitals. In a *New York Times* letter to the editor, Parker called competent and licensed psychologists and social workers "the very quacks who have created the problem." Fishbein's proposal, according to Parker, was "not only a betrayal of medicine, but the public as well." What states needed were modernized laws governing the practice of medicine so that they specifically included "mental and nervous disorders and diseases within the meaning of the law." Further, "any licensing on a purely academic basis, without a simultaneous enlargement of the Medical Practice Act, will give the psychologists just the feeling of medical legitimacy they desire to spread out."[11]

Parker's call for adding "mental and nervous disorders and diseases" to states' statutory definitions for the "practice of medicine" was a novel but not unheard of proposal. Over the past 10 years almost half of the states had at least vague references to mental afflictions in their physician licensing laws. Many of the states that were not contemplating certification or licensing legislation were instead eyeing basic science laws. Since the enactment of Wisconsin's basic science law in 1925, this type of law had spread by early 1949 to a total of seventeen states, plus the District of Columbia and Territory of Alaska. Among them, Connecticut was alone in having both a basic science law, enacted in 1925, and a psychologist certification or licensing law, enacted twenty years later. These laws required individuals to pass basic science examinations before treating the sick. Different states tested doctors and practitioners on different subjects, including chemistry, bacteriology, hygiene, diagnosis, and public health. In 1949, legislation was introduced to establish basic science laws in Texas and Utah. The Texas bill— staunchly opposed by chiropractors and supported by the Texas Medical Association—passed the state senate that July after "one of the longest— and at times one of the bitterest—battles in state legislative history."[12]

To Parker, all of the anecdotes of victims of psychological quacks detailed in Fishbein's article represented "clear-cut medical cases suffering from nervous and mental disorders." These cases included a melancholic and extremely shy college student who killed himself after taking a public speaking class recommended by a quack, and a disobedient eleven-year-old daughter who had a mental breakdown after her mother sent her to a boarding school, as recommended by a charlatan. Parker's stance on the medical nature of these cases—and medicine's claim to exclusivity in the treatment of them—likely stemmed from his training in Vienna in the 1920s. After studying at medical schools in Germany for two years, Parker in 1924 traveled to Vienna to complete his clinical work and to enroll in the Freudian Psychoanalytic Institute. In 1925, while enrolled at the University of Vienna, Parker met the Austrian psychiatrist and psychoanalyst Paul F. Schilder, and a year later the student began an analysis under him.[13]

Schilder's views on the mind-body dichotomy strongly instructed his own position on lay analysis in Europe and Parker's in America. Schilder was closely associated with European phenomenology, which, according to William Roller, "attempts to understand the conditions for our knowledge of the world by paying attention to and describing our very experience of the world." However, Schilder's phenomenology was very different in character from the kind Donald Snygg and Arthur Combs were pioneering in upstate New York in the late 1940s, largely because theirs grew out of Gestalt psychology and his was influenced by Edmund Husserl's concept of "intentionality." Husserl held "that all consciousness, including all thought processes, are directed towards objects in the world." In a 1926 article, Parker noted how Schilder employed a "biological approach to natural phenomena" to bridge the gap in understanding the mind that was created by the intuitive psychological method and the scientific, physical method. Schilder believed "the laws of the psyche and the laws of the organism are identical" and the two could be studied using the same methods. The phenomenological method alone, however, only provided "a description of psychic constellations at rest," but "resting psychic life is but an abstraction and that . . . takes on meaning only in the stream of becoming." Psychogenetic research, such as psychoanalysis, was also necessary for a complete understanding of the psyche, which was not static but "proceed[ed] in time," influenced by the past, and striving into the future. Brain pathology and experimental pathology were also needed, and the combination of these methods resulted in what Schilder called "eclecticism."[14]

In 1929, Parker became the director of psychiatry at the New York City Department of Hospitals. He also served as a senior alienist at Bellevue Hospital and lectured on psychiatry at New York University Medical College. In 1930, amid the Nazis' rise in Austria, Parker arranged for Schilder, a

Protestant Jew, to join Bellevue as its research director and New York University as a research professor. As he had been in Vienna, Parker was again Schilder's assistant in New York. Schilder joined the Psychoanalytic Society of New York, but his membership was later revoked because, according to Parker, "they considered him a maverick and not a real psychoanalyst." Freud, too, had believed Schilder operated in "too wide dimensions." In 1935, Schilder had founded the Society for Psychotherapy and Psychopathology, which was renamed the Schilder Society after his death. Schilder worked at Bellevue until his untimely death in 1940, when he was struck by a car on a city street. However, during his ten years at Bellevue he conducted a vast amount of research and influenced a generation of psychiatrists. He published important papers with psychiatrists such as Parker and Morris Herman, both of whom would play important roles in the following decade's legislative battles with psychologists. Iago Galdston, the New York Academy of Medicine's longtime spokesman, served as the president of the Schilder Society and was another Schilderian physician who would become an important player in the battle of the professions.[15]

Parker's letter in the *New York Times* represented a revival of the question of lay analysis that psychoanalysts—including Schilder—had debated more than two decades earlier after the Reik case. Parker's letter attracted sharp rebukes in the *Times* from psychologists. Grace Rubin-Rabson, a University of Indiana professor, said that by proposing an expansion of the definition of medical practice, psychiatry could "claim as its territory the mildest behavior disorder as well as the severest psychosis with organic components. Further, Parker was "laying on the shoulders of a few competent men in the medical profession a burden which they can never hope to carry." Kosseff, chair of the NYSCP's Public Relations Committee, likewise said it was "utterly impossible to see any virtue in Dr. Parker's argument against state licensing or certification of clinical psychologists. . . . It even leads one to wonder what Dr. Parker is really driving at."[16] That question about the endgame of Parker's proposed amendment—and how psychologists openly challenged and forced the medical profession to publicly defend it—was a key factor differentiating New York from other states that had already included language for mental ailments in their physician licensing laws.

One person who did see virtue in Parker's argument was Samuel L. Greenberg, a World War I veteran and Brooklyn Democratic senator. Prior to joining the senate in 1943, he had practiced law. Less than a month after Parker's letter ran in the *New York Times*, Greenberg introduced legislation proposing to amend New York's Medical Practice Act so the "practice of medicine" covered anyone who sought to "diagnose, treat, operate or prescribe for any human disease, pain, injury, deformity, *mental or nervous disorder*, or physical condition." In justifying the bill, Greenberg cited the position against lay analysis recently declared by Parker, whose Kings County Hospital was in the senator's district. Backing the bill was, among other medical groups, the Kings County Medical Society. "I believe firmly that doctors and doctors only should be permitted by law to treat patients suffering from mental and nervous disorders," Greenberg said. "I am sponsoring this measure in the hope that the quacks and fakers in this field may be eliminated." Greenberg's bill, however, was not the only antipsychologist bill introduced in a state legislature in 1949. In Indianapolis, where the Indiana Psychological Association was on record favoring licensing legislation, a state assemblyman who also worked as a physician drafted a bill that "would have seriously crippled the practice of psychology in the state." While the chair of Indiana's Senate Committee on Public Health saw the need for such a measure to eliminate abuses, psychologists convinced him this was not a good bill. He withdrew it with the understanding that the Indiana Psychological Association would enter its own bill when the legislature reconvened.[17]

The introduction of the Greenberg bill helped unify New York's psychologists in their opposition to it, though they largely fought it outside the public sphere. The *American Journal of Psychotherapy* did note that the NYSCP's new president, Arthur Teicher, had claimed the bill, if enacted, "would deprive emotionally disturbed individuals of the services of trained non-medical specialists and permit physicians who are not experienced in the specialty of psychotherapy to minister to the psychically ill." At thirty-five years old and having only received his master's degree from the City College of New York two years earlier, Teicher was the first in a line of feisty young leaders who were assuming leadership roles in New York's psychology community. During the war, he had conducted psychological evaluations at induction centers, and after his discharge in 1945 he had worked for the VA's New York regional office. When he became the NYSCP's first elected president, he was working toward his doctoral degree in psychology at New York University.[18]

Although the Greenberg bill did not pass the legislature, its introduction was quickly followed by the birth of a politically aggressive sect of psychiatry centered in Brooklyn. On March 7, 1949, more than a third of Brooklyn's psychiatrists banded together to form the Brooklyn Psychiatric Society. Its president was Sam Rothenberg, a borough practitioner, and Parker was its vice president. The bill's introduction was indicative of the changing public debate over the regulation of psychologists, especially from the standpoint of the medical profession. The question was no longer when circumstances would become appropriate for clinical psychologists to use psychotherapeutic methods—which the VA's Daniel Blain and Karl Menninger had said was not in the immediate future; the question became whether psychologists in any field should be allowed to practice psychotherapy at all or at least independently.[19]

As New York's psychologists were busy playing defense against the Greenberg bill, others in Pennsylvania were taking steps to counter the Pennsylvania Medical Society's procurement of a state attorney general's ruling. The attorney general a year earlier had ruled that the licensing of psychologists could fall under the state's Medical Practice Act. Fearing the medical society would use this ruling to severely curtail the practice of psychology, the Pennsylvania Psychological Association lobbied for licensing legislation in Harrisburg. One of the Pennsylvania Medical Society's demands for the bill, which the psychologists adamantly opposed, was the inclusion of the phrase "under medical supervision" in the definition of the practice of psychology. That April, Senator A. H. Letzler introduced a bill with the support of the state medical society. The legislation mirrored Kentucky's clinical psychologist licensing law in that it limited the use of psychological technique to reeducational guidance or readjustment. However, the bill died in committee later that month, and Pennsylvania's psychologists would have to wait two years before the legislature could take up nonfiscal legislation.[20]

A month after the Pennsylvania bill died in committee, the APA passed a resolution that further polarized the debate over psychologists' role in treatment. This action came at a turning point in the three-year-old intraprofessional war between the psychoanalysis-oriented GAP and the more traditional, biologically focused psychiatrists who formed the Committee for the Preservation of Medical Standards in Psychiatry. In the association's May 1948 presidential election, GAP's George S. Stevenson, head of the National Committee for Mental Hygiene, narrowly defeated the traditionalist candidate, C. C. Burlingame. This victory, according to historian Gerald N. Grob, symbolized the split within the APA between "those who emphasized the significance of the social environment, social activism in a community setting, and the importance of psychotherapy . . . [and] those committed to a more traditional institutional setting, and a greater emphasis on the organic aspects of mental disease and somatic therapies." The following May, the APA's council adopted two policies recommended by the GAP's Committee on Clinical Psychology: (1) "The Council is opposed to independent private practice of psychotherapy by clinical psychologists," and (2) "The Council feels that psychotherapy, whenever practiced by clinical psychologists, should be done in a setting where adequate psychiatric safeguards are provided."[21]

Later that summer the GAP committee elaborated on the reasoning behind this policy by issuing a report on the relation of clinical psychology to psychiatry. The committee warned, "The independent operation of clinical psychologists may lead to diagnostic error, the failure to detect serious psychiatric conditions in their early stages, or failure to recognize physical disorder which may be the basis of the maladjustment." Clinical psychologists, therefore, needed to maintain "close, continuous operation with the psychiatrist." It would also be insufficient for clinical psychologists to only associate with general practitioners or medical specialists because such arrangements would provide "medical but not psychiatric safeguards." While the APA's new policy was looser than Parker's position, in that it did not outright bar clinical psychologists from treatment, it did align with the stance of Parker's mentor. Shortly before his untimely death in 1940, Schilder had insisted that physicians physically examine patients before starting psychotherapy.[22]

As the medical profession's stance on psychologists' right to practice psychotherapy swung to one extreme, that of psychologists swung to the other. At the APsychA's annual conference in Denver in September 1949, the association's Conference of State Psychological Associations held a symposium on certification and licensing legislation. When the APsychA formed this conference three years earlier, it had fourteen state affiliates. By the time of the symposium that number had grown to twenty-five, with 2,000 members total. That was only slightly more than the 1,700 psychologists in New York spread across ten psychological organizations. The symposium largely presented academic discussions on psychologists' legislative options, similar to the one featured in the *Journal of Consulting Psychology* in 1941. However, the conference's chair, John G. Peatman, noted the recent emergence of "practical realities to deal with and deal with rather quickly." One of the pressing practical realities was the introduction of the Greenberg bill to amend New York's Medical Practice Act. Wendt, who chaired the conference's Committee on Certification and Licensure, declared, "There is a very healthy swing, today, however, away from certification and toward licensing." He called certification "ineffective" because "the public is not well-informed and tends to go to the person with the lowest fees, regardless of training or certification." By this time, Wendt was also chairing a subcommittee appointed by New York's commissions on mental hygiene and education to study the licensing of psychologists and to draft legislation for it. He believed the licensing bill he was preparing for New York had the potential for influencing efforts across the country.[23]

However, another APsychA conference in Colorado, held before the association's annual conference, would inadvertently complicate those efforts. This Conference on Clinical Training in Psychology was sponsored by the Public Health Service and became known as the "Boulder Conference," due to its location at the University of Colorado. It involved a gathering of seventy-one participants and set the course of clinical psychologist training for the next several decades. As a result of the conference, the group recommended that the title "clinical psychologist" should be reserved for people with a doctoral degree stemming from four years of graduate studies in clinical psychology. The Boulder Conference played a major role in the "scientist-practitioner model" for the clinical psychologist, who was supposed to receive graduate training built around both research and practice and then direct to university psychology departments vast sums of funds from the VA and Public Health Service. This influx of federal training monies, according to historian James Capshew, "prevented a significant increase in the overall completion time for the doctorate, providing a significant advantage over psychiatry with its postgraduate residency training." In laying the foundation for the elevated status of clinical psychologists, the Boulder Conference also emboldened them in wanting to stand out from other fields of psychology, in practice as well as in legislation. For example, in an *American Psychologist* published shortly after the Boulder Conference, Carlyle F. Jacobsen of the State University of Iowa noted how the higher training standards established at the meeting could justify licensing legislation exclusive to clinical psychologists.[24]

Chapter 6
Warning Shots

It was time. Time for him to finally come out from anxiety. By January 1950, nearly five years had passed since Rollo May had visited the Greenwich Village office of Lawrence Frank, who had set the graduate student on a new course for approaching his doctoral thesis on anxiety. During those five years, May had kept a low profile, publishing little and struggling to provide for his family. He had finished attending courses at Columbia's Teachers College in 1946, the same year he opened a private practice as a consulting psychologist, even though he lacked a PhD. In May 1948, May applied to attend lecture and seminar courses at the WAWI, but not for credit. Since the WAWI's first year in 1943, Erich Fromm had been keeping May informed on the development of the school. May spent the summer of 1948 writing and rewriting his doctoral thesis at a family lake retreat. He had anticipated receiving his PhD in the fall, but that actually did not happen until July 1949. Two months later he requested to be registered for three courses at the WAWI. He was eager to continue to work with his old mentor, Fromm, then the institute's chair of faculty.[1]

May was forty when he received his PhD. The heavy debts he had accrued during an extended period of graduate study had compelled him to work relentlessly. It was a drive that would keep his family solvent as much as it would fuel his rise within the city's psychological community. On Sundays he would take his three children for walks along the Hudson River and to the Museum of Modern Art. His daughter Carolyn recalled him being "a very serious, very dedicated and very private man." On top of his postgraduate studies at the WAWI, May was busy preparing for the transformation of his doctoral thesis on anxiety into a book, which was to be published by the Ronald Press. There was the tedious task of satisfying his publisher's demands that he secure permissions for all quotes in his book, *The Meaning of Anxiety*, and that he prepare promotional journal articles highlighting his findings. For the latter task he leaned on his theological roots and published a two-part series on anxiety in early 1950 in *Pastoral Psychology*.[2]

Wendt's time, too, had come. In January 1950, starting in Rochester, where he taught, he began publicly discussing the psychologist licensing bill he had helped a New York State Education Department–appointed committee draft. He had high hopes for the legislation. "We believe," he told the Rochester *Democrat and Chronicle*, "that action by the New York State Legislature could be very important, because other states generally follow the lead of New York in professional matters."[3]

On January 19, at a special NYSPA meeting at Hunter College, on the Upper East Side of Manhattan, Wendt unveiled his legislation. The bill defined the "practice of psychology" as the rendering of "any service involving the professional application of recognized principles, methods and procedures of the science and profession of psychology." The definition also included the undertaking "by whatever means to evaluate, appraise or classify mental abilities, personality characteristics, or personal or interpersonal maladjustment" as well as the performance of "psychological reeducation, psychological readjustment, psychological guidance or counseling." To practice psychology as a "licensed psychologist," a person would need a PhD in psychology and two years of supervised experience. The bill proposed to make the commissioner of education, rather than the commissioner of mental health, responsible for the regulation of licensed psychologists.[4]

An onslaught of opposition from within the profession erupted after Wendt detailed this legislation at the Hunter meeting. One of the most vocal opponents was Theodor Reik, whose legal problems nearly a quarter century earlier had inspired Freud's *The Question of Lay Analysis*. In 1938, Reik had emigrated from Holland to New York City, where he had famously feuded with the Freudian NYPS. The NYPS had extended membership to Reik, who lacked an MD, on the condition that he teach and not practice psychoanalysis. This offer was rescinded when he used his course at the New York Psychoanalytic Institute to speak disparagingly of the NYPS. In 1945, he started teaching at the WAWI, but shortly afterward the school temporarily ceased training nonmedical analysts. Reik took several students displaced by the institute's anti–lay analyst policy under his wing, and in 1948 they organized the National Psychological Association for Psychoanalysis.[5]

May, speaking on behalf of psychologists at the WAWI, similarly expressed concerns over Wendt's bill. May said it "should license a profession rather than a science." He likened the attempt to license psychologists in academia or research to licensing anatomy professors under the Medical Practice Act. May, however, added that the legislation would serve a "useful purpose" and the WAWI's psychologists would support it on the condition it be amended to the licensing of only practicing psychologists. Further, the proposed licensing examining board would have to consist primarily of practicing psychologists, and the bill's grandfather clause would have to be broadened to include psychologists with demonstrated competence in helping people with emotional problems. The *New York Times* identified May as the chair of the WAWI's group of psychologists.[6]

After psychologists criticized Wendt's bill, New York's medical professionals piled on their objections. At the national level, the APA registered its opposition to the draft bill when the APA's legislative consultant, Morris Herman, sought Blain's feedback on it. Blain, the APA's medical director in Washington, DC, referenced the anti–lay analysis policies the association had adopted the previous spring. He noted that Wendt's bill mirrored legislation that the Washington Psychological Association had recently lobbied for in the District of Columbia. Blain had led the effort against that legislation because, among other reasons, he objected to "the implied dichotomy between psychological and organic factors." He also opposed the way psychotherapy "could not very well be completely separated from diagnosis and other forms of treatment and could not, in a practical way, be isolated from total care of the patient." Blain told Herman it would be "very difficult to meet on common ground" and encouraged him to push psychologists toward certification legislation. "I personally do not wish to have any part of it and aid or abet it in any way," Blain said.[7]

Later in January, at a public forum at the New York Academy of Medicine, Iago Galdston, the academy's Schilderian spokesman, declared that psychotherapy was "the treatment of the abnormal" and in the treatment of the abnormal "there cannot be any such thing as lay psychotherapy."

He said that anyone practicing lay psychotherapy was a quack and that he counted clinical psychologists "among the laity," though he acknowledged their resourcefulness in diagnostic work. In some regards, this meeting, sponsored by the medical profession–backed Association for the Advancement of Psychotherapy, was reminiscent of the 1927 symposium on lay analysis, with Reik and Clarence P. Oberndorf again participating. Oberndorf was one of the New York psychoanalysts who had likened Freud's endorsement of nonmedical analysis to a "premature incision of an ugly-looking subcutaneous inflammation which has yet to come to a head." At the time of the symposium, he had been serving as the NYPS's president and believed "only to medicine and its many contributing and allied sciences can we look for the ultimate solution of the mystery of neuroses and the psychoses."[8]

Despite this opposition, on February 21, 1950, Assemblyman Leo P. Noonan, a five-term Republican and former school principal from western New York, introduced Wendt's psychologist licensing bill. It defined the practice of psychology as follows:

> A person practices psychology within the meaning of this act, except as hereinafter stated, when he renders to individuals or to the public any service involving the professional application of recognized principles, methods and procedures of the science and profession of psychology, or when he holds himself out as being able to, or undertakes by whatever means to evaluate, appraise or classify mental abilities, personality characteristics, or personal or interpersonal maladjustment, or to perform psychological reeducation, psychological readjustment, psychological guidance or counseling.[9]

Noonan's bill died in committee, a victim of intraprofessional fratricide. That prompted Arthur Combs's successor as NYSPA president, Joseph McVicker Hunt, the director of the Institute of Welfare Research at the Community Service Society, to recommend the formation of a more inclusive body of psychologists tasked with advancing licensing legislation in Albany. During the summer of 1950, thirty-five psychologists were selected to represent psychological organizations, training centers, geographical areas, and special interests in applied psychology. They were appointed to a newly created Joint Council of New York State Psychologists on Legislation, whose chair was Combs. Its vice-chairs were Harry Bone and Florence Halpern. The vote of each member of the Joint Council had equal weight, regardless of the size of the group they represented. The primary condition on members was that whatever bill the Joint Council decided on, they would make its passage "the number one on every agenda."[10]

The Joint Council set a budget of $15,000, and it sought to raise those funds from the state's seventeen hundred psychologists. While the fundraising campaign was underway, the Joint Council in late summer began discussing and revising Wendt's licensing bill. As the Joint Council's chair, Combs was its executive director and the moderator of its meetings at the Psychological Corporation's building in Midtown. But, more importantly, he was the liaison officer with other interested professionals, such as psychiatrists, and the spokesman for New York's psychologists in Albany. Combs took a leave of absence from his position at Syracuse University so he could spend the remainder of the year briefing various psychology groups around the state on the legislation. The medical profession, though, was left out of these talks because its legislative committee was not scheduled to meet until January.[11]

* * *

Meanwhile, psychiatry, under the direction of the GAP, was moving the APA away from the hard sciences and deeper into the broad sciences of human relations. As psychiatrists made these inroads with psychodynamics, psychologists did not offer much in terms of opposition. Throughout the last four years of NYSPA's lobbying efforts in Albany, psychologists had not contested organized medicine's assertion that psychiatrists' medical training not only made them capable of treating patients with emotional problems but also endowed them with the professional responsibility of overseeing clinical psychologists' limited therapeutic work. Although he was not yet associated with the Joint Council, May began formulating such a challenge to what he viewed as the hard sciences' overreach into the mental health field. May was working on a chapter in *Liberal Learning and Religion*, which would be published in 1951. In this essay, which would also be serially reprinted in *Pastoral Psychology*, May explored a topic that not only would become the theme of his next book but also was an unscientific and humanistic concept that many psychologists and psychiatrists wanted to avoid: the self.

The self, or selfhood, May said, was a dynamic union of "unconscious depths with conscious choices and direction," resulting in a "psychological and spiritual integrity which is characterized by the capacity—and practice—of judging one's actions by one's own inner criteria rather than by the vain and narcissistic standards of public (and parental) acceptance and applause." He acknowledged that some psychologists were "distrustful" of the concept of self because it got "in the way of scientific experimentation" and could not "be reduced to mathematical equations." But he warned against those who dismissed the self as "unscientific," just as others had done with Freud's concept of the unconscious a few decades earlier. May would later argue, "It is a defensive and dogmatic science—and therefore not a true science—which uses a particular scientific method as a Procrustean bed and rejects all forms of human experience which don't fit." What mattered, May said, was not proving that the self was an "object" but showing "how people have the capacity for self-relatedness."[12]

May identified one's alienation from oneself as a common element in nearly all of the problems that drove people to professional psychotherapeutic help. Whether it was a person's anxiety, sadomasochistic sexual patterns, or irrational compulsions that resulted in poor decisions about divorce or remarriage, the individual "cannot affirm himself as a being who has powers and desires, who can take responsibility and move toward self-chosen goals." Paul Tillich, May's mentor, called this estrangement from the self the "present crisis in civilization," which had been centuries in the making.[13]

Medicine and its affiliated disciplines, May said, were a product of this "cultural situation in which there was a dichotomy of mind and body." However, he stressed that an "increased emphasis on one side or the other or on both sides of the dichotomy will never overcome it." That emphasis had contributed to the "irrational" broad authority granted to medicine in modern culture. May deemed this unconditional faith in medicine as a holdover from the Renaissance. "One serious form in which this irrational authority appears is the tendency on the part of many people in our society to assume that emotional problems are medical problems because they happen to be mediated by the neurological and physiological bodily systems," he said. But he attributed these problems to "disturbed forms of an individual's relatedness to himself and to his world"; they involved "the 'whole' person acting and reacting to his environment, not the bodily part of the person." These problems "have more centrally to do with the social sciences, ethics, and religion, than they do with medicine as such."[14]

* * *

As the start of the next legislative session neared in Albany, the Joint Council readied another licensing bill. Rather than challenge what May had called the medical profession's "irrational authority," New York's psychologists tried to ignore it. For this strategy, the Joint Council's chair, Combs, mirrored that of his mentor, Carl Rogers. After introducing the concept of nondirective therapy in the early 1940s, Rogers had notoriously refused to respond to criticisms of his theories. Under the leadership of Combs, the Joint Council similarly avoided conflicts inside and outside of the profession. These political strategies were a reflection of Combs's phenomenological approach, which emphasized the creation of a "non-threatening permissive atmosphere" in which "a greatly expanded portion of the phenomenal field [is] available to the client for more adequate representation."[15]

An example of the Joint Council's intraprofessional permissiveness was illustrated by Combs's description of the bill-drafting process. What for the past several years had been an arduous and contentious task became a smooth process under his leadership, achieved with a "spirit of mutual understanding and respect." He said, "Perhaps no better evidence of this spirit can be pointed to than the single fact that every decision of the Council from the date of its inception to the present has been a unanimous decision." While this spirit likely benefited from the political brokering that Wendt had conducted for earlier versions of the bill, this unanimity suggests the Joint Council sidestepped contentious but important issues that would have created more division.[16]

Shortly before the January 3 start of the 1951 legislative session, the Joint Council began fielding feedback on its bill from the medical profession. By this time the Joint Council's membership had already approved the bill. It was too late in the bill-drafting process for the Joint Council to garner support for the expected contentious amendments that would be proposed by the medical profession. An example of a promedicine proposed amendment that drew staunch opposition from psychologists was one that called for the inclusion of a psychiatrist on a licensing advisory council created under the bill. This advisory council, as defined in the final bill, would have twelve to eighteen members, all of whom had to be psychologists from a variety of fields. A quarter of them were required to hail from training centers, and the rest were to be engaged primarily in practice. Frank S. Freeman, a Joint Council member and Cornell University psychology professor, acknowledged, "It may well be that having one [psychiatrist] on the Board is 'politically' and 'realistically' necessary, [but] I deplore it." He said it would be just as absurd to have a psychologist appointed to the psychiatrists' state advisory board. "We all know that they are constantly using and misusing psychology." Another proposed amendment was for clinical psychologists to demonstrate to the board of examiners created under the bill that "they have established direct contacts in the field of medicine." Freeman objected to this "vague" provision, saying it implied that clinical psychologists need to have medical collaboration or supervision and they "would not utilize medical consultants when the need is indicated, unless they are required to do so."[17]

These proposed amendments were not incorporated into the final draft of the bill, so when Combs presented it to the chairs of legislative committees of the county societies of the NYSMS on February 13, they refused to endorse it. This decision was not unanimous. For example, the chair of the legislative committee of the Westchester County Medical Society described the opposition to the licensing of psychologists as being "based upon stubborn tradition rather than logic." One week after Combs sustained this defeat before the NYSMS, two Republican lawmakers—Senator George R. Metcalf of Auburn, Cayuga County, and Orlo M. Brees of Endicott, Broome County—introduced the Joint Council's licensing bill. Although New York psychologists had spent fourteen years lobbying for legislation for the control of their profession, this was the first time a bill had been introduced in both houses of the legislature.[18]

The Metcalf-Brees bill modified the definition of psychological practice as it had appeared in the previous year in the legislation introduced by Assemblyman Noonan. The new definition defined the practice of psychology as the representation of being able to or undertaking "by whatever means to evaluate, appraise or classify mental abilities, personality characteristics, or personal or intrapersonal maladjustment, or to perform psychological reevaluation, psychological readjustment, psychological guidance or counseling for any person, corporation or association." The key difference between the 1950 and 1951 bills was the substitution of Noonan's language about the rendering of "any service involving the professional application of recognized principles, methods and procedures of the science and profession of psychology" with the broad and vague "by whatever means to evaluate, appraise or classify."[19]

By March, the Joint Council's campaign was in its homestretch, and it had already expended most of its lobbying budget. That left little funds for a final push, but the campaign had already succeeded in securing the support of several key state agencies and a dozen of New York's leading universities. The legislation's sponsors stayed on message, justifying the proposed licensing by pointing to a study that found a third of persons listed in the Manhattan telephone directory as psychologists had no affiliation with any legitimate psychological organization. Irking the medical lobby—and in another example of how psychologists were averse to confrontation—the senate on March 13 passed the bill without subjecting it to a public hearing. Three days later the assembly passed Brees's bill. In the *New York Times*, Combs hailed the bill as the first of its kind to be passed by any state legislature. However, the Joint Council had only 10 percent of its cash reserves left, and it still needed to secure Governor Thomas E. Dewey's approval.[20]

At the time Dewey remained a popular and powerful political figure, but he was no longer the rising star of the Republican Party on either the state or national level. His rise to political prominence started in 1935, when New York governor Herbert H. Lehman appointed him as a special prosecutor for New York County for what became known as the "Racketeer Investigation." Dewey's work in this position made him a national figure with folk hero status as he took on the mob, which had approved a hit on him. Over the next two years he received convictions in seventy-two out of seventy-three prosecuted cases, setting the stage for his 1937 election as New York County's district attorney. A year later he unsuccessfully ran for governor against Lehman, and in 1940 he also was a contender for the Republican nomination for president, but he lost that as well. Then, in 1942, he won New York's gubernatorial election by such a wide margin that he was able to secure the 1944 Republican nomination for president against Franklin D. Roosevelt. Although Dewey lost the presidential election, his 1946 reelection as governor by a record margin again positioned him for the Republican nomination for president. Dewey, however, suffered a humiliating defeat to Harry S. Truman in the 1948 presidential election.

Halsman, *Thomas Edmund Dewey, head and shoulders portrait, facing*, 1946. Photograph. Library of Congress, https://www.loc.gov/item/89708464/

After two failed presidential bids, Dewey, near the end of his second term in 1950, announced plans to return to private practice. His achievements as governor by then included measures that led to the creation of a state university, the eradication of tuberculosis, the construction of the New York State Thruway, and the passage of the nation's first antidiscrimination law. Despite Dewey's lack of interest in a third term, party leaders convinced him to run for reelection. In November 1950, he won by a landslide against a relatively unknown Democratic Bronx congressman. With this election, not only did he become New York's first three-term governor but also a more powerful one, with Republicans expanding their majorities in the state senate and assembly.[21]

Believing Dewey would support the licensing bill, the Joint Council did not develop an aggressive strategy for lobbying him. As Stephen C. Clark, the chair of Alfred University's Psychology Department, said in a letter of support to the governor, "This letter may not be necessary at all, as I judge from your record in the past that you have always stood for the protection of the public interest; however, it sometimes happens that bills are misinterpreted even after passing the legislature, and it would be a great misfortune if such were to happen to this bill." Combs apologetically wrote to the governor's counsel, Lawrence E. Walsh, and attested to it being "a good bill and deserves careful consideration." However, Combs added, "I see no point in harassing you already busy people unless such action serves a useful purpose in clarifying understandings." Between mid-March and early April, only a handful of letters of support were sent to the governor's office. The most prominent supporter was Frank Stanton, who on top of being the president of the Columbia Broadcasting System was the recipient of a PhD in psychology from Ohio State University in 1935. Another letter of support came from the New York–based Association of Analytic Psychologists, signed by Bone, Fromm, May, Donald Slesinger, and Herbert J. Zucker. Although Brees, in a memo to Walsh, claimed a "large number of psychiatrists and members of the medical profession" supported the bill, no letters of support from them were found in the legislation's bill jacket.[22]

Before any official action was taken on the bill by Dewey, the APA scrambled to mitigate the legislation's impacts. About two weeks after the bill passed New York's legislature, the APA's new president, Leo Bartemeier, called APsychA president Robert R. Sears and proposed meeting to discuss "desirable modifications" to it. However, emboldened by his profession's victory in Albany, Sears, the director of the Laboratory of Human Development at the Harvard Graduate School of Education, rebuffed Bartemeier's overture. Sears reminded Bartemeier how the two associations for the past three years had a committee on relations between the professions and it had been blocked from reporting to the APA's board of directors. Sears blasted Bartemeier for this "clear lack of cooperation," and he said the passage of the New York licensing bill could not be blamed on psychologists' unwillingness to cooperate with psychiatrists.[23]

Prior to the start of the Joint Council's April 2 meeting at the Psychological Corporation's headquarters, NYSPA's president, Hunt, relayed news about Sears's call. That set the tone for the discussions that followed. Seventeen Joint Council members gathered in a conference room for what, in some regards, was a victory lap. Combs reported on his meetings with the governor's counsel and representatives from the state Education Department. Several of Dewey's close associates—including his budget director, Cornell University vice president John Burton; Senate Finance chair Walter J. Mahoney; and state Republican chair William L. Pfeiffer—had discussed the licensing bill with the governor. A veto was still possible, though, and Combs days earlier had learned of a letter-writing campaign that the medical profession had launched to block Dewey's approval of the bill. Combs's advisers informed him this campaign could backfire and actually compel Dewey to sign the bill, so under these circumstances the Joint Council's chair was advised to not see the governor. The psychologists could only wait for the governor's signature, and with only $500 on hand, they could not do much else.[24]

Combs congratulated the Joint Council on its ability to overcome "systematic differences and possible conflicts of interests." He informed its members that he had returned to Syracuse University's payroll, but several tasks remained for him. They included doing an interview with *Collier's Magazine* about the problem of quackery, writing for the *American Psychologist* an article summarizing the 1951 lobbying campaign in Albany, composing numerous letters, and making phone calls and occasional visits. Looking beyond licensing, Combs turned the Joint Council's attention to future activities, including changing this federation into a unified state organization, developing a code of ethics, establishing professional policing mechanisms, and setting up policies and procedures for specialty certification.[25]

Prior to adjourning, the Joint Council voted to change the way psychological groups were represented within it. The federation's ten member organizations would each have three association-elected representatives, selected for their ability to represent geographic regions, training institutions, and special interests. The associations included in this federation were the National Psychological Association for Psychoanalysis, the Association of School Psychologists for New York City Public Schools, the New York Society of Clinical Psychologists, NYSPA, the Metropolitan New York Association of Applied Psychology, the Group for Applied Freudian Psychology, the New York Association for Individual Psychologists, the New York Society of Clinical Psychologists in Private Practice, and the Upper New York State Psychological Association. Since its creation, the Joint Council had operated like a senate, with each association having one vote. The Committee on Constitution was tasked with exploring whether that tradition should continue. Bernard F. Reiss, a Hunter College psychology professor, and several other representatives said they did not foresee vote counting being an important issue for the Joint Council, given its track record, at least under Combs, of achieving unanimity. However, Bone, the vice-chair, provided a cutting insight into this purported esprit de corps. He cautioned, "[The Joint Council has] a more severe test ahead of us, when, lacking a common enemy, we may feel more inclined to magnify our disagreements."[26]

Part 3
Battles

Chapter 7
Defeat

It was all coming apart—despite all the meetings, all the miles traveled across the state, the nights away from home, the licensing effort was about to be crushed. It was ten days earlier that Combs had learned about the letter-writing campaign the medical profession had been mounting to dissuade Dewey from signing the psychological licensing bill that the legislature had unanimously passed in mid-March. At the Joint Council's last meeting, Combs had told the group that this opposition could backfire and result in the governor's approval.[1]

Despite having been advised to not directly contact the governor, Combs, on April 9, sent him a telegraph warning about "an organized campaign . . . instituted by small group of psychiatrists to flood your office with telegrams urging veto of Senate Bill 2366 on grounds would permit persons without medical training to treat the sick." The Joint Council chair called the psychiatrists' fears "groundless" and clarified that the Metcalf-Brees bill would neither repeal nor impair New York's Medical Practice Act; the bill instead would control who practiced psychology rather than expand the scope of their practice under the law. Combs's telegram, however, was sent too late. The opposition campaign had largely concluded before he had learned about it. On April 10, Dewey vetoed the bill, delivering the profession of psychology a devastating blow.[2]

The medical profession's letters opposing the Metcalf-Brees bill were mostly sent to the governor on March 20 and 21. While Combs tried to dismiss the campaign as being led by a "small group of psychiatrists," there were three times more letters of opposition in the legislation's bill jacket than letters of support. General practitioners and psychiatrists alike emphasized the threat to the public the legislation posed. One general practitioner from Flushing called the bill a "bare-faced attempt" to open the practice of medicine to anyone other than "properly trained and licensed Doctors of Medicine." Another from Ithaca said, "There is a great danger to the public in permitting unqualified people this privilege [to treat psychiatric cases]." In addition to saying "it would be <u>dangerous</u> for persons, who are not completely trained to attempt DIAGNOSIS and TREATMENT," a Queens physician provided insight into the medical justification behind this political opposition. He said, "The Mind is the function of the Brain, which is an integral part of the Body,—and, the Psychologist, having no complete training or knowledge of the Anatomy, Physiology, Pathology, or Therapeutics,—how can he diagnose and treat the mind without jeopardizing the patient?" This lack of training justified the positions that psychologists, as a Schenectady psychiatrist said, "should only function as an adjunct to a psychiatrist and under strict psychiatric and medical supervision."[3]

The decisive blow to the licensing bill came with a telegram to the governor from Daniel Blain, the APA's medical director. With six thousand medical doctor members nationwide, Blain's opposition carried significantly more weight than the NYSMS county chairs who had also written to Dewey. Blain echoed those county chairs' concerns in his opposition to the independent diagnosis and treatment by psychologists. He also took issue with the "significantly loosely worded" bill and stressed the need for "revision and stricter definition" to prevent psychologists from engaging in independent medical practice. Most importantly, Blain noted his association supported the certification of psychologists and that psychiatrists would "welcome them as associates in the care of the sick." However, such interprofessional collaboration would be contingent on ensuring that psychologists' "functions are clearly delimited and understood." While Blain did not expressly state it, with psychological licensing being a nonstarter with the APA, the only way to achieve such clear delimitation would be through amendments to the state's Medical Practice Act. Blain warned, "It would be particularly disastrous for the Empire State to be the first to open the doors to this threat to sound medical practice."[4]

Ten days later Blain doubled down on his opposition to the Metcalf-Brees bill with a letter to Dewey that eviscerated the legislation and the psychologists advocating for its enactment. Blain dissected the bill's

> **WESTERN UNION**
>
> SYA15
> ST ITA081 LONG DL PD=ITHACA NY 7 213P=
> GOVERNOR THOMAS E DEWEY=
>   STATE OFFICE BLDG ALBANY NY=
>
> AN ORGANIZED CAMPAIGN HAS BEEN INSTITUTED BY SMALL GROUP OF
> PSYCHIATRISTS TO FLOOD YOUR OFFICE WITH TELEGRAMS URGING VETO
> SENATE BILL 2366 ON GROUNDS WOULD PERMIT PERSONS WITHOUT
> MEDICAL TRAINING TO TREAT THE SICK THIS FEAR IS GROUNDLESS
> STOP UNDER EXISTING MEDICAL PRACTICE ACT SUCH ACTIVITY IS
> SPECIFICALLY RESERVED TO PHYSICIANS. METCALF BILL DOES NOT
> REPEAL THAT ACT NOR IMPAIR ITS FUNCTION. BILL WOULD PERMIT
> LEGITIMATE PSYCHOLOGIST NOTHING HE DOES NOT DO ALREADY UNDER
> EXISTING LAW. AT PRESENT ANYONE WHO PLEASES MAY CALL HIMSELF
> A PSYCHOLOGIST AND ENGAGE IN UNCONTROLLED PRACTICE. METCALF
> BILL REQUIRES PERSONS PRACTICING PSYCHOLOGY MEET REASONABLE
> STANDARD FOR PROTECTION OF PUBLIC FROM GROWING BODY OF FRAUDS
> QUESTION AT ISSUE IS SHALL WE HAVE CONTROLLED OR UNCONTROLLED
> PRACTICE. WIDE SPREAD SUPPORT OF COLLEGES STATE DEPARTMENT
> SOCIAL AGENCIES AND PHYSICIANS AS WELL AS UNANIMOUS SUPPORT
> OF LEGISLATURE WHICH SEEM TO FAVOR CONTROL=
>   ARTHUR W COMBS   CHAIRMAN JOINT COUNSEL NEW YORK STATE
>   PSYCHOLOGISTS=

Arthur W. Combs. *Telegram to Thomas E. Dewey*. April 9, 1951. Combs, chairman of the Joint Council of New York State Psychologists on Legislation, sent a hurried message to Governor Dewey about an "organized campaign" instituted by a "small group of psychiatrists" to defeat the psychologist licensing bill that the Legislature had passed. Dewey vetoed the bill the next day. New York Veto Jackets 1951, New York State Library, Albany, New York (Senate Int. 2366 to 2864 Assembly Int. 43 to 838, Reel 3).

definition for the "practice of psychology" and found flaws in almost every other word. The phrase "by whatever means" was "unlimiting and permits the practitioner to go outside his field," and the words "to evaluate, appraise or classify" corresponded to "'diagnosis and prognosis' in medical parlance." More importantly, Blain, in scrutinizing the definition, succinctly laid out the medical profession's claim to the exclusive treatment of mental and emotional conditions. The "personality characteristics" referenced in the definition were "symptoms of underlying conditions due to any number of combinations: physical, endocrine, developmental, imitative or psychological defense reactions." He warned that "personal or inter-personal maladjustments" were undefined terms that were often used to cover all mental ills, including "functional" psychoses, such as schizophrenia, anxiety states, and depression. "It is our belief," Blain added, "that the 'functional' psychoses . . . are medically sick people, totally sick and not just psychologically 'maladjusted.'" While Blain said "there [was] no pure medical condition and no pure psychological condition," he also used the mind-body split to justify a psychologist's subordination to the medical doctor. Further, only physicians were "completely trained to diagnose and treat all conditions with a total approach." This argument echoes Paul Schilder's Cartesian "dual-aspect monism," which incorporated both the mind and body but held that the latter governed the whole.[5]

Highlighting the APA's fears that enactment of the Metcalf-Brees bill could spark a nationwide movement, Blain cautioned Dewey that "other states are eyeing this bill." Blain said legislation previously introduced in New Jersey had been altered to conform to the New York one. Also hinting at the association's nationwide aspirations and the significance of this political fight in Albany, Blain said, "Our effort in New York and all other states to raise the standard of care for 'maladjusted' people, mentally ill people, will be made much harder if this bill is passed." This effort to "raise the standard of care" for the maladjusted would send psychiatry deeper into what Stanley Cobb eight years earlier had called the profession's "borderlands," and it was only four months earlier when the APA's council had approved the blueprint for this incursion: the *Diagnostic and Statistical Manual: Mental Disorders (DSM-I)*. The development of this manual, which the APA's Committee on Nomenclature and Statistics had been working on since 1948, stood as what historian Gerald N. Grob calls a "visible symbol of the transformation of American psychiatry." Whereas just four decades earlier,

American psychiatrists were chiefly interested in somatic nosology, their focus shifted to a more psychodynamic and psychoanalytic nosology in the postwar years.[6]

In his veto message, Dewey attributed his disapproval of the Metcalf-Brees bill to "fundamental arguments against the creation of a new group who can practice their calling only by license of the State" as well as to its "broad language" that would create "uncertainty as to the fields of psychology and psychiatry." Additionally, he cited the "vigorous and impressive objections" by the NYSMS, the APA, many individual physicians, and other medical organizations, as well as his own commissioners of mental hygiene and health. Dewey also claimed there was insufficient information on the extent to which fraudulent psychologists were evading the state's penal laws against false representation as well as on how many persons "having an honest claim to the title psychologist" wouldo be excluded from practicing under the legislation. Ultimately, the legislation's fatal flaw was its definition for the practice of psychology. "The borderline between psychology and psychiatry, although clear enough in the abstract, is very difficult to recognize in practice." The Metcalf-Brees bill's definition was "not helpful" and ran the risk of creating confusion among the public.[7]

Dewey's veto shocked many New York psychologists. After all, during his first year as governor, Dewey had demonstrated a fearlessness in challenging the medical profession. In May 1943, Dewey had ordered a sweeping probe of the state's mental hospital system.[8] And even before the investigation's findings were revealed, Dewey had lamented over the one hundred thousand patients in those facilities and how they were overcrowded by 20 percent. He acknowledged that staffing shortages and other war conditions, including the War Department's takeover of three institutions, had contributed to the decline in their services and capabilities. He had pledged to restore or expand those institutions' capacities and space after the war.[9]

Dewey's wilingness to investigate the mental health system may have contributed to psychologists' belief that he "always stood for the protection of the public interest." They expected he would unwaveringly support them in their fight against quacks. However, during the years between the assembling of this commission and the governor's veto of the Metcalf-Brees bill, the Dewey administration had become substantially more invested in its mental hospital system and the psychiatrists who ran them. Between the 1942–43 fiscal year, when Dewey took office, and the fiscal year in which he vetoed the licensing bill, the Mental Hygiene Department's annual budget increased by 160 percent to $106.4 million. During that period, the number of people employed by those mental hospitals increased by 20 percent to 25,652. With twenty-seven facilities, New York's mental hospital system was the world's largest, and the changes implemented by Dewey since he had taken office were "so gigantic," he said, that the deficiencies highlighted by the 1943 probes were "now a matter of history."[10]

***

A storm was brewing. Harry Bone, the Joint Council's vice-chair, was losing sleep thinking about it. It was mid-July 1951. On top of struggling with their legislative strategy, New York's psychologists were attempting to create a more unified front through the merger of NYSPA with the state's eleven other psychological associations. At a May conference in Harriman, New York, a committee, chaired by Florence Halpern, was formed to revise NYSPA's bylaws. At another conference at Vassar College in July, a second committee, chaired by Harold Seashore, was formed to propose divisional structure. Meanwhile, the medical profession, emboldened by its surprise victory in Albany, was mounting a major offensive against the profession of psychology; only this one would not be led by the APA or NYSMS. Instead, this new campaign was being organized by the much larger and more politically influential AMA.[11]

In May 1951, in response to a question from J. W. Holloway, director of the AMA's legal bureau, the association's Committee on Clinical Psychology met in Cincinnati and discussed drafting a formal report on the certification or licensing of clinical psychologists. Involved in these discussions were George Raines, who was also finalizing the *DSM-I*; former APA vice president Spafford Ackerly; Blain; and Francis J. Gerty, head of the AMA committee and of the College of Medicine at the University of Illinois. Referred to as the Gerty committee, it was divided over the question of permitting psychologists to privately practice psychotherapy, with Raines, Ackerly, and Blain insisting such practice be conducted under psychiatric supervision. These doctors, however, could not answer "how to provide for supervision that will realistically and actually meet the requirement of satisfying good medical psychiatric standards."[12]

Gerty's committee presented its findings at the meeting of the AMA's Division of Nervous and Mental Diseases in Atlantic City in June. There the

Cleveland psychiatrist Louis J. Karnosh warned the attendees of the threat that "untrained" psychologists posed to the general public through their private practice of psychotherapy. He said that danger was being made greater through their pursuit of licensing legislation. Following Karnosh's presentation, a committee was formed and tasked with making recommendations to the division on this issue. The next day those recommendations were reported and unanimously approved. They included support for certification but not licensing legislation and the requirement that psychologists' practice of psychotherapy be done under "the direct supervision of a psychiatrist." The committee also called for a review of medical practice acts across the country as they related to psychotherapy. Of particular interest were the states that had already passed psychologist certification or licensing laws. The division urged the AMA's Legislative Committee to "work towards a tightening up of legislation if it does not adequately control psychotherapy."[13]

By the time of the July 7–8 Vassar conference on NYSPA's expansion, friendly sources within the VA and psychiatric community had already tipped off the Joint Council's leadership to the AMA's actions in Cincinnati and Atlantic City. After hearing about these developments while at Vassar, Bone told Harrower that it was "urgent for the J. C. to have a clear policy" regarding the relation of psychology to medicine and psychiatry. But the development of such a policy would draw the Joint Council into a confrontation with the medical professions, and that was what Combs had gone to great lengths to avoid during his tenure as chair. And in the waning days of his term, Combs was not interested in pursuing that task. When the Joint Council met two days after the Vassar conference and adjourned without even addressing the policy issue that Bone had been pressing for weeks, he was left speechless. A few days later, though, he accosted Combs because the Joint Council had "not tackled and thrashed out and formulated its position in regard to the relations of Psychology with Medicine and Psychiatry." He stressed that the defeat of the licensing bill, coupled with efforts to see whether an agreement could be reached with the medical and psychiatric representatives, "means that we must, by adequate discussion achieve and formulate a clear-cut, unified conviction as to what we will have and what we will not have." Without knowing the Joint Council's position on what could be compromised and what was nonnegotiable, Bone said psychologists would have to go to the physicians and psychiatrists and say, "What do you want of us?" rather than, "This is how we see it—how do you see it?"[14]

Bone was not alone in fretting over the Joint Council's temerity before organized medicine. After attending the Atlantic City meeting of the Division of Nervous and Mental Diseases, Bernard Locke, chief clinical psychologist of the Mental Hygiene Unit of the Brooklyn VA Regional Office, informed Combs of the activities there. Locke cautioned Combs about dismissing what happened there as "a last gasp of the AMA to hold back the irresistible tide of psychology." He warned, "To the AMA with its resources, political strength and size we are not a tide but a tiny puddle which must be blotted up quickly to avoid a nuisance. I argued against complacency while our New York bill was awaiting Dewey's signature but was shouted down—Do nothing, I was told by members of the Joint Council. Dewey is for us and he'll sign the bill without question. Then came the AMA!" Locke implored Combs to ready the Joint Council for "the restrictive legislation which is bound to be introduced." He believed psychology's "last hope for a licensing bill lies in having one ready for the opening days of the legislature before the machinery of the AMA gets rolling—once it is in high gear. I can't see how we can beat them!"[15]

These urgent warnings were not heeded by Combs. To Bone, what was more troubling than the Joint Council's passivity was Combs's successor: Harrower. Harrower was elected chairwoman at the Joint Council's July 10 meeting. She was supposed to share the responsibility with Carleton Scofield of the University of Buffalo, with the former being in charge of medical affairs and the latter tasked with lobbying for legislation. Scofield, however, had to decline the co-chair position just before the election due to a new job with the government. Scofield's sudden withdrawal left the Joint Council without a person dedicated to the push for a revised licensing bill that addressed Dewey's concerns. Although he had not yet admitted to not favoring the licensing legislation, Combs told the Joint Council there was insufficient time to work on a bill that year and there were not enough funds for another lobbying campaign. He proposed postponing the legislative effort until an agreement with the medical profession was reached. While the Joint Council was unanimous in being "full steam ahead on obtaining an agreement with medicine," Bone cautioned that if no deal was reached then a "vigorous committee" would be needed "to oppose any possible restrictive legislation sponsored by opposing groups."[16]

When Harrower had interviewed with the Joint Council for the chair position in June, she acknowledged opposition to her appointment due to her being perceived as "too conservative." She, however, believed not only that she was the ideal candidate to represent psychologists before the medical profession but also that her appointment was "inevitable." She believed her fellow psychologists' resentment of the phrase "medical supervision" stemmed from a "misunderstanding." Through her "enlightenment" they would be more welcoming to the types of relationships with physicians and psychiatrists that had helped her private clinical psychology practice thrive for the past six years. Physicians, too, needed her enlightenment, and she declared it was one of her major life aims to deliver it. While Harrower's close academic and professional relations with physicians and medical organizations had lifted her name to the top of the list for the Joint Council's chair, Bone believed "these very assets carry a liability . . . for the negotiation job." With the medical lobby having "ruthlessly destroyed a long-continued and burdensome effort of the unified psychologists of the state," Bone argued it was more important for psychology's representative to "be unambiguously willing to fight Medicine if Medicine is unreasonable in its demands on us." Harrower's business relations with referring physicians, Bone feared, could compromise her willingness to oppose and disagree with their representatives in negotiations and put her in the position in which she "could not stay with the J. C. in the fight because she either agreed with their position or did not want to jeopardize her relationships with them." That would result in a "disastrous situation" for the cause of psychology in not only the state but also the nation. "It takes little imagination," he warned her, "to picture what our opponents would make of a situation in which our own freely chosen official representative would be, or appear to be, for their side and against ours."[17]

Even before Harrower assumed her position as Joint Council chairwoman, her interactions with psychiatry had raised red flags. For example, in a letter to Bernard Wortis of Bellevue's Psychiatric Division, she had told him, in what Bone described as a "chummy, confidential way," that a faction within the Joint Council had opposed her appointment. This admission had ingratiated her with the psychiatrist at the expense of the Joint Council, "incidentally informing him that we were not united," Bone said. She had likewise conveyed such disunity to Theodore J. C. von Storch, Montefiore Hospital's chief of the Division of Neuropsychiatry.

Von Storch had recently been appointed to head the NYSMS's committee charged with addressing the psychologist licensing issue. With him, Harrower began hosting a series of informal meetings between select Joint Council members and medical representatives. These meetings, held in Harrower's apartment, afforded psychologists the opportunity to gain insights into the position of physicians and psychiatrists—something that traditionally had been largely unattainable until their formal committees met at the start of the legislative session. Through the meetings, however, Harrower either intentionally or inadvertently amplified these opposing parties' positions by creating a forum where they made demands, albeit in a friendly manner. As Bone had feared they would, psychologists were left reacting to these demands. These medical representatives commonly pledged support to psychologists' practice of psychotherapy with the caveat that, despite their personal positions, they would not oppose the stance of the groups they were representing. For example, prior to the July 17 meeting at Harrower's apartment, von Storch had made such claims to her. When she reported that to the Joint Council, Bone was shocked how she had been "very happy" with the doctor's stated belief that psychologists should not be supervised and how she was "not disturbed" with his assertion that he would not contradict himself with the NYSMS if it believed otherwise.[18]

The July 17 meeting, attended by six Joint Council members and NYSPA president Louis Long, was significant not because of what von Storch said—a reiteration of what Harrower had already reported—but because of what happened after he left. Harrower, who had just assumed leadership of the Joint Council, told the group she "personally did not think it was the time for licensing" but she would campaign for it if that was the majority's opinion. Additionally, following this meeting and through von Storch's facilitation, Morris Herman of Bellevue Hospital and the New York Society of Clinical Psychiatry, became Harrower's primary medical liaison on the licensing issue. While Herman shared von Storch's pretense of interprofessional cooperation, he had played an integral role in rallying the medical profession's opposition to Senator Desmond's 1948 psychologist certification bill.[19]

Harrower trusted these medical representatives, even though Lawrence Kubie had warned her about psychiatry's quest to control and limit the practice of psychology. After serving on the APA's Committee on the Relationship between Psychiatry and Psychology for three years, Kubie, earlier in April, had stepped down from it. He had "gradually become convinced that the APA does not want to have any relationship to clinical psychology." To Kubie, the committee's activities were "perfunctory and insincere," with each of its reports, despite making "every possible concession to the entrenched APA biases," being rejected on trivial grounds. He told the committee's chair that the group should be renamed the "Committee on Abolishing Relationship between Psychiatry and Clinical Psychology." The Joint Council, however, did not embrace Kubie as an ally, despite his severance with the APA committee and his willingness to provide Harrower with recommendations for a revised licensing bill. The Joint Council's members adamantly opposed Kubie's assertions that psychiatrists should serve on the board of examiners and advisory council called for in the legislation. And Freeman, the Cornell University psychologist, said, "I would rather have no licensing bill at all than have one that incorporates the views of Kubie, Herman, or Wortis."[20]

The summer passed with the Joint Council making no decision as to what type of legislation it should push for in the next legislative session. At its annual conference in Chicago, the APsychA delivered some guidance to New York's psychologists, with its Committee on Relations with Other Professions issuing a report urging members to maintain psychology's integrity as an independent commission and to resist restrictive regulations. Shortly after the conference ended on September 5, the Joint Council did agree to a budget of $5,000 to support the "rapprochement with medicine" from October 1 to January 1. This attempt at conciliation had to wait until the fall because Harrower had to travel to Denver for a teaching assignment, Princeton for a conference, and Montreal for lectures. That left little time for interprofessional and intraprofessional negotiations for a bill. By the time Harrower started interviewing leaders from the major national, state, and local medical and psychiatric associations in early October, the leaders' positions on the profession of psychology had already become further entrenched. At the same time, a clearer picture of the medical profession's next legislative move was emerging. Harrower's report to the Joint Council on her findings offered few surprises, other than that the AMA was on the verge of announcing its official position against the licensing of psychologists and for their certification. Additionally, Samuel Parker, the architect of the 1949 Greenberg bill, was involving himself in von Storch's NYSMS committee on licensing.[21]

After painting licensing as a dead end, Harrower continued to advocate for certification legislation. Backing her was Combs, who pointed to the AMA's and APA's lack of opposition to such legislation. That made it "worth a try." While the former's official declaration of support for certification would not be published until January 1952, the latter announced the same through the November 1951 issuance of a joint statement from its Committees on Clinical Psychology and Legal Aspects of Psychiatry. On top of stating that the APA "fully supports the desirability of designating by legal certification," the committees stated clinical psychologists working with physical or psychological illnesses needed to "work under the continuing direction of a licensed physician." Further, the association did not believe the licensing of psychologists constituted sound public policy, and it was "impossible" to "define and delimit the practice of psychology for the purpose of licensure." Although this position echoed the opposition that New York's psychologists had been encountering for the past several years, Harrower continued to describe the New York Academy of Medicine as a potential ally. Despite this mounting opposition, Harrower took comfort in Herman's assurance that "we might feel some moral pressure [to adopt the APA's position], but we would be in no way bound."[22]

In Harrower's efforts to steer the Joint Council away from licensing, she recruited Herman to address the group in mid-November so "they would be interested in turning toward certification." When that did not happen, she griped to him about "skeptics" on the Joint Council and its unabated interest in again pursuing a licensing bill. Undeterred by its chair, the Joint Council agreed on amendments to the licensing bill. One major concession was the inclusion of language requiring clinical psychologists to establish "direct contacts in the field of medicine and, where available, in psychiatry for the purpose of medical appraisal, consultation and referral." In addition to this clause was the proposed placement of a psychiatrist on the advisory committee created under the bill. With the next legislative session less than two months away, Harrower told Herman she felt "considerable pressure" to introduce a bill in Albany. She believed another joint meeting between a larger group of medical and psychological representatives was needed to "allay the mistrust and suspicion which still permeates the group as a whole if there is a chance for an open discussion of these suggested clauses."[23]

* * *

As Harrower sought to bring psychology closer to medicine, May was expounding the advantages of the former in relation to the limitations of the latter. Although he was not yet involved with the Joint Council, May was rising in prominence at the WAWI, where Bone also worked. Earlier that spring, May had received an invitation from Clara Thompson, the president of WAWI's board of trustees, to teach a seminar for ministers in the winter. When Bone was transferred to a curriculum for teachers near the end of 1951, she tapped May to succeed him as the person in charge of the minister curriculum.[24]

By November 1951, May was finalizing his theories on the self and humankind's dilemma that he had written about in *Pastoral Psychology*. As preparation for his next book, *Man's Search for Himself*, he presented these theories at Mills College's Centennial Conference in Oakland, California. With his lectures that November, May was moving toward what he would later acknowledge to be a seemingly "rash" conclusion. In *The Meaning of Anxiety*, he had said that "physical illness may relieve psychological troubles by giving some focus for 'floating anxiety.'" May took this conclusion a step further by claiming that, so long as scientific progress strove to eradicate bodily diseases "*without* helping people address their anxiety, guilt, emptiness, and purposelessness, sickness [was] only forced into a new channel." He likened this "compartmentalized way" of addressing disease to Hercules fighting the many-headed Hydra, with a new head emerging each time one was cut off. "The battle for health must be won on the deeper level of the integration of self." Medical discoveries were welcome, but "lasting progress in health" required more than "finding means of killing germs and bacilli and external organisms that invade the body"; it required discovering the "means of helping ourselves and other people so to affirm their own beings that they will not need to be sick."[25]

Chapter 8
Threats

The room was crowded. Eleven men, three women. It was the night of December 21. Harrower's long-promised meeting between the members of the Joint Council and representatives from New York's psychiatric groups was unfolding in her Upper East Side apartment. Frances Alexander, a clinical psychologist at New York University, kept wondering why more people were not in the room. There were eleven Joint Council members to three psychiatrists. The New York Society of Clinical Psychiatry's Morris Herman stood with two colleagues from a psychiatric committee examining the psychology licensing issue. Herman apologetically explained to the psychologists that he had told more psychiatrists from the committee to come, and Alexander was "struck" by the fact that they had not. Their absence made her "somewhat suspicious of the avowed statements that they wish to work collaboratively with us."[1]

Alexander, who had worked at McGill University with Harrower in the late 1930s, was not alone in viewing the medical representatives skeptically. Emanuel Schwartz, a psychoanalyst at the Postgraduate Center for Psychotherapy, concluded that the men in Harrower's apartment represented a group that was "motivated, perhaps understandably, almost entirely out of self-interest." Harrower had hoped this meeting would smooth relations between the professions, especially with Herman addressing the Joint Council with other psychiatrists beside him rather than individually, as he had done earlier in the year. However, the meeting sowed more distrust than it settled, and the impressions it left on the psychologists in the room would influence the Joint Council's direction for the year to come. The Joint Council's former chair, Combs, "liked the friendly atmosphere in which this meeting took place" and perceived Herman as "a fine gent and a man who is a real statesman." However, Combs had to admit that Herman was "the most enlightened of the group" and not a representative figure.[2]

The psychiatrists' mantra for the night was that New York's psychologists needed to do something during the coming legislative session in Albany, and their only viable option was to pursue certification. With the psychiatrists insisting on the impossibility of adequately defining the practice of psychology, the prospects for licensing dimmed, even among its strongest advocates. Even though she viewed certification as a "'sop' or stop-gap that [had] little value for the profession or the public," Halpern believed it would be a "waste of time and effort" to pursue licensing legislation. NYSPA's president, Louis Long, favored certification because psychologists could "apparently get it without much trouble." Combs was in no rush to pursue legislation, saying, "We can afford to let the matter ride for another year without doing ourselves irreparable harm."[3]

After making their opposition to licensing unequivocal, the psychiatrists made a bombshell disclosure: they would lobby for legislation adding "nervous and mental disease" to the definition of medical practice under New York's Medical Practice Act, similar to what Senator Greenberg had proposed in 1949. Herman explained that these terms would encompass clear-cut psychoses and anxiety states, leaving to psychologists what one of his colleagues described as "minor neuroses" and "character disorders." This disclosure triggered panic in several Joint Council members. They proposed declaring a moratorium on any definitive legislation, but the psychiatrists said they would not pause efforts to amend the Medical Practice Act. One suggestion that piqued the psychiatrists' interest was an omnibus bill that would be jointly sponsored by the two professions and both expand the Medical Practice Act and grant licenses to psychologists. However, to Joint Council members such as the Columbia University Teachers College vocational psychologist Albert S. Thompson and Herbert J. Zucker, a Columbia clinical psychologist, the psychiatrists were "illogical in their reasoning." They were hypocrites for holding that psychology was "too amorphous to permit definition of the psychologist's function" but "it apparently is clear enough to permit definition of their own." The more the psychiatrists pressed the Joint Council to pursue certification, the more Zucker suspected they wanted to postpone "any legal formulation" of the practice of psychology, giving them "time to define areas of function unitarily." As Thompson saw it, psychologist licensing would "preempt" a Medical Practice Act amendment. Schwartz, likewise, worried psychologists were being "sucked in by the cooperative offers of the psychiatric profession" and risked backtracking "in their rightful demand for professional equality."[4]

When the psychologists left Harrower's apartment that night, the Joint Council was more divided than when its members had walked into it. The conference had done little to change psychologists' positions on the pursuit of a certification or licensing bill, but it had introduced a new topic of division: whether a legislative battle between the professions was inevitable. The most ardent advocates for certification were also the ones who believed a high-stakes confrontation was avoidable. To Long, certification was a better alternative to a "knockdown drag-out fight with psychiatry" that would "do a great deal of harm to psychology and psychologists." Combs was actually more concerned about a knockdown, drag-out fight between psychologists. Shortly before the conference, he had told Harrower that "certification would suit me fine," but he wanted to limit discussions about it in the Joint Council. In another example of his aversion to confrontation, Combs said, "I cannot seem to get over the uneasy feeling that it is possible to talk too much and in the process wake up a number of sleeping dogs that are better to be left asleep for a while longer."[5]

Harrower tried to assuage the Joint Council's members over the threatened restrictive legislation by assuring them that any confrontation would only be with a small sect of psychiatry. She said the "medical profession at large does not favor a change in the Medical Practice Act." And Carleton Scofield, who since October had been acting as the Joint Council's legislative chair, tried to convince his colleagues that there could be no confrontation because "there are no funds." To other Joint Council members, however, that was not a compelling argument for resting "at the tender mercies of medicine in general for a narrow interpretation of 'nervous and mental disease,'" said Clement Staff. Alexander believed psychologists, allied with other professionals in social work and education, "could put up a very good fight and perhaps successfully defeat such legislation." In such a fight, Zucker believed, psychologists would be "knit" together and financial support would "be readily forthcoming."[6]

* * *

On a January afternoon, the phone rang in the Midtown office of Walter P. Anderton, the secretary of the NYSMS. Harrower awkwardly waited in the room after Anderton picked up the phone to talk to Samuel Parker, the Bellevue psychiatrist and mastermind behind the 1949 Greenberg bill. Anderton had invited Harrower to his office after she had called him in the morning—at the suggestion of Herman. She wanted to find out how seriously the state's psychiatrists and other medical doctors were pushing for the introduction of legislation that would insert language for "nervous and mental disease" in the Medical Practice Act. When Harrower had posed that question to him over the phone, Anderton had reacted with "considerable incredulity." He said he doubted the medical profession would lobby for such an amendment with it being so late in the legislative session, though to be sure he would have to talk to Parker. Anderton had planned to talk to Parker over the phone before Harrower's visit, but that call had come after her arrival. After several minutes, Anderton hung up the phone and told Harrower that Parker had expressed interest in the amendment but would not commit to lobbying for it. There was considerable dissention among psychiatrists about its advisability. Anderton said psychologists did not need to be overly concerned because legislators tended to avoid bills when there was conflict within a profession over them. As an example, Anderton pointed to a recent attempt by a faction of the profession in the state to pass legislation that would limit the interpretation of X-ray slides to medical doctors. Due to "considerable opposition" to the bill, it had "immediately died." In 1950, New York's highest court, the Court of Appeals, had ruled "the taking or reading of an X-Ray did not constitute the practice of medicine," likely prompting the introduction of the bill referenced by Anderton.[7]

Harrower's interviews with Herman and Anderton strengthened her belief that "there is certainly no general organized or widespread attempt on the part of medicine or psychiatry to alter the Medical Practice Act." She reported her findings and this conclusion to the Joint Council. While Parker remained a wildcard and a "sneak attack" remained a possibility, she said that if he pushed for an amendment, "it will once again be his baby" and be "regarded as an extreme and rather undesirable measure by a large number of the medical and psychiatric profession." She optimistically reported that Anderton personally believed it was unnecessary to amend the Medical Practice Act because it was "perfectly sufficient to prevent non-medical people from practicing medicine in any area." However, she failed to grasp that this position assumed "nervous and mental disease" were medical conditions. This assumption was one of two key factors that distinguished the threat of a Medical Practice Act amendment that psychologists faced from the one radiologists had faced. Whereas the Court of Appeals had ruled that X-ray interpretation was not a medical practice, the court had not afforded psychologists any such clarification. Another factor was that the amendment threatened against New York psychologists aligned with new policies set by the AMA and the APA.

Additionally, Harrower's emphasis that there was "no general or widespread attempt" to alter the Medical Practice Act belied the trends that were playing out in the profession of psychiatry. In less than six years, the GAP had substantially changed the course of psychiatry toward social activism, despite failing to muster enough of a majority of membership to reorganize the APA. In this regard, according to historian Gerald N. Grob, the GAP "lost the battle, but surely they won the war." In the 1950s, the GAP won the war within its profession by transforming the association's structure for committees—and Lawrence Kubie had called one of them the "Committee on Abolishing Relationship between Psychiatry and Clinical Psychology." The GAP's victory also came because of the elevated stature of the APA's medical director, Daniel Blain, who viewed New York as a key battleground state for spreading the reach of psychiatrists nationwide.[8]

Herman had even admitted to Harrower that "there is an element in psychiatry which cannot or will not compromise with regard to the question of psychologists doing therapy." This "element" was a cause of great concern for the Joint Council's hawkish members, such as Bone, Halpern, Zucker, Albert Ellis, and Jesse Zizmor. Up until mid-January, the Joint Council was still undecided as to whether it should go on the offensive with another licensing bill or play defense and mount a campaign against an amendment to the Medical Practice Act. While there was little question that a licensing bill introduced at that time would be nothing more than a "token bill," Zucker pressed for reintroduction in the legislature. That would "have the effect of letting psychiatry know that we are not in the position of merely agreeing to take what medicine will give us." Ellis, who in addition to having a small private practice in New York City was also New Jersey's chief psychologist, argued that licensing would make it harder for psychiatrists to expand the Medical Practice Act. Further, certification would put psychologists "in an ancillary position" and reduce their chances of opposing such an expansion. At the end of its January 14 meeting, the Joint Council approved a $3,000 budget for the "vigorous opposition to any restrictive legislation."[9]

As the Joint Council waited for the medical profession's offensive, one was already underway in France. On December 4, 1951, French prosecutors began a trial against Margaret Clark-Williams, a US expatriate who became the center of the most sensational news story about lay analysis in Europe since Theodor Reik about a quarter century earlier. The Joint Council closely monitored this case involving a former New Yorker, Clark-Williams, who had undergone psychoanalysis in the early 1940s with Raymond de Saussure, a founding member of the Paris Psychoanalytic Society. After moving to France in 1945, she studied psychology under Daniel Lagache, a physician and psychoanalyst who had taught at the Sorbonne in Paris. She received her clinical training under Georges Heuyer, a physician who pioneered child psychiatry in France. In 1950, she became one of the first graduates at the Sorbonne to receive a license in psychology that Lagache had established, and she was also admitted to the Paris Psychoanalytic Society. She worked as a child psychotherapist at the Centre Claude Bernard in Paris, but in March 1950 the Order of Physicians sued Clark-Williams for the illicit practice of medicine because she practiced "psychoanalysis, and, therefore, medicine." Although the trial would end in March 1952 with the charges being dropped against Clark-Williams, she was found guilty a year later after the case was appealed.[10]

* * *

There was a new face among the seventeen psychologists who gathered in a room of the Psychological Corporation's Midtown building on Fifth Avenue on the night of January 28, 1952. May likely sat next to Bone, the Joint Council's vice-chair. The two psychologists' relationship had just come full circle. Twelve years earlier Bone had written the introduction to May's second book, and May had recently succeeded him as the WAWI's ministry curriculum head.[11]

Increasingly concerned about psychiatrists' interest in amending New York's Medical Practice Act, the Joint Council pressed its chair, Carleton Scofield, to act as its "watchdog" for legislation threatening to the profession of psychology. It was a charge Scofield did not want to accept. He kept trying to explain that he had agreed to serve as chair to lobby for legislation, though he disagreed with the Joint Council's leanings toward a licensing bill. He had not accepted this job so he could serve as the Joint Council's capitol sentry. Harrower, who also sat at the table, found it "disturbing . . . to see how impossible it was for the group to understand what you [Scofield] were trying to tell them." To her, all this was unnecessary. Harrower not only dismissed the possibility of a Medical Practice Act amendment being introduced in the legislature; she also believed the proposed insertion of the phrase "nervous and mental disease" seemed to be "a legitimate and not a threatening addition."[12]

Scofield was at his wit's end with the Joint Council. From his perspective, the "personal interests of a relatively small group [i.e., private practitioners] are dominating its deliberations." He believed the last five moths had been wasted by focusing on "the struggle with medicine" and "negative action" that "raised hostilities anew." He joked to Harrower, one of his closest allies in the group, that "the Council is ripe for a therapeutic analysis." So, on January 28, after delivering to the Joint Council a list of recommendations, which included no legislative action that year and the creation of a legislative watchdog committee, Scofield declared his intention to resign from his chairship. May's attendance at the meeting suggests the Joint Council had already lined him up to become Scofield's successor. Even though Scofield agreed to retain his chairship until March 3, the leadership shakeup came in the middle of the legislative session and prompted the Joint Council to vote to not pursue legislation that year. It also voted to create, as the outgoing chair had recommended, an Emergency Committee on Legislation, with its members including Zizmor as chair, Staff, Long, and Harrower.[13]

Within two weeks, Zizmor's committee was first put to the test, and Scofield's claims that there was no credible threat to amend the Medical Practice Act were proved wrong. The legislation, however, threatened the profession of psychology in a way the Joint Council had not been expecting. On February 12, Wheeler Milmoe, an assemblyman from the Syracuse area, introduced a bill to amend the Medical Practice Act to provide for the suspension of the medical license of a physician who "aids or abets a person not licensed to practice the profession." Milmoe, a Canastota Republican and newspaper publisher, had drafted the legislation at the request of the NYSMS's Medical Grievance Committee. Zizmor flagged this bill as "potentially dangerous" because it could prevent physicians from consulting with or being consulted by psychologists. Scofield had brought the Joint Council's concerns to the attention of Milmoe, who assured him he would hold the bill until the issue was further clarified. Despite this promise, the bill passed not only in the assembly but also the senate. When Milmoe advocated for the bill on the assembly floor, he emphasized the bill was not aimed at psychologists, though that did not make the Joint Council any less concerned. They found cold comfort in Governor Dewey's April 7 veto of the bill because it had also been strongly opposed by osteopaths, physiotherapists, and the New York State Board of Medicine.[14]

In addition to coming in the middle of the legislative session, the Joint Council's leadership transition came amid a low point in morale, especially among its academic members. Their complaints, raised frequently by Scofield, were that the Joint Council had lost touch with the profession's grassroots and that private practice psychologists were dragging out the legislation issue. He also blamed them for perpetuating "the threat of the psychiatrist," which was self-defeating because it detracted from a "positive program" in which psychology could work with other professions to protect the public. However, underlying these complaints, a shift was happening within the Joint Council that would see the academic psychologists lose their stronghold on leadership. Since its inception, the Joint Council's chairs had heralded from academia, with the exception Harrower, whose research and close association with psychiatrists put her in a class separate from the private practitioners. The shift was not lost on May, who noted at the Joint Council's April meeting that the split in attitudes toward legislation was "potentially dangerous." He said the academicians needed to realize "that the future of the science of psychology is bound up with that of practicing groups." He observed that the NYSCP, then headed by Arthur Teicher, would have "to take the lead in supporting legislation." Toward the end of that meeting, May was nominated chair of the Joint Council. In accepting the nomination, May declared the Joint Council was "no longer merely an ad hoc committee but is concerned with policy and long-term planning for psychology as a profession."[15]

This broader scope for the Joint Council led to three major changes in its operations. The first major change was a heavier reliance on committees and the appointment of legislative hawks as their chairs. The formation of Zizmor's Emergency Committee on Legislation was only the beginning. There was also a Committee on Certification vs Licensing, chaired by the

Brooklyn clinical psychologist Solomon Machover; a Committee for Nominating New Officers, chaired by Zucker; and a Medical Liaison Committee, chaired by Zizmor, with Combs and Bone as members. Harrower, who had served as the Joint Council's chief medical liaison since its inception, would serve this committee only as a consultant. After years of unsuccessfully trying to steer the Joint Council toward the psychiatrist-preferred option of certification, Harrower declined to sit on this committee. She had found meetings convened by its predecessor as being "unnecessarily time consuming." A Committee on Public Education, initially chaired by May and also including Bone and Long, was the most important new committee. One of its first successes was an article placed in the *New York Times* and *Herald-Tribune* announcing the installment of May as the Joint Council's new chair. Lending key support to this committee, which would later be renamed the Public Relations Committee and be chaired by Long, were the noted social psychologist Gerhard Wiebe and Wallace H. Wulfleck. In addition to being the Joint Council's treasurer and a former NYSPA president, Wulfleck was also the vice president of the New York advertising agency William Esty Co.[16]

The second major change was the Joint Council's heavier reliance on professional services, such as lawyers and public relations specialists for the Public Relations Committee. May, a nationally renowned author and public speaker and regular *New York Times* contributor, brought to the Joint Council a substantial amount of public relations savviness that had been lacking as much in the Joint Council as in the profession of psychology.[17]

However, as psychologists were launching their public relations efforts, the AMA was refining its new messaging apparatus following several serious missteps with the press. In 1949 it had launched $3.5 million fundraising campaign to build a "political war chest to fight socialized medicine." Half of the campaign's budget, which had been supported through the imposition of a $25 membership assessment, had gone toward "defense and attack," with the other half going toward strengthening the voluntary health insurance system that the AMA had held out as the better alternative to government insurance. To keep the campaign's momentum, the House of Delegates, the AMA's policy-making body, made the membership assessment permanent in late 1949. The following year, in the run-up to the congressional elections, the AMA expended $1.1 million on newspaper advertisements, radio time, and magazine space to further stoke public opposition to compulsory health insurance. By 1950, the AMA had cemented its reputation as the "most powerful legislative lobby in Washington," spending more on lobbying at the federal level than any other group. By 1952, compulsory health insurance was a dead issue, and the funds that had been used to fight that were redirected to "fringe" legislation.[18]

The third major change in the Joint Council was its pursuit of legal battles outside the capitol in Albany that addressed practical matters related to private practice. They included seeking a ruling from the Internal Revenue Service (IRS) on whether fees paid to psychologists were deductible from federal income tax. Other issues needing clarification were the requirements on psychologists to pay the federal social security tax and the state unincorporated business tax, with both stemming from psychology's nonrecognition as a profession. This lack of recognition also meant psychologists could not be excused from jury duty. Leading this fight was Zizmor's legal committee, with one lawyer on retainer and another serving as a consultant. This committee's work was significant because the APsychA's executive secretary, Fillmore H. Sanford, had told Zizmor that the national association was not prepared to participate in the IRS case. This only continued the APsychA's reluctance in entering the fray. At the APsychA's annual meeting that year, its Advisory Committee on Legislative Matters emphasized that psychologists "must move slowly, carefully, and thoughtfully, if at all," toward the stating of an APsychA policy. Consequently, without any official policy on the independent practice of psychotherapy, the APsychA's Committee on the Relations of Psychology to Psychiatry concluded it would "operate on the general policy that rational discussion is good, and good communication is necessary."[19]

To help take the Joint Council in this new direction, May sought the support of the APsychA's current and former leaders. He found a willing ally in APsychA president Laurence Shaffer of Columbia University's Teachers College but not in the first president of the reorganized association, Carl Rogers. May had never met Rogers, who was then teaching at the University of Chicago. His *Client-Centered Therapy* had been published the previous year, outsizing his influence over the profession. But when May called him, the Joint Council chair was "taken aback" by his statement that he did not know whether it was in psychologists' best interest to be licensed. May could not understand Rogers's hesitancy in supporting licensure.[20]

Filling this leadership void on the national level created by the APsychA was May's Joint Council. For example, in June, May and Bone "strenuously endeavored" to dissuade the California Psychological Association—under pressure from a daily parade of sensational news stories about quack psychologists—from pushing for a certification bill. May acknowledged psychologists' public image crisis was worse in California than New York, but he believed the bill for which his West Coast counterparts were lobbying would "give up a crucial aspect of psychological autonomy" and would "do harm possibly to the profession in the long run." Here, as with the IRS case, May positioned the Joint Council to represent the national interests of the profession of psychology, even though doing so fell far outside the Joint Council's scope of representation. In fact, the Joint Council's members were even torn over the scope of their own representation and mission on the statewide level. For example, Long and Combs, both former NYSPA presidents, believed the Joint Council should become a committee of the statewide group when NYSPA's reorganization was complete in the coming months. Others saw NYSPA as being "not yet sufficiently differentiated to deal effectively with legislative problems" and the Joint Council as better off being a council of affiliated associations. To May, this question of integration or affiliation was not an immediate problem, and by fall 1952 he honed the Joint Council's focus on the "next six months."[21]

At its October meeting, the Joint Council had been, as May observed, "diffuse and at cross purposes, and many of the old foci of anxiety seemed to reappear." However, this confusion, May later assured the group, related less to "what we were discussing" and more to "where we're going." He was applying a major theme of his forthcoming book, *Man's Search for Himself*, to the Joint Council's search for itself. Members told him the group was "disintegrating because we don't have a program into which we can throw ourselves"; they were caught in a "frustration reaction," with no bill to push and mounting doubts as to whether doing so was worth the trouble. Since Dewey's veto, they had "been merely rolling with the punches," and they were "afraid of growing up." They were overly concerned with getting information from other groups rather than striving "to sit down and make up our own minds what we want." The Joint Council's "trouble" was, in one member's words to May, "that we don't take advantage of our own strength and assets." May saw this confusion over goals as underlying the Joint Council's feelings of being "buffeted about" and reacting defensively.[22]

Wanting to "clear the decks on what our present purposes are," May reminded the members that they did not appoint him to maintain the status quo and limit the Joint Council's role to that of a mere legislative committee. The Joint Council was already more than that, with it serving as the only "field headquarters" for the different psychological groups in the state, one that was capable of dealing with various professional emergencies as they emerged. This "automatic broadening" of the Joint Council, May said, was "instinctively sound." He warned, "It is dangerous policy to have a Council promoting legislation which is not intimately connected with the long-term planning of policy for the profession. Legislation is obviously not an end in itself, but is only a codification, a formalized step in the long-term development of the profession." He urged the Joint Council to not rush and harm the profession with precipitous legislation and encouraged it "to lead from strength rather than weakness." Reminding them that New York accounted for a sizeable portion of the APsychA's membership, he said: "We have a responsibility to the future development of the profession which is obviously greater than other states. Psychology will continue to grow in size and we hope in quality, and our job as I see it is to steer it into as constructive and socially useful channels as we can."[23]

After taking a month to digest May's vision, the Joint Council met in November to set its course. There would be no legislation campaign. New York psychologists lost one of their key allies in Albany when Assemblyman Brees, who had sponsored the 1951 licensing bill, lost his seat in the elections earlier that month. At least George Metcalf, the bill's senate sponsor, held his seat and offered to reintroduce the bill. James Allen, the deputy commissioner of education, also encouraged the psychologists to pursue legislation, but only a certification bill. This intelligence came from Combs, who spent a substantial amount of time in Albany following his election as vice-chair of the Joint Council in September and appointment to its Albany Liaison Committee. Although Alexander and the clinical psychologist Roger Lennon were also appointed to this committee, Combs was the most active and became the Joint Council's chief lobbyist in the capitol. The Joint Council decided to continue on a "stand-by, low-level-of-operation basis," meeting every two months. However, May emphasized that the Joint Council would be an "active organization" during the next six months. The Joint Council approved a $6,000 budget, which was slightly higher than the previous year's due to a new line item for legal expenses. While appealing to the state's psychologists for financial contributions, May justified the Joint Council's existence by saying its work on several new fronts "are important as—or more important than—getting a bill itself, for on our success on these fronts will hang the questions of whether the bill we eventually do get will be sound and whether it will work effectively or not." He identified the Joint Council's watchdog function as its most important job. However, as 1952 ended, no legislative threats were seen on the horizon.[24]

Chapter 9
Blitz

They were under attack. They saw the offensive maneuvers, but they did not know what was coming. In January 1953, the NYSMS's county affiliates—following the lead of the APA—had started passing resolutions stating that psychologists should only be permitted to practice under medical supervision. Separately and a month earlier, the AMA's Committee on Mental Health had published a report in *JAMA* in which it declared that "the primary motivation of clinical psychologists is to be recognized by law as qualified to enter the private practice of psychiatry under the guise of psychotherapy." The committee had urged the AMA to adopt a policy that defined "the practice of psychotherapy as an integral part of the practice of medicine."[1]

With this proposal, the medical profession sought to align New York's Medical Practice Act with those of twenty-seven states, mostly in the Midwest and West, which covered both mental and physical ailments. New York was among nine states with medical practice acts that were ambiguous as to whether they covered both conditions, and an additional twelve states clearly did not cover mental conditions. The enactment of bills giving recognition to psychologists had introduced conflicts with medical practice acts in twenty-five to thirty-two states that would need be resolved through legislative action or court decisions.[2]

The NYSMS's activities prompted an emergency meeting of the Joint Council and its preparation of a statement, which May delivered at NYSPA's annual meeting. During his speech at New York University, May framed the issue in the context of a war. He reiterated his belief that the Joint Council, as the unifying body of thirty-four member groups representing training centers and associations of private practitioners, was the "field headquarters" for dealing with "the front-line problems of psychology in this state." He called the APA's opposition to psychologists' practice of psychotherapy "the front-line problem now... because of the tremendous need of persons in our society for competent psychological help. In this age of anxiety, this period of upheaval and radical change in values and moorings past, people of all sorts vitally need help in emotional integration."[3]

May told the audience that the APA's antipsychologist resolution "is not a solution to the problem, and also is not in the public interest." He described "psychological therapy" as a "very broad term" that applied to marriage, vocational, and school counseling as well as problems with accepting or giving love and the inability to work. All dealt with "emotional re-education." May used the words of psychiatrists to emphasize "that many forms of psychotherapy are not to be defined as parts of medicine." He noted how Franz Alexander, the Hungarian American founder of the Chicago Institute of Psychoanalysis, had described psychotherapy as "more an educational process than a therapy in the original sense" and how Thomas French, the associate director of the Chicago Psychoanalytic Group, said that "psychotherapy indeed becomes a process of emotional reeducation." May also referenced Freud's *The Question of Lay Analysis* and how it demonstrated that "psychoanalysis is a form of psychology." May asserted that psychologists' training made them competent to deal with personality disorders, which "underlie a great deal of unhappiness, isolation, emptiness and anxiety in our own society." However, rather than pursue a "premature law [that] may do more harm than good," he said New York psychologists' "over-present job" was to police their profession through the establishment of an accreditation program for competent therapists and diagnosticians and set their own higher standards through the formation of an ethics and grievance committee. Laying out the task at hand, he said:

> We are engaged in the birth pangs of psychology as a profession. We are in the odd position of having to preside at our own birth and to be our own midwives. A profession lives and grows depending upon its self-discipline. If it cannot regulate itself, the public sooner or later kills the profession and its functions are taken over by other groups. We cannot expect to survive unless we

can discipline ourselves and grow and develop along constructive lines. Let us devote ourselves to the building of our science and profession with far-sightedness, dedicated energy and courage.[4]

Despite the increased activity among the county medical societies, when the Joint Council met on February 9, it was reported that there did not appear to be "any danger of a restrictive bill in the legislature this year." The only bill on the Joint Council's radar was one introduced by Senator Metcalf, who had sponsored the 1951 licensing bill, providing $25,000 for a study of the licensing of professional practices involved in the diagnosis of mental and physical disease. Both the Joint Council and several county medical societies favored the bill. The medical profession, however, viewed it as a means for blocking chiropractors' bid for licensing. "There are a number of groups pounding on our doors for licensure and I think we ought to find out about them all at once so we will know how to act," Metcalf said. "At present, we have before us chiefly the claims of rival interest groups." The next meeting was scheduled for March 16, and it was agreed that at it the Joint Council should "deal specifically with the problem of developing a positive rather than merely a defensive, program."[5]

* * *

On November 4, 1952, Wheeler Milmoe was elected to the New York State Senate after serving nine terms in the state assembly. The newspaper publisher had sailed into office, garnering 77 percent of the vote. It was likely sometime after his election win that the fifty-four-year-old Milmoe received a visit from James Beasley, an Albany lobbyist representing the NYSMS. Beasley had presented to either Milmoe or his staff a proposal to insert six words into the Medical Practice Act, amending the definition of the "practice of medicine" to read: "A person practices medicine within the meaning of this article, except as hereinafter stated, who holds himself out as being able to diagnose, treat, operate or prescribe for any human disease, pain, injury, deformity, physical condition *or mental condition*, and who shall either offer or undertake, by any means or method, to diagnose, treat, operate or prescribe for any human disease, pain, injury, deformity, physical condition *or mental condition*."[6] During the previous legislative session, it had been Milmoe who had sponsored the NYSMS-backed bill to amend the Medical Practice Act and penalize physicians who aided or abetted persons not licensed to practice the profession. Milmoe's willingness to sponsor such legislation in the face of opposition from other professions, coupled with his election to the upper house, had likely attracted Beasley to him. However, unlike the similar Greenberg bill in 1949, the one Beasley lobbied for in the capitol would not be limited to the senate, referred to as a one-house bill. Alonzo L. Waters, a western New York Republican, was tapped to sponsor the bill in the assembly. Like Milmoe, Waters was a newspaper publisher, owning the *Medina Daily Journal-Register*. He was a World War I veteran and entering his third term as an assemblyman. His wife of twenty-nine years had died less than two weeks after his reelection the previous November. With legislation requiring passage in both the senate and assembly, in addition to the governor's approval, the Milmoe-Waters bill would have sponsors in both houses who could help push it through the committee process and work to resolve differences between the versions that emerged from them. At the least, the Milmoe-Waters bill was more than the type of symbolic gesture represented by a one-house Greenberg bill.[7]

Milmoe introduced his bill on February 17. New York's psychologists received no warning. The APA's February newsletter, however, had stated that the association's Executive Committee declared that "medical practice acts in the states should include a statement that the practice of medicine includes the diagnosis and treatment of all mental and physical ills." At the time of the bill's introduction, the Joint Council was trying to develop a "positive program" for interprofessional relations. To do so, they were considering sending letters to medical journals, sending a *NYSPA Bulletin* to physicians, or having members personally reach out to them. At the national level, the APsychA's Committee on Relations with Psychiatry was working with the APA's Committee on Clinical Psychology. The members of the latter were, according to the Fillmore Sanford, "doing their rational best to confront interprofessional problems constructively." Indicative of just how caught off guard New York's psychologists were by the bill's introduction, it took them two weeks to muster a public response to it.[8]

The Joint Council likely learned of the bill's introduction in late February. May had entertained the "naïve illusion" that his duties would slacken as the Joint Council's program got going in January and February. Then, suddenly, he found himself canceling almost all of his other work. Night and day, for the next two weeks, psychology's "crisis" consumed him. He needed answers. How could this have happened? The medical and psychiatric committees that had been "calmly discussing" definitions and other matters. There had been reassurances that no restrictive legislation was forthcoming. Either from his own outreach or from reports from the Joint Council's Medical Liaison Committee, May learned that these medical and psychiatric counterparts "were as much double-crossed as we were." It became clear, May later told the Joint Council in a briefing, that the "liberal" physicians and psychiatrists serving on these committees did not "have much to do with the seats of power in the medical and psychiatric hierarchies." May said he had been "authoritatively informed" that the Milmoe-Waters bill was linked to a "group of old-lined institutional psychiatrists." In the AMA, NYSMS, and APA, they represented the "reactionary groups" that held their respective associations' power, but they lacked "effective contact with the rank and file." He said, "We realize that so far as politics go, our adversaries are these reactionary hierarchies."[9]

With these adversaries in its sights, the Joint Council on March 3 returned fire. The result was arguably psychology's most forceful retort to the medical profession since Freud's *The Question of Lay Analysis*. On that night, the Joint Council organized an emergency mass meeting at the New Yorker Hotel, a forty-three-story art deco hotel. On top of attracting more than nine hundred psychologists, the meeting was open to reporters, including those from the *New York Times* and *New York Herald-Tribune*. Standing in one of the New Yorker's conference rooms, May savored a "marvelous morale." The event's lineup of speakers included the Joint Council's chair and co-chair, May and Halpern; Joseph G. Keegan, a Fordham University pastoral psychologist; and Laurence Shaffer.[10]

It was only hours before the mass meeting started that the APsychA's board of directors passed a resolution condemning the Milmoe-Waters bill. The resolution, which Shaffer read at the meeting, stated that the board was "opposed to legislation restricting to any one profession the application of psychological techniques and knowledge. Public welfare demands that such services be the joint responsibility of many professions, including psychology, medicine, education, the ministry, and social work, and should not be limited to any one of them." This resolution, however, only reiterated the APsychA's long-standing position on restrictive legislation and failed to call organized medicine out for its sneak attack. It also failed to challenge the validity of physicians' claims to exclusively diagnose and treat mental conditions. Although Sanford, acknowledged it would be "an immorally weak submission to arbitrary authority" to allow "mental conditions" to be added to the Medical Practice Act, he believed it was "undesirable" to "wage a public fight," hence the resolution's tame language. May, however, believed a public fight was what the profession needed to survive.[11]

At the New Yorker, according to May, there was a "terrific tension." He thrived off it, knowing "we shall never be the same again." The Milmoe-Waters bill, he told the crowd, was "part of a nationwide movement among reactionary groups in the psychological and psychiatric hierarchies to prevent the work of other professionals in helping people with emotional and personality difficulties." Touching on themes from *Man's Search for Himself*, he warned that enactment of the bill "would set the clock back one hundred years. What our society needs for its survival is not new drugs or methods for curing physical ailments, important as these are. What is needed, rather, is that people be helped to learn to live together harmoniously. If we simply continue emphasizing that man is a physical machine, we produce only more effective soldiers and our civilization will indeed be threatened." In a statement distributed to the news media, the Joint Council also called it "obviously inconsistent and illogical" for physicians to define the mental field as wholly part of medicine when Governor Dewey three years ago had vetoed the licensing bill, saying it was impossible to adequately delineate where psychology ended and psychiatry began. The Joint Council also stated that "mental conditions" was a term that spread to the work of teachers, social workers, the clergy, and psychologists. The term's broad scope made the bill administratively impossible to enforce. As an alternative to the Milmoe-Waters bill, the Joint Council urged the legislature to pass Senator Metcalf's proposal for a study of professions seeking licenses.[12]

Away from the public eye, the Joint Council remained active as well. Harold Seashore, the vice president of the Psychological Corporation, joined Combs on the Joint Council's Albany Liaison Committee. The two spearheaded a lobbying campaign that targeted key legislators, including the bill's sponsors. They encountered legislators who were "ready to see our viewpoint and desirous of learning more about what psychologists are and do." While Senator Milmoe had claimed he had not realized the implications of his bill, the Joint Council's former chair, Carleton Scofield, had warned the senator the previous year of the impacts his proposed aiding-and-abetting amendment to the Medical Practice Act would have on the profession. Meanwhile, the Joint Council had allies in medicine, psychiatry, religion, social work, and education pass resolutions and send telegrams to the legislature. Even Harrower, who before leaving the Joint Council had warned May about psychologists' habit of underestimating "the strength of medical opposition," joined the opposition campaign to the Milmoe-Waters bill. In her capacity as president of the NYSCP, which had four hundred members in the New York City area, Harrower warned Milmoe that "properly trained psychologists" would be, if his bill became enacted, "deprived of their livelihood." More important, "the community would be deprived of services in an already overburdened field with a scarcity of trained workers."[13]

The mass meeting's success was beyond what the Joint Council had hoped, especially in terms of public relations. Prior to the introduction of the bill, the Joint Council's Public Relations Committee had been focused on long-term projects, such as defining psychology and surveying college students on attitudes toward psychology. The bill's introduction drove a shift from this long-term approach toward public education to what the committee chair, Louis Long, described as an "intensive immediate one." The mass meeting resulted in full-length articles the next day in the *New York Times* and *New York Herald-Tribune*. The latter, a few days after it ran that initial report, wrote an editorial in support of the psychologists. The editorial demonstrated the Joint Council's success in framing the emerging public debate over the amendment and portraying it as a power grab pursued by the medical profession.[14]

The *Herald Tribune* editorial described the bill as "an extremely exclusive amendment" and "much too sweeping." The newspaper said the psychologists had "a case" for opposing the bill because it would "restrict competently trained psychologists from treating individuals for mental disturbances." With it looking unlikely that the licensing debate would be "easily or intelligently resolved in ordinary floor debate," the paper said the "sensible solution" was for the legislature to pass Metcalf's bill, though lawmakers might be reluctant to do so because it was suspected that that proposal was designed "only to block the chiropractic licensing measure." While May was enthused by the mass meeting's media coverage, he was discouraged that the press had confused "the fight" as being between "psychologists and medicine rather than between medicine and society." Either way, psychologists could not give up, because "it was entirely clear that we could not let this bill pass without surrendering our fundamental belief that psychology is an independent science and profession, and has its own important and essential contribution to make to human welfare." The introduction of the Milmoe-Waters bill had handed the psychologists what they had been lacking for years and what Bone had predicted a year earlier: a unified message. May said, "We know much more clearly where we stand and what needs to be done for our future development." On top of having a message, they had someone who could forcefully deliver it in May. It was a marked change from psychologists' previous attempts at public relations, which, as a newspaperman had told May, had been "incredibly bad."[15]

Ten days after the mass meeting, Senator Milmoe wrote to May to inform him that he had withdrawn his bill, believing "the whole problem needs considerable more study before any legislation should be framed or proposed." Later that day, May informed the Joint Council of Milmoe's withdrawal and said, "The time has come when we can emit a collective 'whew!'" Although he believed "there seems no reason for longer anxiety," he cautioned, "We are not living on faith, however, but are remaining hourly vigilant." May's call for vigilance was justified because the APA then joined the fray and asserted public pressure against the psychologists. In the *Herald-Tribune*, Theodore R. Robie, an East Orange, New Jersey, psychiatrist who chaired an independent, voluntary Committee for the Preservation of Medical Standards in Psychiatry consisting of APA members, claimed May "maligns our medical schools" when he, at the mass meeting, said ordinary physicians were untrained in psychotherapy. Robie, who was a staunch advocate for electroshock therapy and the sterilization of those with mental defects, said the 1951 licensing bill had revealed psychologists' intent to "seek the same privileges and responsibilities of practicing physicians," without the same requirements in training.[16]

Next, the APA issued a statement declaring psychotherapy the province of medical practice, and its president, D. Ewen Cameron, expressed support for the Milmoe-Waters bill. He said psychologists' licensing attempts represented an "ominous trend." The association's medical director, Daniel Blain, said, "All psychological illnesses react on the physical body. The sick individual had to have both psychological and organic medicine." In *The Annals of the American Academy of Political and Social Science* that month, Blain continued to disparage psychologists' independent practice of psychotherapy. He said those who use this technique must "assume full responsibility when working alone." He framed the practice in the context of Cartesian duality, saying psychotherapy was "an attempt to influence the illness of the patient through his intellect and emotions by means of an interchange of ideas and attitudes in an orderly, planned, and responsible way."[17]

May recognized that the APA's repeated attempts to assail psychologists in the days after Milmoe pulled his bill was nothing more than an attempt to bait psychologists into the type of public debate in which they would assume their customary defensive posture. But Robie's letter in the *Herald-Tribune* went unanswered, and deliberately so. "We did not answer the statement from the psychiatrists in the *Herald-Tribune* for temporarily sound reasons from Albany," May told the Joint Council. He added, "We can be sure in the future that this reactionary group basically speaks only the language of power, and we shall gain nothing from them by being defensive. As a matter of fact, if we wanted their respect, we could get it only by showing our power." And it was through such a show of power, May said, that the psychologists "won the battle of publicity hands down in this crisis."[18]

The Joint Council's success in causing Milmoe's bill to die in committee was not an isolated incident. It was only the beginning. Amid the legislative battle that March, the New York State Department of Taxation and Finance issued an opinion stating psychologists were exempt from the state's unincorporated tax so long as 80 percent of their gross income was derived from personal service. This decision was significant because it recognized that APsychA associates were "practicing a profession," as defined by New York's tax law. The IRS also delivered a ruling stating that the federal income tax exemption applied to fees paid to qualified psychologists. Although these rulings, which the Joint Council had fought for over the past year, were "not as dramatic as legislative activity," May believed, they were "just as significant in the slow and steady building of our profession."[19]

On top of these public relations, legislative, and regulatory victories, there was a financial one as well. The mass meeting proved to be a fundraising boon for the Joint Council. Between March 1 and March 15, it raised $3,003 in contributions, almost matching the $3,196 raised between September 1952 and March 1, 1953. However, the Joint Council had incurred significant expenses in its response to the Milmoe-Waters bill. The group also needed to increase May's salary to compensate him for the even greater amount of work he had been performing as chair, which had been 30 percent more "than bargained for." As chair of the Public Relations Committee, Long stressed the need for a part-time worker to establish and maintain media contacts, prepare material, create media lists, and organize reporters interested in Joint Council activities. It was becoming clear that the organization needed to "operate as professionals from here on out and not as amateurs," May said, and that meant it needed a bigger budget supported by a wider fundraising base and contributions based on proportion of income rather than a fixed rate. That would make psychologists in private practice contribute more than those in academia, and rightly so, May believed, because "their livelihood is immediately at stake." "It makes me laugh," May told the Joint Council, "after this last two weeks, to recall that we contributed our $15 or $20 checks, when our whole profession could have been wiped out overnight."[20]

In the aftermath of the Milmoe-Waters bill's failure, the APA attempted to distance itself from what had become a debacle in New York. In late March, "embarrassed" APA officers met with their APsychA counterparts to negotiate what Sanford described as a "'cease fire' arrangement." Cameron and Blain later proposed forming a joint study commission to investigate the legislative situation, even though the two groups had committees that had been doing that for years. May told Sanford that the Joint Council had "little confidence" in the APA's conciliatory statements and that "we must demonstrate the power behind our efforts" with a bill the next year. While the Joint Council sought to assert its power, the APsychA minimized its own. Its board agreed to confer with the APA to avoid "pushing them into restrictive legislation." Only after such legislation was passed would the APsychA support psychologists' attempt to legally challenge it. Later, May was informed that the backers of the proposed Medical Practice Act amendment were "very angry and offended that these servile psychologists should rise up and dare to hit the press." The psychiatrists "came out especially for this stupid bill, which shows publicly where they stand," and May planned to capitalize on this blunder. He advocated for more public relations events like the New Yorker mass meeting, where psychologists could "set right the loose ends from the present struggle, *e.g.*, pointing out that we have no quarrel with medicine or psychiatry as such, but that the theory of absolute medical responsibility (as in the psychiatrist's release) is false." As the APsychA and APA continued their talks to maintain interprofessional peace, the fight for psychology's legal right to independently practice therapy was escalating in New York and being waged by these national groups' proxies.[21]

Even before the legislation session was over, with the threat of the Medical Practice Act amendment behind them, May began pushing the Joint Council to pursue a licensing bill for the next session. "Offense is in general the best tactic from now on," May said in a March 11 letter to the state's psychologists. He was not as skeptical as others on the Joint Council that such a bill would not pass, pointing to expressed support from the state's Education Department as well as the "much good political capital" that the psychologists had built in Albany since February. He said it stood "a good chance of passing." In fact, the Joint Council was already quietly laying the foundation for this legislative campaign. On May 5, Harrower sought the assistance of Jean Stralem, a prominent philanthropist and the wife of a New York City investment banker, in learning whether Dewey had made "an irrevocable decision that a licensing bill for psychologists cannot be passed." Despite having been born into the Lehman investment banking family—a member of which Dewey had defeated in the 1942 gubernatorial election—Stralem had influence on the second floor of the capitol in Albany, where the governor's administrative offices were located. Her letter to Dewey resulted in May and Seashore scheduling a meeting with the governor's counsel, George Shapiro, in June, though there are indications this meeting was pushed back to August. Regardless of when the meeting was held, Harrower encouraged Stralem to follow up with Dewey after the Joint Council representatives independently met with Shapiro.[22]

As the Joint Council worked to determine whether Dewey would support a licensing bill, May set out to build the interprofessional alliances needed for the lobbying campaign. May reached out to several prominent progressive psychiatrists. One of them was Carl Binger, the best-selling author who had sat on the New York Academy of Medicine's Subcommittee on Certification of Psychologists. Binger had provided a promotional blurb for *Man's Search for Himself*, saying it was a "fine and courageous book." Although Binger had been critical of psychologists' pursuit of certification when he sat on that subcommittee in 1948, he was receptive to

May's entreaty. "It is apparent that clinical psychology is becoming a kind of Korea or Kashmir," Binger said. [23]

May also reached out to John A. P. Millet, chief of Presbyterian Hospital's Psychosomatic Clinic and president of the New York Society of Clinical Psychiatry. Importantly, Millet had ties to one of psychologists' leading adversaries: the APA's Blain. In 1938, the two had established the Tratelja Farms Sanitarium in upstate New York. Millet told May he viewed himself as a "moderate" in the "knotty problem" over licensing. He believed the APsychA's and APA's committees discussing the issue would not achieve any consensus. Consequently, the best option was "to whack away at it on the local level through joint conferences," which was what the Joint Council had been attempting. He said the licensing of psychologists could "prove to be the best solution" so long as the APsychA could guarantee psychologists' medical collaboration. Lawrence Kubie was less than pleased with May's outreach. Kubie had watched with dismay the recent partisan flare-up between the professions. There had been "a complete mistrust of the motives and purposes of the other side," and he felt May was "as guilty as anyone else." Kubie reprimanded May for painting the AMA and APA positions as being "purely mercenary," even though the psychiatrist, too, disagreed with them. He refused to even meet with May, saying, "I will not try to work with anyone who approaches this problem in this spirit."[24]

As the Joint Council headed into the summer, the unknowns were many. Would they introduce a revised licensing bill? Would Dewey veto it? Would the AMA and APA attack again? Adding to these questions was, Who would lead them? In April, May had announced plans to resign as chair. That would free him for an even greater leadership role within the profession: NYSPA president. In his last address to the state's psychologists as the Joint Council's chair, he said:

> The crises of this fateful spring are part of the "frontier struggles" of the development of psychology as a profession. We have to be pioneers whether we want to or not, for history places us in the particular point in evolution when the science of man is being born. To be on the growing edge of history does not make for security or comfort, to be sure. It does not provide one with an external, ready-made status. And it requires a special self-discipline and integrity in developing our own standards and training facilities. But to be on the edge of history also has its compensations—it calls forth our creativity and challenges us to make the most of our potentialities. Furthermore, we have some inspiring w—

William James, Tichener, Dewey, Freud, G. Stanley Hall, and the others who had to be pioneers in the birth and development of their periods in psychology. Not at all a faint-hearted company![25]

Chapter 10
The Calm before the Storm

Money had stopped coming in. The Joint Council had less than $1,800 in its treasury, and it would be expended by the fall. The June meeting with the governor's counsel had been postponed. There was the "spontaneous development" of Albany and Brooklyn psychologists organizing regionally, and if they did not align with the Joint Council then they could detract from, rather than advance, its planned legislative activities. In Illinois, the Illinois Psychiatric Society had persuaded the Illinois Psychological Association to drop its campaign for certification legislation and instead "attempt to draft legislation or determine action acceptable to both organizations." A study conducted by the Southern California Society for Mental Hygiene concluded Los Angeles was a "breeding ground" for quacks and charlatans posing as psychologists, with 30 percent of 544 individuals and organizations offering psychological services in the city lacking any recognized psychological training. Problems on top of problems were mounting on May's desk, and his tenure as the Joint Council's chair was becoming shorter and shorter. Then there was the phone call he received in early June.[1]

The call came from a psychologist who had attended the AMA's annual conference in New York City at the invitation of a medical colleague. The psychologist had attended a meeting of the section on nervous and mental diseases to hear a paper, but before it had been presented, a short business meeting had been held. The psychologist told May that Hans Reese, a University of Wisconsin psychiatry professor, had reported that the AMA House of Delegates had recently addressed the issue of psychologists' licensing pursuits. Reese said the AMA had accepted the recently adopted position of the APA that psychotherapy required medical supervision. He warned that if psychologists became licensed then physicians would have to participate in their training, as they did with osteopaths. He said the AMA must immediately launch a broad educational program to block the licensing efforts of psychologists and other technicians who might have followed their lead, such as bacteriologists. Reese then held up a copy of the April issue of the *American Psychologist* in which Sanford had summarized organized medicine's winter lobbying blitz in Albany. The psychiatrist said the positions stated in the journal were not tantamount to a formal protest and physicians still had time to move forward with their plans to block the licensing of psychologists.[2]

May conveyed this information in a confidential memorandum to Sanford and the APsychA's outgoing and incoming presidents, Shaffer and Orval H. Mowrer of the University of Illinois. Mowrer had been elected APsychA president in 1952, but as he assumed that role in summer 1953 he fell into the deepest depression of his life. That fall he admitted himself to a psychiatric institution. He was suicidal and convinced he had "lost [his] mind" and that he could "never function intellectually and professionally again." Mowrer's institutionalization created a leadership void at the APsychA just as the AMA was mounting a second strike against the profession of psychology in New York.[3]

While the APsychA inherited a shaky leader, the Joint Council inaugurated one who was solid and not only ready for political fights but a veteran of them. In June 1953, the Joint Council elected Stuart W. Cook as its chair. He was a forty-year-old social psychologist who was known as being "infinitely patient" and "an exceedingly decent, low-key person." That, however, did not mean he was not bold. After receiving his master's degree in psychology from the University of Richmond, he had hitchhiked to the University of Minnesota in 1935 to work toward his doctorate. Over the next decade, he worked in a variety of fields, conducting experimental research with B. F. Skinner and serving as a clinical psychologist at the University of Minnesota Hospital. During World War II, he developed tests to identify potential pilots, bombardiers, navigators, and airborne radar operators for the army's aviation psychology program. After the war he focused more on social psychology, initially in 1946 by researching ways to counter anti-Semitism for the American Jewish Congress's Commission on Community Interrelations. In 1949, he moved to New York University, where he had founded the Research Center for Human Relations. There he honed his attention on Black-White issues, such as the psychological impacts of segregation and racial prejudice.[4]

Through these positions at social science institutes, Cook had gained insights into state politics, and his experiences had likely drawn the Joint Council's Nominating Committee to him. For example, in February 1949, he had addressed the New York State Senate Committee on Discrimination in Housing. Three years later, Cook, with Kenneth B. Clark and Isidor Chein, drafted a pivotal appellant's brief for *Brown v. Board of Education*, which the US Supreme Court would rehear in December. This "Social Science Statement" illustrated the effects of segregation on African American children and would later be cited in the court's landmark 1954 decision. Clark, an African American professor at City College, later said Cook's involvement in the drafting process was "just wonderful because he brought the appearance of white, Anglo-Saxon dispassionateness to our task where I had a tendency sometimes to be a little strident. Stuart would say, 'Well, now, we don't want to lose our point by overstatement.'"[5]

With another political storm heading toward New York, Cook's on-point character was just what the Joint Council needed. When he oversaw his first Joint Council meeting in September, however, everything presented seemed to want to throw him off point. A mid-August meeting with Dewey's personal counsel, Shapiro, had been as disappointing as it was confusing. Freeman, Combs, and Seashore had attended the meeting, and each had left it with different impressions. Combs believed Shapiro had indicated the governor would be more open to legislation for certification rather than licensure; Freeman was less optimistic and believed the lawyer had indicated any type of legislation from psychologists would be viewed unfavorably; and Seashore left the meeting thinking that psychologists were simply caught in a nationwide trend in which lawmakers were increasingly reluctant to license any new group. Cook had told the Joint Council that "the Governor's position is a deciding factor in legislation," and these conflicting reports did not lend themselves to a well-informed decision. Making matters worse was the fact that the trio had failed to ask Shapiro about psychologists' need for protection from revisions to the Medical Practice Act. That month's edition of the *New York State Journal of Medicine* included a copy of a resolution that the NYSMS's House of Delegates had recently passed. It stated the society would petition the legislature to amend the Medical Practice Act to include "nervous and mental disorders as a part of the duties and responsibilities of duly licensed practitioners."[6]

An attack was coming. Unlike the previous summer, there was no question within the Joint Council about that. It began preparing for battle. May, as chair of a newly formed Interprofessional Liaison Committee, began building alliances with social workers, ministers, and educators. His background as a pastor and a teacher of pastoral psychology ideally positioned him for recruiting allies in the ministry. The same was true for Bone, who also sat on the committee, as did Harrower, who returned to the Joint Council after a hiatus of several months. May stressed that such alliances would be integral in helping the Joint Council "prepare for a long struggle." For ammunition in this battle, Max Siegel, who had established a vocational and psychological counseling center at Brooklyn College, oversaw the preparation of informational materials that would be distributed to state legislators. Assisting him on his Committee on Legislative Kits was Avrum Ben-Avi, who, like Cook, had helped develop tests for identifying potential army pilots and bombardiers during World War II. By October, the Joint Council's financial war chest had shrunk to $195.50. A major fundraising initiative would soon be launched to satisfy the Joint Council's $20,000 budget, which was 33 percent higher than its budget in 1951. However, the Joint Council voted to only seek funds from psychologists in New York. This decision to limit the financial influence of out-of-state sources had been proposed by May, whose relationship with the APsychA's leadership was tested that month.[7]

October should have been the month in which the Joint Council's legislative aspirations gained momentum. The APsychA revisited the subject of certification and licensing with a series of papers on the topic that were published in that month's *American Psychologist*. A year earlier the APsychA's Council of Representatives had requested this study on legislative matters. The hope was that the symposium would help the board of directors in overcoming the hesitancy that had impaired the APsychA's ability to "take a stand." The October issue featured an introduction from New York psychologists' stalwart ally Sanford and papers from two Joint Council members, Albert Ellis and Combs. In addition to sitting on the

APsychA's board, Cook had recently been appointed as an advisory editor to the *American Psychologist*.[8]

Also, psychologists in Tennessee earlier that year had proved licensing legislation could still be enacted, though at a cost. In April, Governor Frank Clement signed a psychologist licensing bill into law. Tennessee's psychologist licensing law was modeled after those in Kansas and Georgia, but it deviated from them by, among other ways, dividing practitioners of psychology into two categories: "psychological examiner" and "psychologist." School, vocation, industrial, and clinical psychologists were primarily covered under the definition of psychologist, which focused on professionals who rendered services involving "the application of recognized principles, methods and procedures of the science and profession of psychology, such as interviewing, or administering and interpreting tests of mental abilities, aptitudes, interest and personality characteristics." They were not licensed to practice psychotherapy but could test for people who should be selected for it. Psychological evaluators, in contrast, were licensed to practice psychotherapy, as well as conduct personality appraisals or classifications, engage in personality counseling, or use personality-adjustment techniques. However, they could only engage in these practices "under qualified supervision," and they could not practice any form of psychotherapy that infringed on the practice of medicine under state law. Psychological evaluators were required to "maintain inter-communication with a psychologically oriented physician, usually a psychiatrist, to make provision for the diagnosis and treatment of medical problems by a physician with an unlimited license to practice the healing arts in the State." The Tennessee law did represent a new movement toward professional licensing, though. Certification remained a valid option, as demonstrated in Maine, which earlier that year also enacted a law similar to Connecticut's.[9]

Before the October issue of the *American Psychologist* could be published and help the APsychA Board set its legislative policy, its ad hoc Committee on Relations between Psychology and Other Professions made that decision about the recommended type of legislation. Included in that month's issue was the ad hoc committee's report exploring the implications of the recommendations it had made in the May 1952 issue of the *American Psychologist* on psychology's relations with other professions. Although not exclusively focused on legislative matters, the older report did address several. For example, the ad hoc committee had called on the APsychA to support state associations' legislative efforts so long as they were to certify qualified psychologists. The APsychA was not to support state associations' attempts to "specify the activities of psychologists," as in a licensing bill, or to "limit these activities to persons designated as psychologists," as in a hybrid bill. In his introduction to the October issue, Sanford noted that the inclusion of this ad hoc committee's report in the October 1953 issue made the symposium on legislation "somewhat out of date before it appeared to the public."[10]

May had not served on this committee when it issued its initial report in 1952, but he was later appointed to it, likely due to his new role as NYSPA president. That made him the committee's second Joint Council member, with the other being Combs. Joseph McVicker Hunt, the Joint Council's founder, also sat on the ad hoc committee. May's name was accidently included at the end of the committee's subsequent October 1953 report, which expounded its recommendation for certification legislation as opposed to licensing or hybrid bills. Although May agreed with the rest of the report, he could not endorse it because of the certification recommendation. May later clarified his position in the *American Psychologist*, saying bills such as the one Dewey vetoed in 1951 and another in Tennessee were the recommended type. He continued to maintain the position that "we need to be in no hurry to get legislation for psychologists," and he cautioned that the ad hoc committee was overlooking each state's "immediate, dynamic aspects of the problem which must be struggled with day in and day out in the political arena and in the market place of public opinion."[11]

Unlike Combs, who had recently claimed in the *American Psychologist* that "so long as we cannot write a definition . . . we cannot be picked out as a subject of special attack," May believed it was unwise to hold to the belief that "principles carry their own power." Having withstood the political might of the AMA at the Joint Council, May recognized how "truth could be buried for decades or centuries unless it is allied with democratic power." That was why he continued to emphasize building alliances with "farseeing physicians and psychiatrists," artists, social workers, clergy, and others who shared with psychologists "a unique perspective of man." That may also be why, in his introduction to Mowrer's *Psychotherapy*, May described psychotherapy as broadly as possible: as "social learning," with "social" not referring to social adaption but to the process of relating "*to one's own self as a person as well as to others.*" This "new view of man" represented "the understanding of and dealing with man as a psychological and social being rather than chiefly a biological being."[12]

While May made this entreaty for a new view of man, old views prevailed outside New York. In April, the state attorney general of Michigan ruled that "the practice of psychotherapy by non-medically licensed people" constituted a violation of Michigan's Medical Practice Act. The medical profession's aggressiveness even rattled the APsychA's new president-elect, Lowell Kelly of the University of Michigan. A private psychiatrist visited Kelly's university clinic and intimidated the psychologist by referring to his clinic's lack of psychiatric supervision in "a clearly threatening fashion." In New York that fall, the NYSMS's House of Delegates referred its resolution to amend the Medical Practice Act to the organization's Committee on Legislation. By mid-November, Cook learned this committee was taking "preparatory action" toward implementing the resolution in Albany. Separately, the APA budgeted $20,000 for a public education campaign on "the desirability of restricting the practice of psychotherapy to physicians." That amount was ten times greater than the Joint Council's public education budget. Harrower continued to try to assure the Joint Council that there were prominent psychiatrists who desired a "compromise solution," but already one New York City hospital—under pressure from the Bronx County Medical Society—was prohibiting clinical psychologists from practicing psychotherapy. At the Joint Council's November meeting, Zizmor warned that if this policy became more widespread then it could become the "most serious of threats to psychology" because "it would slowly choke off training facilities." Elsewhere in the city, several psychologists were denied office space in a residential area because they did not practice recognized medical specialties covered by zoning regulations.[13]

In response, the Joint Council began preparing legislative kits to help psychologists counter the impending attack, and it struck cooperative action agreements with the American Association of Social Workers, New Jersey Psychological Association, APsychA, and Federal Bar Association. The kits included talking points and outlined which legislators volunteers should visit. The talking points referenced published declarations of the NYSMS's plans to amend the Medical Practice Act and discussed how the Joint Council represented more than three thousand psychologists in New York. The talking points further warned that the Medical Practice Act amendment would "cut out vital public services from professions other than medicine or place non-medical workers under severe harassment." On November 10, Herbert J. Zucker, the Joint Council's associate chair, reported, "Our campaign to contact members of the legislature in regard to restrictive legislation and future licensing is now under way." More than one hundred psychologists would participate in this lobbying campaign over the next two months, visiting 140 legislators. The effort became, in Cook's words, "the largest enterprise of this sort ever attempted by psychologists."[14]

Regardless of what psychologists would learn from legislators about the prospects for licensing, the Joint Council was in no position to launch an offensive in Albany. Had it not been for several creditors' willingness to postpone payments, the Joint Council would have been running at a deficit. At May's recommendation, the Joint Council voted to not pursue a bill. This decision against a bill coincided with the off year of several other states with biennial legislatures that were interested in certification or licensing, such as North Carolina, Texas, Utah, and Wisconsin. That meant the AMA and APA would have to devote fewer resources to attacking pro-psychology bills in those states as well as New York in 1954. Instead of legislation, the Joint Council would pursue the NYSPA-based certification option that New York psychologists had previously dropped. With Assemblyman Noonan's 1950 certification bill as a model, NYSPA, according to Seashore, would attempt "to do ourselves what the state apparently was not ready to do for us and with us." NYSPA planned to make clear in its directory of certificate holders that certification did not demonstrate specialty competence.[15]

Less than three weeks before the 163rd legislative session was to start in Albany, Cook delivered disheartening news to the Joint Council: his Research Center for Human Relations at New York University had sustained an unexpected cut in federal funding, and he would have to substantially curb his Joint Council work so he could focus on fundraising. Cook offered to resign or continue serving as chair in a limited capacity, mostly to conduct high-level negotiations, such as with the New York state education commissioner, Carroll V. Newsom. That option left Cook's associate chair, Zucker, to handle the rest of his duties. The Joint Council, at May's recommendation, moved to reactivate its Nominating Committee, though no replacement could be found, leaving the chairship split between Zucker and Cook. However, the leadership shakeup did not take the fight out of the

Joint Council. More so than the previous year, it would be a public fight. It would be a fight in which psychologists, Cook proposed, would "challenge the competence of physicians in psychology instead of confining ourselves to a defensive position." It was also a fight that psychologists wanted to be fought professionally, by a public relations specialist.[16]

After debating whether to contract with a public relations specialist for two years, the Joint Council in January 1954 finally voted to retain one. Members had debated whether to hire a small, inexpensive organization that would likely "give more active attention to our account than a large one." However, according to Zucker, they also wanted someone who was "in a position to exert pressure rather than merely to solicit influence as a small organization or a free lance [sic] person would." With these objectives in mind, the Joint Council opted for the latter option and retained the services of Edward L. Bernays, the sixty-two-year-old nephew of Freud whose reputation as the "father of public relations" and "the father of spin" had long been sealed.[17]

Bernays was a Viennese native who had come from Austria to New York when he had been less than a year old. As a young man, he had gravitated toward journalism, the field into which he entered after graduating from Cornell University in 1912. Shortly afterward, his career took an unexpected turn while he had served as the editor of the *Dietetic and Hygienic Gazette* and associated *Medical Review of Reviews*. Wanting to support an actor who had been struggling to find sponsors in New York to produce Eugène Brieux's *Damaged Goods*, Bernays used the *Review* to mobilize public opinion for the play's production. *Damaged Goods* included the controversial themes of sexually transmitted diseases and infidelity. To further build support for the play "on the grounds of social and public interest," Bernays created a sociological fund whose members financed the production and were given tickets to a performance. His success in campaigning for this production began his career in public relations. To Bernays, public relations was "a vital tool of adjustment, interpretation, and integration between individuals, groups, and society." It also was "an implementing factor in many and varied competitive battles for public opinion in our country." Following the success of *Damaged Goods*, Bernays became a press agent for a theatrical firm in 1913 and a publicity agent for the Metropolitan Musical Bureau in 1915 as well as the Diaghilev Russian ballet. After the United States entered World War I, he joined the Committee on Public Information that Woodrow Wilson had created to garner domestic support for the war effort. After leaving this committee in 1919, Bernays formed a public relations firm with Doris E. Fleischman, whom he later married. His early work as what he described as a "public relations counselor" included, on behalf of the War Department in 1919, garnering public support for servicemen transitioning back to civilian life; helping the Lithuanian National Council overcome American indifference toward their country and receive official recognition from the United States in 1919; helping the Beech-Nut Packing Company boost its bacon sales in the mid-1920s by publicizing doctors' statements endorsing hearty breakfasts; and making Procter & Gamble's Ivory soap more popular among children by organizing a National Soap Sculpture Competition in 1924. Presidents, including Calvin Coolidge and Herbert Hoover, had retained his services for their reelection campaigns in 1924 and 1932, respectively.[18]

Jule Nydes, the vice president of the National Psychological Association for Psychoanalysis, raised questions over whether Bernays's unorthodox public relations practices "would violate principles of the Joint Council" and whether he would accept guidance from it. However, Bernays's offer to provide public relations services to the Joint Council at the low rate of $5,000 per year was too good to pass up. Zucker noted that Bernays appeared to be "motivated more by an interest in the issue than a desire for profit." Bernays's interest may have stemmed from his uncle, Freud, who twenty-eight years earlier had opposed medicine's stranglehold on psychoanalysis in Europe, similar to how the Joint Council was opposing its hold on psychotherapy in New York. One key differentiating factor between the opposition faced by Freud and the Joint Council was the former favored physician supervision of lay analysts, whereas the latter did not. While it is not clear whether Bernays was aware of his uncle's position in *The Question of Lay Analysis*, the two appeared to have been corresponding since 1919. That was the year Bernays had launched his public relations practice and seven years before the publication of *The Question of Lay Analysis*. Bernays frequently bragged about his connections to Freud, and he attributed his early success in the social sciences to his famous uncle and to how he had been "exposed at home to discoveries about the mind and individual and group behavior." In return for a box of Havana cigars that Bernays had delivered to his uncle in 1919, Freud had sent his nephew manuscripts of lectures he had delivered in Vienna between 1915 and 1917. A year later, Bernays oversaw the publication of their English translation in Freud's

Introductory Lectures on Psychoanalysis. Bernays later tried to persuade his uncle to go on a six-month lecture tour in America and write a series of articles for $1,000 each, though Freud declined both opportunities.[19]

Later in January 1954, at its annual business meeting at Hunter College, NYSPA officially inaugurated May as its president and approved the establishment of the New York Board of Examiners in Psychology. In February, NYSPA planned to appoint nine people to this board, which would be responsible for evaluation applications for and issuing certificates to psychologists. The swift decision to revive certification was more of a reaction to the threatened Medical Practice Act amendment than an indication of the Joint Council's lack of interest in licensing. "We as psychologists will be in a poor position to defeat this bill if we are not able to show the public, the legislators, the state departments in Albany, and the Governor's office that we have taken steps to set up standards to discipline our own profession," the New York Psychological Corporation's board of directors explained in a memorandum to its membership. This action was specifically designed to counter criticisms from officials in the governor's office, who had "pointedly asked why we do not take steps within our own profession to set standards."[20]

In his January 30, 1954, president's address to NYSPA's membership, May described one of the greatest challenges before them as correcting "an error of great over-simplification" that psychologists and psychiatrists had committed in the 1920s and 1930s in "seeking to divorce psychotherapy from its ethical and philosophical sources in the past." Consequently, people believed they could separate their problems from their ethical outlook, and they "unconsciously and uncritically" adopted the mores and values of American culture without consciously examining their ethical presuppositions. This resulted in 1920s-era concepts such as "success" and "social adjustment" that were "generally not nearly as good as the values developed in man's long ethical historical quest." For May, the science of psychotherapy existed in those philosophical and ethical traditions of the past. He saw, as Nietzsche did in the age of the Greeks, that philosophical thinking's pursuit of "those things worth knowing," and its ability to "legislate greatness," could tame science's "blind desire to know all at any cost."[21]

Chapter 11
The Last Stand

To May, it was a familiar scene. Another winter night. Another nine hundred psychologists packed into a room, with worry on many of their faces. The setting was different, though; the grandeur of the New Yorker Hotel's conference room in which last year's emergency mass meeting had been held was replaced with the coarser brick and limestone Roosevelt Auditorium of 100 East Seventeenth Street, once known as Tammany Hall. At 8:30 p.m. on February 15, a Monday, the psychologists began the meeting.[1]

Five days earlier, Senator Samuel Greenberg had introduced the long-threatened bill to amend the Medical Practice Act. Just as he had proposed in 1949, Greenberg, with his new bill, sought to insert the phrase "mental and nervous disorders" into the definition for the practice of medicine. Whereas the Joint Council had been slow in its response to the Milmoe-Waters bill the previous year, the organization's response to Greenberg's was swift. One day after the bill's introduction, there were announcements for the emergency meeting at the Roosevelt Auditorium. "A CALL TO ARMS" read a flier for the event distributed by the NYSCP. In its own flier, the Joint Council said Greenberg's bill "represents a distinct threat to the profession of psychology and must be stopped at all costs." However, the Joint Council was not prepared to incur those costs. By mid-February, it had raised less than half of its $20,000 budget. Harry McNeil, the chair of its Finance Committee, warned that more than $10,000 needed to be raised immediately "for the advancement and defense of psychology in New York State." In a more urgent plea, Max Siegel, the president of the

NYSCP, told his membership, "Psychology as a profession is fighting for its very life in the State of New York. This fight costs money, and will continue to cost money until our professional status has been securely established via the defeat of restrictive legislation and the passage of a licensing bill for psychologists."[2]

Even with a shoestring budget, the Joint Council had been able to prepare for this attack. From the Joint Council's volunteer lobbying campaign, Cook had received psychologists' reports of visits to forty-six legislators. That accounted for less than a quarter of the lawmakers in the legislature. While a few were noncommittal about changes to the Medical Practice Act, none were hostile to psychologists. The chairmen of the senate and assembly committees on public education both promised Cook and Zucker that they would have an opportunity to testify about the amendment if the bill ever went to a public hearing. The Emergency Committee, headed by the former *NYSPA Bulletin* editor Roger T. Lennon, had prepared several letters advocating for the defeat of restrictive legislation. The letters were intended for legislators, psychologists, and the press. Action plans with allied professions were set. Social workers, who in the past had felt slighted by psychologists, agreed to provide support even though they lacked the resources to launch a rapid response. May had procured pledges of active support from Protestant, Catholic, and Jewish members of the clergy, and within a year he expected the powerful National Council of Churches to join the fray with psychologists. The New York State Bar Association said it would oppose only aspects of a bill that were technically deficient, and the Federal Bar Association offered more positive support, though its influence in Albany was marginal. The Joint Council had also extended its alliance outreach to labor unions, and by January it had forged ties with several labor groups. That may explain how the emergency meeting ended up being held in an auditorium owned by Local 91 of the International Ladies' Garment Workers' Union.[3]

May came to the emergency meeting armed with letters, which he read to the audience. One was signed by five Jewish and Christian leaders. They warned that the Greenberg bill, if passed, would restrict the counseling performed by members of the clergy and religious social workers. One of them, Rabbi Henry E. Kagan of Mount Vernon, New York, was the chair of the Central Conference of Rabbis' Committee on Religion and Psychiatry. Another was the Reverend Benjamin Priest, who was in charge of counseling at Trinity Church, near Wall Street. This opposition letter was so significant that it overshadowed the rest of the emergency meeting in the Associated Press's coverage, with its headline reading, "5 Clergymen Balk at State Mental Bill." May's other letter came from Lawrence Kubie, a clinical professor of psychiatry at Yale University. He said, "I believe the official position of the American Medical Association . . . in opposition to the further training of the clinical psychologist for psychological diagnosis and psychotherapy is scientifically, humanly and practically indefensible. . . . It would be unwise to place all psychological diagnosis and all psychological therapy under the Medical Practice Act. This would block the development of psychological services urgently needed in day nurseries, kindergartens, primary schools, churches, social agencies, pediatric clinics and hospitals, high schools and universities." Kubie had sent this letter to Harrower, and May appears to have selectively read from it. May appears to have omitted Kubie's statement that "neither clinical psychologists nor psychiatrists are adequately trained today." Kubie thought "any legislation," meaning restrictive or licensing, would be "premature" because it would "shut the door to the future development" of facilities for the doctorate of medical psychology for which he had been advocating for the past several years.[4]

In his emergency meeting address, May continued to frame the fight as not being psychologists against psychiatrists but psychiatrists versus society. The struggle was over "whether the benefits of psychological knowledge [are] extended to as many people in our society who need them, or [they are] strictly limited." He continued to stress the importance of psychology's alliances, saying it was a "struggle with leaders of church, social workers, educators and liberal physicians and psychiatrists, against that segment which would fence off benefits to [the] privileged few." He regretted that this "political fight is forced upon us," detracting from their counseling, research, and teaching, "but none of us will shirk a fight if it is for what we believe in, and we shall sacrifice in time and energy." "Furthermore," he added, "when some new advance in society is born, [it] almost always involves a struggle. What is occurring is the birth of a new approach to human problems, understanding and dealing with man as a psychological, social and ethical being rather than centrally a biological being."[5]

May then elaborated on what he believed to be physicians' and psychiatrists' "real motives" behind their push for restrictive legislation. He did not believe they were "chiefly economic," but if they were then it was "illusory" because "there is plenty of work to go around for every competent person." The motives, instead, were "power and prestige." He said, "The physician is heir to tremendous authority and prestige in our society. This is partly rational authority, because the physician is the mediator of vast scientific progress since the Renaissance: our great technical advances touch ordinary people's lives through the drugs and activities of their doctors." What the psychologists were questioning was the physicians' "irrational authority." May called this the "physician's narcissism" that drove the thinking that "nobody can treat anybody for anything except a physician." He said the backers of the Greenberg bill were exhibiting "amazing arrogance"—and contradicting Freud himself—in trying to pass psychotherapy as a form of medicine. May urged the psychologists in the auditorium, as he had the Joint Council, to "not succumb" to "a minority state of mind"—to "not become defensive, fighting where there is no fight; or neurotically anxious, and waste our strength; or vindictive, and damage our own profession." If psychologists could see clearly what they stood for, then they would find "the confidence both to fight strongly and not succumb to minority feelings." "We must not, ourselves, fall unconscious victims to that irrational prestige of medicine, and try to be second-class doctors."[6]

May assured the psychologists that someday they would be licensed, but more important than that was "inner discipline," which NYSPA was demonstrating through its new certification board. This inner discipline, he said, was "more creative, flexible, can grow easier, [and] avoids being pegged statistically at the level of licensing." With this inner discipline came responsibility—one that was different from the AMA's "brash" "medical responsibility," by which doctors acted as though they were the "only one[s] who knew what responsibility was." Psychologists' responsibility would be different: one that was "rarely *for* the person, only when incapacitated" and "rather responsibility *with* the person." This meant psychologists primarily needed to empathize with their clients and help them navigate the world as they experience it. Rather than assuming authority over these non-incapacitated clients, psychologists worked *with* them on this journey.[7]

A Joint Council press release highlighted statements made at the emergency meeting by May and the other speakers, such as Cook and the APsychA's executive secretary, Sanford, and previous president, Shaffer. The press release, through its selected quotes from these psychologists, was designed to sow doubts over the effectiveness of the Greenberg bill and the competence of physicians. May's quotes in the press release emphasized how "this bill would not keep quacks out but would hurt only the legitimate professions." Sanford's statements were the most pointed. He noted how one in ten Americans at some point in their lives had suffered from mental difficulties and millions more suffered from "crippling psychological ailments" that prevented them from reaching their potential. "Who is going to help these millions of people," he asked. "Ordinary physicians? They know little more about psychotherapy than a clinical psychologist knows about taking out someone's tonsils." On top of that, with the nation only having seven thousand psychiatrists, Sanford added, "There really are not enough of them." Despite these strong words, many psychologists in the audience, especially the students, believed the Joint Council was not being aggressive enough. Two days after the emergency meeting, one of May's colleagues at Columbia told him that the students she encountered believed that "since the Amer. Psychiat. Ass. is playing dirty, we should too." They said that because "there is nothing more the AMA dislikes more than poor publicity and since publicity in this struggle cannot hurt psychology in the public's eyes, we should make it dirty enough so that the AMA tells the Amer. Psychiat. Ass. to cut it out."[8]

The "dirty" campaign, however, was already underway, and it would be waged on the editorial pages of newspapers across New York, though most prominently in the influential *New York Times*. Major themes of the campaign would be psychiatrists' insufficient amount of personnel to meet the public's demands and an appeal to parents and spouses by emphasizing the adverse impacts the Greenberg bill could have on families, children in particular. In most cases, the psychologists avoided using psychological terminology and instead employed simpler terms, such as "troubles" and "difficulties." Over the next month psychologists and psychiatrists fired off several volleys of letters to the *Times*; the newspaper also provided its own coverage of the controversy. Just before the introduction of the Greenberg bill, Bernays had been trying to hone the Joint Council's focus on these issues. But it was only on February 8—two days before the introduction of the Greenberg bill—that Cook had briefed the Joint Council on the formal agreement with Bernays. That left no time for the Joint Council and Bernays to finalize a strategy. New York's psychologists had to fend for themselves in the public relations battle with the AMA and APA.[9]

May fired the opening shot with a letter dated February 12, two days after the introduction of the Greenberg bill. May warned how "no one has yet succeeded in defining 'nervous and mental disorders' beyond the obvious nervous illnesses such as epilepsy and organic psychosis, which should admittingly be under the scope of medicine." Playing on the fears of parents, May cautioned that a child's nail biting or truancy, or students' stress-related underachievement, could be regarded as indications of mental disorders under Greenberg's bill. Further, the bill's "broad and undefinable terms" would "produce chaos among the legitimate facilities in the state for helping people with their emotional and psychological problems." Needing to provide an alternative solution to the problem of quackery, May called for the formation of a "commission representing all of the professions which work with the people." With this proposal he may have been referring to draft legislation that Assemblyman Gould Hatch, a Rochester Republican, had approached Cook about earlier that winter, which called for an investigation into the professions involved in mental hygiene.[10]

May's letter to the *Times* elicited a response from Samuel Parker, the director of psychiatry of New York City's Department of Hospitals. Parker, who had been the driving force behind Greenberg's similarly restrictive 1949 legislation, was the first of many in the medical profession to disparage the "frenzied propaganda drive of psychologists." Those psychologists, he claimed, sought to thwart the bill "entirely on the single fact that they want to practice psychotherapy on people suffering from well-defined nervous ailments." Parker claimed May was drawing red herrings in claiming teachers or ministers would be persecuted under the bill because it would apply only to "those who set themselves up to treat nervous or mental disorders for a fee." He added, "Free advice is the prerogative of every American." However, Greenberg's proposed definition for the "practice of medicine" made no reference to fees for services. Parker warned that lay practitioners were "ganging up to destroy" the high medical standards that enabled psychiatrists to evaluate and treat "complex and fearful nervous disorders" and concluded that "Senator Greenberg's bill will put them back where they belong."[11]

As the debate in the *Times* raged, the Joint Council learned that their lobbying in Albany had convinced leaders of the Senate Public Education Committee to delay a vote on the Greenberg bill by two weeks. All but two or three noncommittal senators had already expressed to Joint Council officers their opposition to the bill. Senate majority leader Walter J. Mahoney, a Buffalo Republican, made it clear he would not vote for the bill if it came to the floor. There would be no companion legislation introduced in the assembly, though the Joint Council continued to press psychologists to lobby legislators in the assembly, especially those on that house's Public Education Committee. Cook warned that if Greenberg's bill passed, the senate could transmit it to the assembly for action there. Meanwhile, the Joint Council's allies, such as the newly formed Brooklyn Psychological Association, were making an "intensive effort" to acquaint Greenberg with "the inherent dangers in his proposal." The *Brooklyn Daily* and *Brooklyn Eagle* both published editorials opposing the bill. On or around February 20, Greenberg told the *Times* that he did not plan to push for the bill's passage that year and he had only introduced it to provoke discussion and flush out a possible solution agreeable to all parties. However, New York's psychiatric leaders continued to publicly advocate for the bill's passage for weeks after the senator made this admission, and the APA ran a quiet yet aggressive lobbying campaign months after the debate in the *Times* ceased.[12]

Support for the psychologists' cause also came from within the medical profession. Several eminent physicians, such as Kubie, Lawrence Crawley, and Ephraim Shorr, informed legislators about their opposition to the proposed amendment. The Brooklyn Association for Mental Health, whose sponsors included the Brooklyn Psychiatric Society and Brooklyn State Hospital Psychiatric Forum, also wrote to Greenberg to oppose his bill. However, even psychiatrists who supported the bill were upset with how the APA rushed it into the legislature without their input. For example, Sidney L. Green, the chief psychiatric consultant for the Community Service Society of New York's Division of Family Services in Brooklyn, told the APA's secretary that while he supported the amendment's restrictive intent, the bill "aroused serious concern of bona fide Family Service agencies because it was too broad to give them unqualified assurance that their legitimate functions would not be jeopardized." Green added it was "most unfortunate" that the APA had "failed to provide us with the necessary minimum of leadership, facts and encouragement with which to carry out a positive and vigorous campaign which would acquaint the lay and professional community with the facts which would win full support for the passage of such an amendment."

Daniel Blain, the APA's medical director, explained to Green that his association had entered the situation in New York at the official request of local psychiatric organizations, and by the time that had happened "the work of getting this amendment written and placed had already been accomplished." To improve the APA's local outreach, the association assigned its public information chief, Robert L. Robinson, to the lobbying campaign and to assist the New York Society of Clinical Psychiatry and the alumni association of the New York State Hospital System. To further mend relations at the local level, APA president Kenneth E. Appel personally requested that disgruntled psychiatrists, such as Green in Brooklyn, petition for the association's new Assembly of District Branches to take up the matter. The first speaker of the assembly, Joseph Abramson, had been elected the previous year and was also based in Brooklyn.[13]

In the face of mounting opposition, the APA doubled down on its efforts to pass not only the Greenberg bill but also similar amendments to medical practice or healing arts acts in all states where the statutes did not specifically cover the diagnosis and treatment of nervous disorders. The APA claimed about half of the states lacked such provisions. On March 7, its executive committee approved a statement supporting the proposed amendment to the Medical Practice Act on the grounds that "this provision will help safeguard the mentally ill from diagnosis and treatment at the hands of untrained and unqualified non-physicians." The APA continued to refute May's claims that the bill, if passed, could put those who provided counseling to nail biters or struggling married couples under the threat of prosecution. The association challenged the assertion that Greenberg's bill used overly broad language, noting that "mental illnesses are well-defined disease entities and are clearly described and delineated" in the AMA's *Standard Nomenclature of Diseases and Operations* and the APA's *Diagnostic and Statistical Manual of Mental Disorders*. The APA maintained that "it is a basic tenant of modern medicine that the psychological and physical components of an illness cannot be separated in diagnosis and treatment." Further, the "association is firmly convinced that the public wishes to confine responsibility for the diagnosis and treatment of mental illnesses to the medical profession."[14]

The APA's escalation of the Greenberg bill fight to a national concern prompted psychologists to similarly respond at that level. Through the parent organizations of the New York chapters allied with the Joint Council, a new coalition of national mental health groups emerged. This alliance overshadowed anything the APsychA had managed to muster on this issue and included the following organizations: the American College Personnel

Association, American Personnel and Guidance Association, American School Counselor Association, National Association of Guidance Supervisors and Counselor Trainers, National Vocational Guidance Association, Student Personnel Association for Teacher Education, and APsychA. On March 17—three days before the end of the legislature's regular session—these organizations issued a joint statement warning that the Greenberg bill was "gravely against the public interest" and would "deprive millions of individual Americans of the help they need and seek in contending with their personal problems of adjustment and emotional well-being."[15]

If the AMA's public image had not suffered by the end of winter, it was thoroughly tainted by spring. In May, the *Yale Law Journal* published a scathing assessment of the AMA's "Power, Purpose, and Politics in Organized Medicine." This eighty-four-page report by the journal's editor in chief, David R. Hyde, and a fellow law student, Payson Wolff, exhaustively explored the AMA's structure, the sources of its power and influence, and the application and limitation of its power. Their study illustrated how situations such as the psychologists' battles in New York were driven by the AMA's "actively controlling group," which was no more than "a self-perpetuating minority" whose viewpoint was "readily accepted by the passive majority." Hyde and Wolff said, "This acquiescence assists that governing minority in excluding dissident opinion from organized medicine." Their article sounded alarms over the "dangers inherent in . . . the AMA's monopoly position." Even though the AMA's county societies were democratically organized, member participation was extremely low, owing to doctors' busy schedules. Twenty-five percent member attendance for a business meeting in New York was considered high. "Thus, the few doctors who are interested in medical politics can easily wield power and influence out of proportion to their numerical strength." Further, the physicians who yielded great power within these county societies tended to be urban practitioners and specialists who earned more than general practitioners and could devote more time to politics. Ninety percent of AMA officers were specialists.[16]

Hyde and Wolff said this governing minority enjoyed the "consent and loyalty of an overwhelming majority of physicians" because "doctors may believe rivalry between competing professional associations would be injurious to both public and practitioner." Even potential dissenters often decided to "remain silent in the belief that the interest of the profession is best served by presenting a united front to the public." And those dissenters who chose not to remain silent often found no forum for voicing their opposition, with *JAMA* rarely printing opinions that contrasted with those of the House of Delegates or board of trustees. If dissident groups did emerge, as the Physicians Forum had in 1941 to challenge the Medical Society of the County of New York, they were usually short-lived. Individually, dissenters could be professionally ostracized through sanctions or exiled through a denial of membership. Such actions could severely handicap their practices, making them ineligible for specialty boards or ratings or denying them referrals or consultations. These were among the perils that physicians knew they could face if they were to publicly ally themselves with psychologists in the fight against the Greenberg bill. Harrower had likely not taken into account these intraprofessional perils when she dismissed the threat posed by medicine and repeatedly assured the Joint Council that her medical contacts were sympathetic to the psychologists' cause.[17]

The regular session of the legislature ended in mid-March with the Greenberg bill dying in the Senate Public Education Committee. That, however, did not mean New York's psychologists were in the clear. Lawmakers commonly reconvened in Albany a few months after the regular session for a special session to vote on major legislation for which deals were not struck prior to the end of the regular session. That special session came on June 10 and it lasted only one day, with the proposed Medical Practice Act not being among the handful of bills that went to the floor for a vote. About two weeks later, Cook and Zucker penned a report for the *American Psychologist* summarizing the campaign to defeat the Greenberg bill. "We are publishing this report," they said, "in the unhappy conviction that our experience in New York will be repeated in other states and in the hope that our colleagues in those states may find of value this account of the countermeasures we employed." When Bernays and Cook finally reconnected after the end of the regular session, the public relations specialist was torn over the Joint Council's performance throughout the campaign against the Greenberg bill. "I think that the numerous letters that were published pro and con rather obfuscated than clarified the issue for the people," Bernays said. "On the other hand they would create greater interest in the general subject and a base of greater interest than there was before they were published."[18]

In addition to detailing the lobbying efforts before the bill's introduction and the alliances the Joint Council had forged, Cook and Zucker laid out psychologists' plans for the 1955 legislative session. The Joint Council would likely attempt to introduce a bill, though that course of action largely hinged on the success of conferences with psychiatrists and government representatives scheduled for later that year. Coinciding with this lobbying effort would be a statewide public education campaign spearheaded by Bernays's firm. If the conferences failed, the Joint Council could move forward with introducing a bill "in the hope of mustering enough support to overcome the opposing influences which would be brought to bear on the Legislature and the Governor." Alternatively, the Joint Council could advocate for the type of legislative commission that Assemblyman Hatch had proposed, one that would study the challenges of regulating groups working in the mental health fields. "In the event of failure in the conferences there can be little doubt that a new attempt to amend the Medical Practice Act will be made." Looking at psychology's long-term outlook, Cook and Zucker concluded, "The problem of legislation will be with us for a number of years." While the Joint Council's "defensive action" earlier that year had been "relatively effective," they did not see it solving psychology's "long-range problem." At the least, Cook and Zucker held out the hope that, through the Joint Council's "show of strength," psychiatrists would eventually realize the issue could not be "resolved by unilateral action on their part," improving "the chances for rational discussion."[19]

In the wake of the June 10 one-day special session, Governor Dewey ended months of speculation about his political aspirations and announced he would not seek a fourth term as governor. His decision, he said, was "definite and irrevocable." Although Dewey would play an important role in helping US senator Irving M. Ives win the Republican party's gubernatorial nomination in September, the end of his administration signaled an opportunity for the Joint Council. Dewey's anticipated veto would no longer keep the Joint Council's aspirations for licensing legislation in check. In Washington, DC, the APsychA followed NYSPA's lead in creating an intraprofessional certifying body called the American Board for Psychological Services. The board was responsible for certifying qualified psychologists, who were then listed in a national registry. Looking back at the Joint Council's evolution over the past five years, from the unification of diverse psychological groups to the bonds forged with individual psychiatrists to fight the Greenberg bill, Zucker told a colleague, "In all of this there were and are explosive moments, but I think it is fair to say that a fair degree of stability has been established at this writing."[20]

Chapter 12
Victory

After sustaining an embarrassing defeat in New York with the demise of the Greenberg bill, the APA attempted to move the battlefield over legislation from the state to the national level and to halt all activities on that front. On October 31, 1954, the APA's council approved a joint resolution that had been prepared by its Committee on Relations with Psychology and the APsychA's Committee on Relations with Psychiatry. Under the resolution, the two committees agreed to a five-year moratorium "on all legislative actions regulating the relations between psychiatry and psychology except as such actions may be acceptable to both Associations." During that time, the associations hoped that "many questions may be worked out to the public benefit as well as to our mutual satisfaction."[1]

By this time, the industrial psychologist Raymond A. Katzell had assumed the position of the Joint Council's chair, succeeding Cook, who was in line to take May's role as NYSPA president. After receiving his master's degree from New York University in 1943, Katzell assisted the Adjutant General's Office with the training and selection of army personnel. After the war, he taught at the University of Tennessee and Syracuse University, but in 1951 he left academia to cofound the consulting firm of Richardson, Bellows, Henry and Company. Katzell took the helm of an expanded Joint Council. Its membership had grown to seven psychological societies in New York, seven associations of consultants, five major colleges and universities, and a host of upstate and downstate institutions that granted master's degrees in psychology. Cook urged Katzell to accept the APA's and APsychA's joint recommendation "in principle" but to oppose "the suggestions made for carrying [it] out." Cook called the provision of the proposed moratorium "unnecessary," maintaining that "serious discussions over a period of a few months could lead, either to a resolution of the problem or to the knowledge that it cannot at present be resolved." Cook said state associations "should proceed in accord with the spirit of the joint recommendation . . . but without binding them to a designated year or a specified duration of time during which they should negotiate with one another." He warned Katzell against trying to "outmaneuver the psychiatrists with such tactics as delay and confusion" and cautioned the new chair to not be overconfident in psychologists' "legislative strength." While Cook believed psychologists in most states could defeat amendments to medical practices acts, he did not believe they could secure licensing legislation anywhere in the country, with a few exceptions, "in the face of medical objection."[2]

When news about the joint resolution became public in mid-December, Katzell told the *New York Herald-Tribune* that the agreement would not be binding on state associations. The Joint Council, however, did not plan to act on a licensing bill for the upcoming legislative session. Psychologists were still trying to get a feel for the new political terrain in Albany. In the November 1954 elections, W. Averell Harriman, a Democrat, defeated Dewey's handpicked successor, Ives, for the governorship. The Republican US senator Jacob K. Javits also defeated Franklin Delano Roosevelt Jr. in the race for state attorney general. Although Republicans retained control of the assembly and senate, when Harriman took office on January 1, 1955, it was the first time in a dozen years that a Democrat was governing New York. Edward Bernays played an important role in assessing the new landscape and making connections with the new leaders in it. For example, just before the elections, Bernays had interested Javits in psychologists' regulatory concerns. The attorney general later told him, "It is a matter of which I would like to know a great deal more." After the elections, the Joint Council's next steps remained uncertain in terms of introducing legislation. The Joint Council did authorize its Public Relations Committee to distribute to leaders and molders of public opinion statewide thirty thousand informational brochures, with support from Bernays. However, as Katzell said in the Joint Council's first newsletter, "One thing is certain: psychologists must be prepared to take advantage of favorable opportunities when they occur to mobilize vigorous opposition if and when threatened by restrictive legislation."[3]

* * *

"You can count on me."

May held the telephone receiver to his ear, and as he heard those words, the cloud of anxiety that had been surrounding him suddenly started to part. On the other end of the line was Lawrence Frank, the man with whom May had met at a Washington Square office a decade earlier. All those years ago Frank had helped May salvage his doctoral thesis, which became his book *The Meaning of Anxiety*. Frank was now stepping up to save an even more important project that May had undertaken: a national conference planned for December that would clarify the fields of psychotherapy and counseling.[4]

When they had met in 1944, Frank had been serving as the director of the Caroline B. Zachry Institute of Human Development. His tenure there had ended in 1950, and since then he had devoted much of his time to writing books on child and social psychology. He planned to retire in 1955, and as that date approached, his contributions to the social sciences were recognized through his receipt of the Lasker Award in Mental Health in 1947 and the Parents' Magazine Award in 1950.[5]

It is likely that sometime in early 1954, after his inauguration as NYSPA president, May had started to organize several commissions featuring leaders in medicine, psychology, social work, ministry, counseling, and guidance. The idea for a conference featuring these commissions had grown out of discussions between May and Florence Powdermaker, a psychiatrist with the WAWI. They had concluded "that the best step for us as psychologists would be to clarify all the different branches of psychotherapy." They had formed an Organizing Committee that included Harry Bone, from the Joint Council; Nevitt Sanford, a Vassar College psychologist; Exie Welsch, a psychiatrist with Columbia University's College of Physicians and Surgeons; Frances M. Wilson, the director of guidance at the New York City Board of Education; and Luther E. Woodward, a psychologist and coordinator of the New York State Mental Health Commission. Each commission met bimonthly and addressed several questions posed to them by the Organizing Committee, which was chaired by Frank.

The conference's objective resonated strongly with Frank: initiating interprofessional discussions on the training and practice of psychotherapy and counseling across the five fields: medicine, psychology, social work, ministry, and counseling and guidance. Just one year earlier, in his essay on "The Promotion of Mental Health," he had said, "A community program for mental health, if it is to have meaning for people and is to draw on the strengths of our culture, must be presented as more than a psychiatric proposal; indeed, it must enlist much of what people mean by their religion." While acknowledging the implications of psychosomatics on mental health, Frank had maintained people are "capable of becoming healthy, fully functional, and responsible if provided with the loving care, nurture, education, and interpersonal experiences that evoke and develop these essentially human potentialities." Aligning with themes from May's *Man's Search for Himself*, Frank said, "We are seeking a way to social planning that fosters responsibility and freedom, avoiding the authoritarian pattern that relieves people from responsibilities." And it was not just psychologists and psychiatrists who were needed to implement such social planning; it was also "parents and families, teachers, religious leaders, recreational workers, physicians and nurses." Mental health was a "community-wide goal."[6]

It is not clear how far along the conference planning process was when Frank assured May over the phone that he could count on him. That call, however, could not have come any sooner. Late in life, May recalled that up until that point, "plans for the conference were on a stormy sea and looked as though they would be ship-wrecked after a good deal of effort on the part of some of us." With Frank at the helm, May knew "the ship would sail through the storm regardless of the difficulties." One of those challenges may have been the medical profession's unrelenting quest to claim psychotherapy as its exclusive domain. In the months leading up to the conference, the AMA, APA, and American Psychoanalytic Association released a joint statement in which they attempted to define psychotherapy before the commissions could do so at the conference May and Frank were planning. The medical groups defined psychotherapy as "the systematic application of methods of psychological medicine to the treatment of illness, particularly as these methods involve gaining an understanding of the emotional state of the patient and aiding him to understand himself." Psychotherapy was "a form of medical treatment and [did] not form a basis for a separate profession." The groups maintained that the nonmedical professional groups participating in the conference—psychologists, ministers, social workers, and vocational counselors—could, "of course, use psychological understanding in carrying out their professional functions." However, these groups needed to operate "in contributing roles in settings directly supervised by physicians."[7]

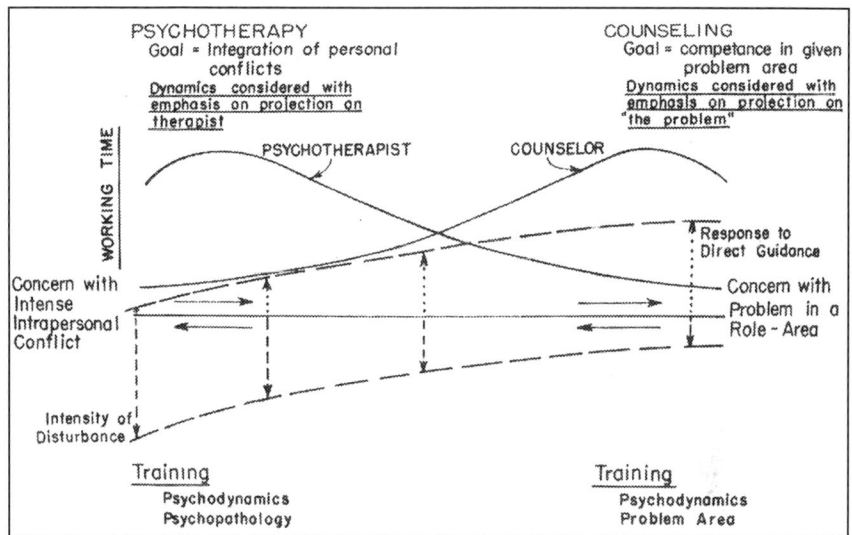

William G. Perry Jr. *Psychotherapy and Counseling*, 1955. In 1954, May and Lawrence Frank organized the Conference on Psychotherapy and Counseling. May believed the conference was more important "than any other single thing in making counseling and psychotherapy the province of the human sciences and arts rather than merely medicine." Perry, Jr, W. G. 1955. The Findings of the Commission in Counseling and Guidance: On the Relation of Psychotherapy to Counseling. Ann. N.Y. Acad. Sci. 63(3): 396–407. © The New York Academy of Sciences.

Several psychiatrists did break ranks with the AMA and APA and collaborated with Frank's Organizing Committee in helping the conference come to fruition. Among these "far-sighted psychiatrists," whom May later singled out for their contributions, were Frederick Allen, chair of the Commission in Medicine and a clinical professor in psychiatry at the University of Pennsylvania Medical School; Carl Binger, who that year had left his clinical psychiatry teaching position at the Cornell University Medical School to become a psychiatry consultant at Harvard Medical School and Massachusetts General Hospital; and Lawrence Kubie. The Conference on Psychotherapy and Counseling was held under the auspices of the New York Academy of Sciences on December 3 and 4 at the Barbizon-Plaza Hotel, a thirty-eight-story art deco building on Central Park South. On top of the thirty-five commission members, there were ten discussants who provided additional commentary on each commission's findings. Each commission, to varying extents, addressed the questions that the Organizing Commission had posed to them.[8]

The most influential report was written by Sanford on behalf of the Commission in Psychology. The report drew distinctions between the therapeutic methods of the set of groups. He said: "Psychotherapy, which is concerned with changing the internal organization of the person, differs rather sharply from those forms of social case work that seek to improve the individual's well-being by modifying his external environment, and from those forms of counseling which, without going into the inner life of the individual, put the expert's knowledge and wisdom at the disposal of the individual's attempts to deal intelligently and realistically with his environment." Sanford stressed that the psychologist practicing psychotherapy, unlike the physician, "does not assume responsibility for the total well-being of the client, nor does he claim the privileges that go with such responsibility." The psychologist's psychotherapeutic work was only effective with autonomous individuals with "*psychological* problems," though Sanford acknowledged more research was needed to determine at what point psychological impairment compromises that autonomy. Attempting to steer the APsychA in the direction opposite from what the APA had taken with the *Diagnostic and Statistical Manual*, the Commission in Psychology said it applauded psychologists' resistance to the Aristotelian thinking "that goes into classifications of mental diseases and leads to speaking of people 'having' this or that disease." In fact, Sanford described "psychological well-being" as meaning a "state of relatively advanced development" rather than the "absence of disease." In that same vein, "psychological maladjustment" was a "relative failure with respect to the diverse goals of development."[9]

In the months following the conference, May served as the contributing editor of the published version of its proceedings in the *Annals of the New York Academy of Sciences*. That summer he also purchased a cabin in Holderness, New Hampshire, not far from Frank's summer home there. Before its publication, May saw great promise in the publication: "There are many indications that these proceedings will do a great deal to structure training and other developments in these five fields in the next years." The publication's significance, however, extended beyond academic considerations. Years later, he stated, "When legislatures of other states had to face similarly proposed laws restricting psychotherapy to medical practitioners, the Attorneys General of these states often referred to these *Annals of the New York Academy of Science*."[10]

One of those attorneys general was Thomas M. Kavanagh of Michigan, who cited the *Annals* report and Orval H. Mowrer's *Psychotherapy* in overturning his predecessor's opinion from three years earlier that held psychotherapeutics were a form or medical practice under the state's Medical Practice Act. Kavanagh emphasized the aspect of autonomy that the Commission in Psychology had identified as a defining quality of psychotherapists' clients. "Psychotherapy, as defined and discussed in the two sources cited above, differs basically and recognizably from any part of the practice of medicine in that the person *receiving psychotherapy surrenders no authority to the therapist*." May later added, "I do not know how many states made concrete use of the published results of the conference; I can only say that from that moment on, the fact [is] that psychotherapy was conducted by psychologists and each of the above groups was then accepted in various legislatures and around the country." In 1965, May told Frank the conference they had organized was more important "than any other single thing in making counseling and psychotherapy the province of the human sciences and arts rather than merely medicine."[11]

* * *

One month after the Conference on Psychotherapy and Counseling, at NYSPA's annual meeting in Rochester, May delivered his swan song: his final president's address. Over the past year, NYSPA's membership had surpassed one thousand, and several grassroots associations, from the Albany area to Long Island, had affiliated with the statewide organization. But the one "radical" milestone that NYSPA had passed over the previous year and that May called special attention to was that "we, as psychologists, no longer need to be defensive. . . . Our days of inferiority are over—if we can fulfill our rightful potentialities. What happens in psychology in New York State, and I think incidentally in the nation, depends hereafter not so much on the factors outside ourselves, or what other professions may or may not think about psychology, but rather on internal factors." Chiefly among those internal factors was the training of psychologists, and the task of addressing them was left to Cook, who succeeded May as NYSPA's president.

No longer pressed to be defensive, New York's psychologists were not compelled to be offensive either, so the Joint Council did not push for the introduction of legislation during the 1955 legislative session. Midway through the session, intelligence gathered by Bernays found that, while there was "no important change of sentiment from the 1951 attitude as regards proposals to license psychologists," it was likely that any new licensing bill would be "sidetracked in the feuding between the Republican legislature and the Governor." Elsewhere in the country, however, psychologists made legislative inroads in the states of Arkansas, which passed a licensing law modeled after Tennessee's, and Washington, which passed a certification law.[13]

The summer saw psychologists make unprecedented headway in negotiations over legislation with the APA and the NYSMS, largely because of the work of Cook. In July, the APsychA's Committee on Legislation, in collaboration with its counterpart committee of the Conference of State Psychological Associations, completed a joint report reexamining the association's policies on legislation and social controls. Cook chaired the APsychA committee, and his fellow former Joint Council member Zucker sat on the conference's committee. At its September 1954 annual meeting, the APsychA's board of directors had created this Committee on Legislation and requested this report. The report signaled an end to the association's yearslong reluctance to provide state affiliates with clear recommendations on the types of legislation they should pursue. However, before making their recommendations, the two committees adopted new classifications for legislation, replacing the terminology the APsychA had used for more than a decade. The four old categories of legislation—permissive certification, mandatory certification, nonrestrictive licensing, and restrictive licensing—had "proven confusing and misleading" in part because "the question of whether a certificate or license is issued varies from state to state, and is due to factors over which psychologists have no control." For example, under the proposed mandatory-certification bill being prepared in New York, qualified psychologists would receive a document called a "license." A certificate was issued under Kentucky's licensing law, and Georgia's licensing law was in fact a mandatory-certification law.[14]

The three new general categories of legislation included the following:

1. Voluntary legislation (old permissive certification): Restricted the use of a specific title, such as "certified psychologist," to people who met certain training and experience requirements.

2. Nonrestrictive legislation

    a. *By title only* (old mandatory certification): Restricted the use of a general title, such as "psychologist" or other terms "tending to imply that such a person is practicing as a psychologist." Placed "all persons claiming to be members of a profession under the control of minimum standards established by the profession but does not interfere with the work of other professions even though they may be using psychological techniques."

    b. *By title and function* (old mandatory certification with a definition): Similar to nonrestrictive legislation by title but also included a definition of practice that could either be general, as in "rendering services to individuals or the public for renumeration," or specific by listing the methods and procedures applied.

    c. *By title and/or function* (old nonrestrictive licensing): Defined practice and restricted its use to qualified individuals, regardless of their title, but also exempted members of other professions who were legally using psychological techniques.

3. Restrictive legislation (old restrictive licensing): Defined a profession by its functions and controlled anyone involved in such activities, regardless of his or her title.

In the report, the Committee on Legislation stressed "the importance of similarity of state standards throughout the nation" because "unless the states are to grant reciprocity to one another, the national image of what a psychologist is and does will be blurred." In what would amount to one of the APsychA's most forceful challenges to the independence of state affiliates, the committee declared, "We cannot subscribe to states' rights isolationism in the matter of professional standards," and, "There are issues of vital concern to all psychologists which transcend local considerations, such as standards for employment in federal institutions." The committee strongly favored nonrestrictive legislation by title and/or function because it could "be used to control the activities of the unqualified no matter what his title." However, the committee decided not to make this type its primary recommendation for the sake of "maintaining amicable relations with related professions." Deeming "these relationships . . . important enough to be given determining weight in the decision on [the] preferred form of legislation," the committee made the following recommendation to the APsychA: "For the time being, states seeking legislation regulating the practice of psychology should attempt to develop laws falling in the category of nonrestrictive legislation by title only, or by title and function (with a general rather than a specific definition). Where local situations permit and with full interprofessional communication, the kind of law known as nonrestrictive legislation by title and/or function should be encouraged."[15]

At its September 1955 annual meeting in San Francisco, the APsychA's Council of Representatives adopted this recommendation, as well as several others relating to legislation. The other recommendations were as follows:

1. The inclusion of a disclaimer that the certification or licensing "does not confer the right to practice medicine."
2. The term "psychologist" should be reserved for individuals with a doctoral degree and no less than one year of supervised experience, though two years were preferred.
3. Terms such as "psychological examiner" or "psychological technician" should be reserved for individuals at the sub-doctoral level.
4. The term "consulting psychologist" should be reserved for individuals satisfying the competence and experience requirements for a diploma from the American Board of Examiners in Professional Psychology.
5. Legislation regulating the practice of psychologists or consulting psychologists should not attempt to differentiate psychological specialties based upon function or locale;
6. Any legislation governing the practice of psychology should hold individuals to the same code of ethics established by the APsychA.[16]

By October 1955—one month after the APsychA council adopted this new legislative policy—the legislative outlook in Albany had improved significantly. Further, in addition to mounting a $16,000 fundraising campaign, the Joint Council already had a licensing bill ready for the upcoming legislative session. Katzell described the bill as mirroring the 1951 licensing bill that Governor Dewey had vetoed but was "revised slightly to bring it in accord with the type of bill favored by the [APsychA] as an outgrowth of its negotiations last spring with the American Psychiatric Association." In addition to having terms agreeable to the APA, the bill was viewed favorably by the NYSMS. That spring, the Joint Council's Legislative Policy Committee, also chaired by Cook, met twice with a NYSMS committee and secured its support for the revised version of the 1951 licensing bill. The NYSMS House of Delegates endorsed the committee's report and forwarded it to the organization's executive committee, which referred it to a lawyer for further negotiations with the Joint Council. Efforts "to get a crystallization of those negotiations," according to Katzell, were ongoing up until at least a week before the bill's introduction in the legislature.[17]

The, bill, however, would be unlike any other passed in the nation. Under the new classifications developed by the APsychA's Committee on Legislation, the bill was nonrestrictive legislation by title and function, with a general definition of practice. Rather than define the "practice of psychology," as the 1951 version did, the new one would define "psychologist." The core requirements for the license would be the licensee would have to be twenty-one years old, of good moral character, and a US citizen or someone having declared the intent of becoming one and have a doctoral degree in psychology and two years of supervised practice in psychology. The administration and enforcement of the bill's provisions, when passed, would fall on the New York State Education Department. The bill called for the creation of a board of examiners of psychologists, whose seven members would be licensed psychologists appointed by the New York State Regents, as well as a twelve-to-eighteen-member advisory council.[18]

Compared to previous years' legislative campaigns, the 1955–56 one was relatively quiet, at least in the public sphere. With Bernays's help, the Joint Council had prepared a brochure about psychology for a series by the nonprofit Public Affairs Pamphlets. At the end of 1955, fifty thousand brochures of *Psychologists at Work* were published, with the APsychA underwriting thirty thousand copies, NYSPA five thousand, and the Joint Council fifteen thousand. Although the Joint Council renewed Bernays's contract and its Public Relations Committee had plans for a public information campaign, the legislative push received scant coverage from the press. The major New York papers made no mention of the Joint Council when the bill was introduced on February 21, 1956, by Senator Walter Van Wiggeren of Herkimer and Assemblyman Anthony P. Savarese Jr. of Queens. Both legislators were Republicans, aligning with a recommended legislative-sponsorship strategy that had come from Bernays. The Joint Council may have opted to not pursue media attention to avoid antagonizing the medical profession. Within a week, however, the Joint Council was quietly mobilizing the support of psychological organizations and allied professions. Katzell and his Joint Council co-chair, Albert S. Thompson, urged NYSPA's members to write their legislators and target the chairmen of the Senate Finance and Assembly Ways and Means Committees by March 2 because the legislative session was expected to be short. "DO IT NOW!" Katzell and Thompson said. "This is the moment we have been working toward for over five years."[19]

The bill defined a "psychologist" as a person who "holds himself out to the public by any title or description of services incorporating the words 'psychological', 'psychologist' or 'psychology', and under such title or description offers to render or renders services to individuals, corporations, or the public for renumeration." This definition's emphasis on the rendering of services for a fee limited the bill's reach to practitioners. Terms such as "psychoanalyst," "psychotherapy," and "psychodiagnosis" fell outside the scope of regulation. As required by the new APsychA policy on legislation, the bill included a disclaimer specifying that "nothing herein shall authorize any person to engage in any manner in the practice of medicine as defined in the laws of this state." There was a provision granting psychologist-client communications the same confidentiality privileges afforded to attorneys and clients. There was also a grandfather clause that allowed the board of examiners to waive a license-examination requirement for psychologists who, as of July 1, 1957, had lived in the state for at least two years and either had a doctoral degree in psychology with five years of professional experience or a master's degree in psychology with at least eight years of professional experience.[20]

When the legislature passed the Van Wiggeren-Savarese bill during the night of its last regular session day on March 23, there were no headlines noting the psychologists' hard-fought victory. In the *New York Times*, passage of the bill was reported in a single twelve-word bullet point: "Set up a licensing system for psychologists in the State Education Department." The fight was not over, though. The bill still needed the governor's signature, and the Joint Council and its allies did not take that action as a given, as it had in 1951, even though Harriman had indicated he would support such legislation. Psychologists flooded the governor's office with letters of support, which in several cases were accompanied by memoranda outlining the needs, history, and costs associated with the bill. The only organizational opposition came from the American Mental Health Foundation, though this nonprofit group later stopped its letter-writing campaign against the bill after Katzell and its research director, Stefan de Schill, reached a mutual understanding about the legislation's scope. Then, on April 17, Harriman signed the bill. In his approval message, he described the legislation as "the result of the joint efforts" of the commissioner of mental hygiene, the New York State Education Department, the Joint Council, the NYSMS, the APsychA, and the APA.[21]

Harriman also cited "numerous eminent psychologists and educators" who had urged for the bill's approval. However, probably more important than these endorsements were those that came from the medical profession. Harriman's counsel, Daniel Gutman, had requested the NYSMS provide its position on the bill, and the executive officer of its legislative bureau, Harold B. Smith, said the group had no objections to its enactment. The APA's Blain, whose telegram to Dewey had likely dealt a fatal blow to the 1951 legislation, sent to Harriman the strongest endorsement for the Van Wiggeren-Savarese bill. The bill, Blain said, "has the full support of this association. It is the product of many months of interprofessional consultation between psychologists, psychiatrists, and physicians in New York, and of similar collaboration between committees of the APsychA and American Psychiatric Association. This legislation is a desirable and important step in the strengthening of interprofessional relationships. It will assist the public in recognizing those [who] are professionally qualified in the field of psychology."[22]

The law took effect immediately, though violators, who were guilty of a misdemeanor punishable by up to six months' imprisonment and a fine up to $500, could not be prosecuted until July 1, 1958. Under the law, $40,000 was appropriated to the Education Department for its administration. On March 31, 1958, the department issued the first certificates under the law to the inaugural seven members of the Board of Examiners of Psychologists. Five of them were former Joint Council members: Frank S. Freeman (chair), Florence Halpern, Harry McNeil, Harold Seashore, and Jesse Zizmor. The other two members were William J. E. Crissy of Queens and Sidney D. S. Spragg of Rochester.[23]

* * *

One year later, Theodor Reik—the psychoanalyst whose Austrian legal case had inspired Freud's *The Question of Lay Analysis*—made a final contribution to the debate. Reik's National Psychological Association for Psychoanalysis, as well as himself individually and several other psychoanalysts, sued the University of the State of New York in New York County Supreme Court. Like Reik, the other plaintiffs, Nandor Fodor, Edward Frankel, and Saul Gurevitz, were refugee psychoanalysts who had been practicing in New York for more than a decade. However, they could not provide the state's Education Department with the documentary evidence of their foreign training needed to receive a certificate, though one managed to submit that documentation postfiling. They claimed the 1956 law was defective in that it had failed to define the profession, "psychology," or "psychological services." Further, the law's requirement that certificates go to psychologists who received degrees from US institutions unfairly denied refugees the right to practice. Defending the bill were NYSPA's former presidents, Katzell and Thompson, along with the secretary of the Board of Examiners of Psychologists, Joseph R. Sanders.[24]

Sanders, in an affidavit, acknowledged that the plaintiffs were well-known among psychologists, as was their inability to provide documentation of their foreign training. He estimated there were fewer than fifty people in New York who were in the plaintiffs' predicament. By being denied certificates, Gurevitz claimed that the state university system, "by unwarranted administrative legislation, ruled out our doctoral training abroad before we came to these shores as fugitives from foreign oppression, as the 'substantial equivalent' of the American Ph.D." Consequently, "the public will now class us with the quacks and charlatans that the statute is supposed to drive out of the profession, and will be deprived of our 'respected' services." However, in dismissing the case, Judge Edgar J. Nathan said, "It should be observed parenthetically here that the article in question does not touch upon the fundamental problem in connection with the plaintiffs' specific field of activity—that is, whether or not the practice of psychoanalysis or psychotherapy constitutes or should be determined by legislation or otherwise to constitute, the practice of medicine. That question is referred to obliquely in plaintiffs' papers, but since it is not raised in this action, it is mentioned here solely as an important matter of public interest."[25]

In the end, the important question was not, What is lay analysis or a lay analyst? "It is entirely immaterial whether or not any person is in fact a psychologist or is practicing psychology or is rendering psychological services," Nathan said. "The test is: Does he hold himself out to the public under any title or description using the words 'psychological', 'psychologist' or 'psychology' and does he render any services for remuneration under such title or description? For that purpose, it is sufficient under the law that the words are used, whatever they may mean."[26]

Conclusion
Frontiers

The publication of the APsychA's new legislation guidelines for state affiliates in the November 1955 issue of the *American Psychologist*, along with the publication of the proceedings of the Conference on Psychotherapy and Counseling that same month in the *Annals of the New York Academy of Sciences*, provided psychologists nationwide with a road map for regulating the practice of psychology. Then, when Governor Harriman signed the Van Wiggeren-Savarese bill into law in April 1956, psychologists nationwide received a clear message: the roadblocks that the medical and psychiatric professions had long erected to stymie the profession's legislative efforts would be far less insurmountable. However, there would still be opposition. For example, in 1957 the APA withdrew its support for certification. The AMA also issued a statement declaring its board recommended opposition to the licensure of psychologists. When the APsychA pressed the AMA on whether this meant that it did not oppose certification, the AMA clarified it had not taken any position on that issue.[1]

During that same year, California, Maryland, and New Hampshire passed laws regulating psychology. The last two enacted nondirective legislation by title and function, though New Hampshire's law, like New York's, had a general definition for practice. In contrast, Maryland's law established a more specific definition of practice by adding to the otherwise general definition of "psychologist" language describing the services offered or rendered as "involving the application of principles, methods and procedures of the science and profession of psychology to individuals, corporations or the public for compensation, or other personal gain." On top of featuring a definition for "psychologist" similar to New York's, California's law featured a general definition for "psychological services" as well as a specific definition for the "practice of psychology." California psychologists paid a steep political price supporting this law because it prohibited "the use of therapeutic measures in the diagnosis or treatment of mentally ill except in collaboration with a physician or surgeon." The New York psychologist Cynthia P. Deutsch criticized this restriction as accomplishing "for the medical hierarchy exactly what they have been unable so far to accomplish for themselves: it in effect makes psychology ancillary to medicine, inasmuch as there are no complementary restrictions on medicine in regard to psychology."[2]

From the enactment of the nation's first certification law in 1945 in Connecticut to 1955, a total of nine states acted to regulate the profession of psychology. From the Joint Council's victory in New York in 1956 to 1966, twenty-one states did the same. By 1977, with the passage of law in Missouri, all fifty states had enacted legislation regulating psychologists. Among them, only five passed nonrestrictive legislation by title.[3] Twenty-nine states passed nonrestrictive legislation by title and function.[4] Seventeen passed nonrestrictive legislation by title and/or function.[5]

Only one state, New Hampshire, followed New York in enacting nonrestrictive legislation by title and function with a general definition of practice. However, there are traces of the New York act in the overwhelming majority of subsequent laws regulating the profession. A total of twenty-six states borrowed language from New York's definition of "psychologist" in their own definitions for this term. However, only seven of those states had "psychologist" definitions that were identical to, or that strongly mirrored, New York's.[6]

Regardless of whether states were enacting nonrestrictive legislation by title and function or by title and/or function, after 1956 almost all were in agreement over how psychologists could publicly represent themselves. Prior to 1956, only Tennessee and Arkansas had established controls on the use of the terms "psychology," "psychological," and "psychologist." After New York's definition of "psychologist" established restrictions on the use of these terms, thirty-four of the forty laws passed through 1977 covered "psychology," "psychological," and "psychologist."[7] Six states added "psychologic" to the trio of covered terms.[8]

In many states, the added specificity through definitions for "psychology" and "practice of psychology" came at a cost—one that New York psychologists had sought to avoid. Michigan and Nevada required psychologists practicing psychotherapy on mentally ill persons to provide that service under the direct supervision or in collaboration with a physician or psychiatrist. Laws in a dozen other states generally required psychologists who practiced psychotherapy to maintain effective intercommunication with a physician or psychiatrist.[9] Concessions in Louisiana's definition of "psychology" left little for the science, describing it as "the study and application of the principles of behavior but it is not to be interpreted as meaning 'psychiatry' which is the branch of medicine that diagnoses and treats disorders of the mind or psyche, especially psychoses, but also neuroses."[10]

* * *

This accelerated rate of laws regulating psychologists following New York's in 1956 coincided with a significant divergence in the direction of psychology and psychiatry. For psychologists, there was the movement away from the mechanical view of people, which had been established under stimulus-response behaviorism, and toward a more humanistic psychology. For psychiatrists, there was the shift away from the psychodynamics, which had pulled them out of mental hospitals and into the community, to a more biologically oriented psychiatry with a greater emphasis on drug therapy and the biochemical factors underlying psychiatric illnesses.

While historians of the two professions have attributed the rise of these movements to a host of factors, ranging from cultural to scientific, the changing legislative landscape on which these trends unfolded has largely been overlooked. It is important to remember that throughout his tenures as the Joint Council's chair and NYSPA's president, May framed the yearslong fight against restrictive legislation as a fight against the view of man as a physical machine. While the goal of licensing or certification laws was not to advance a more humanistic psychology, May made clear that the fight against the types of restrictive legislation pursued by the APA and AMA was to ensure organized medicine did not legally box in psychology and prevent them from exploring their profession's frontiers. It was on psychology's frontiers where May hoped psychologists could find a "human model," as opposed to a purely scientific one, by which people could be studied and understood.[11]

In 1957, just one year after the enactment of New York's law, a group of psychologists met in Detroit and began preparing for a movement toward that frontier through the development of a journal devoted to explorations in humanistic psychology. The next year saw the publication of *Existence: A New Dimension in Psychology and Psychiatry*, edited by May, Ernest Angell, and Henri Ellenberger. *Existence* was the first book for general readers in America on existential psychology. It was followed a year later by a symposium on the topic at the APsychA's annual meeting in Cincinnati, with May, Abraham Maslow, and Herman Feife serving as presenters and Carl Rogers and Gordon Allport as discussants. There May explained existentialism as meaning "centering upon the existing person; it is the emphasis on the human being as he is *emerging, becoming*." He stressed that rather than representing a new school, existentialism was an "attitude" or "approach." May did not reject Western science's essentialist character that embraced mathematics as the "ultimate pure form." He instead acknowledged that "the more absolutely and completely you formulate the forces or drives, the more you are talking about abstractions and not the existing, living human being." The *Journal of Humanistic Psychology* launched in 1962 to explore the "human capacities and potentialities that have no systematic place in positivistic or behavioral theory or in classical psychoanalytic theory, e.g. creativity, love, self, growth, organism, basic-need gratification, self-actualization, higher values, ego-transcendence, objectivity, autonomy, identity, responsibility, psychological health, etc." The journal promised to "speed up the emergence of a more adequate—a more scientific—picture of the full possibilities inherent in the nature of man and ways in which those possibilities could be actualized."[12]

As Amedeo Giorgi notes, the rise of the humanistic psychology movement was greatly influenced by the cultural milieu of the early 1960s. It was "a time of hope; of unbridled optimism; of belief in change." The hope was that psychology "could flow with the cultural tide, and at least bring personal fulfillment to the masses if not a social utopia as well." While the legislative gains that psychologists were making across the country at the same time did not fuel these aspirations, their statehouse victories did provide the legal framework and a less strained interprofessional environment in which these hopes could be pursued almost unfettered. Psychiatrists' inability to control the practice of psychology—illustrated through the spread of certification and licensing laws throughout the 1960s—contributed to their waning interest in psychodynamics. With the two professions competing less in the psychodynamic arena, there was less pressure on psychologists to maintain the scientific rigor that had shielded them throughout the 1940s and 1950s against the attacks of the AMA and APA, who held themselves to be scientifically superior.[13]

Here the humanistic psychologists failed to heed the warnings of the Commission on Psychology at the 1954 Conference on Psychotherapy and Counseling. In his report on behalf of the commission, Nevitt Sanford identified psychologists' most important characteristic as being their "orientation toward research" and the "advancement and application of scientific knowledge." It was "not only false but mischievous" to split psychology between "'cold' science and the 'warm' human relating that moves psychotherapy forward." By the early 1960s May was already sounding alarms over antiscientific tendencies in parts of American existential psychology and the "wild eclecticism" of its proponents, who acted "as though [psychotherapeutic] techniques did not matter." In 1964, Rogers similarly warned that humanistic psychology could amount to no more than a "protest group of temporary value." He acknowledged that humanistic psychologists justifiably protested "against the view of man as completely mechanical," but to become more viable they needed to "make *positive contributions*."[14]

Although cognitive psychology, which had emerged in the 1956–58 period, was well on its way toward making such positive contributions in the field of research and entering the mainstream, existential psychology stood in its shadow. As the humanistic psychology movement got "swept up" in the 1960s counterculture, with its "irrationalist, transcendental, antinominal, and drug-oriented features," some academic leaders abandoned the movement, according to Giorgi. May stood by it, even as he lamented some of his colleagues' attempts to equate existentialism with Zen Buddhism and claim lysergic acid provided a pathway to satori. While the movement delivered on its promise to help individuals reach their potential through the development of growth and therapeutic techniques, such as encounter groups, primal scream, and Gestalt therapy, its "meta-psychological promise" for a human model compatible with the scientific model fell flat. What remained, Giorgi says, was "the tension between being adequate to the human person and being adequate to science." Owing to this "lack of significant humanistically oriented research," Rogers declared in 1985 that "humanistic psychology has not had a deep or significant impact on mainstream psychology in the United States, as it exists in our universities and colleges."[15]

In light of these undelivered promises, it is hard to imagine this "third force," as Maslow coined humanistic psychology, as being as effective a deterrent against the legislative aggressions of the APA and AMA in the 1960s as it was in the 1950s when brandished by May at the head of the Joint Council and NYSPA. Psychology's first two forces—psychoanalysis and behaviorism—had afforded psychologists a degree of scientific respectability among their medical counterparts. The primary argument for the certification or licensing of psychologists was their foundation in science, though physicians and psychiatrists were fast to point out the limitations of its scope. By stressing this third force, through his arguments against the treatment of man as a machine, May had advanced a position that the medical profession at large could not scientifically accept or refute. As cracks in the scientific foundation of humanistic psychology became more evident, the profession of psychology would have been more susceptible to the types of attacks the AMA and APA had waged in New York from 1949 to 1954. However, by the early 1960s, psychiatry's movement away from psychodynamics had already begun.

Psychiatry's "inability to maintain hegemony over psychological therapies," according to historian Gerald N. Grob, was just one of the factors driving a biological resurgence in the profession. Others included the "development of more effective drugs, a growing disillusionment with purely environmental ideologies, and the improvement of technologies in the biological and neurosciences that promised fundamental breakthrough." That expansion of the drug armamentarium started to gain significant momentum with two studies on drug treatments for severe mental disorders that began in 1961—one year before the launch of the *Journal of Humanistic Psychology*. One was a double-blind study by the National Institute of Mental Health's Psychopharmacological Service Center that showed the effectiveness of new phenothiazines and chlorpromazine on schizophrenic patients. In the other study, Benjamin Pasamanick found schizophrenic patients could be effectively treated in home care settings. This latter study came at a time when most psychiatrists were being trained in psychodynamic concepts that were "already obsolete, utilizing knowledge and skills which daily approach obsolescence."[16]

Psychiatry's quest for "magic bullets" that could cure mental diseases had gained momentum as the battle of the professions waged in New York, according to Robert Whitaker. For example, in 1952, French psychiatrists began administering the major tranquilizer chlorpromazine, to psychotic patients. They described it as a "neuroleptic" that commandeered the nervous system, though psychiatrists acknowledged that rather than treating a disease, they were "using a neuropharmacological agent to produce a specific effect." Two years later, Smith Kline and French began marketing chlorpromazine in the United States, where it was known as Thorazine in the United States. It quickly gained its reputation as a "Wonder Drug" that freed patients from confusion and turned untreatable ones into "rational human beings." A year later came another magic bullet in the form of meprobamate, a minor tranquiller marketed by Wallace Laboratories as Miltown. It was followed by the introduction of a drug for depressed patients in 1957: the "psychic energizer" iproniazid, marketed by Hoffmann-La Roche as Marsilid. As these magic bullets were rolled out, Whitaker notes, the AMA gave up its role as a medicine watchdog and partnered with pharmaceutical industry to promote these "wonder" drugs, as it did with Smith Kline and French to jointly produce The March of Medicine television program in 1951.[17]

As more syndrome-specific drugs were introduced, Grob notes, diagnosis and classification took on new meaning within psychiatry, which under its psychodynamic orientation had been more concerned with the interpretation of symptoms. The nosology shift was reflected in the third edition of the APA's *Diagnostic and Statistical Manual of Mental Disorders*, published in 1980—three years after Missouri became the fiftieth state to pass a law regulating the profession of psychology. Biological reductionism, from neuropsychological and neurophysiological research to genetics, resurged in psychiatry. As this happened, May continued to advocate for "dealing with human beings rather than with some absurd and truncated creatures reduced to isolated parts with no center whatever, parts that we can test since they fit our machines."[18]

By the *Journal of Humanistic Psychology*'s twenty-fifth anniversary in 1987, the movement that this publication had heralded was facing an existential crisis. Humanistic psychology remained a minority position within the profession, and its prospects of becoming a dominant third force looked bleak. Giorgi questioned, "What if we [humanistic psychologists] are not here to dominate, but only to call forth a different presence for those who seek it? What if it is in the nature of our task not to force our vision on others, but merely to offer our view, and to accept refusal with equanimity?" In 1991, at the California School of Professional Psychology, where May taught a seminar to seniors about to graduate, he was aghast when not one student mentioned dreams or free association when presenting on a case. More and more, May kept thinking about Rogers and how he had refused to assist the Joint Council in its licensing efforts in the early 1950s. "I think he [Rogers] foresaw that we psychologists could be as rigid as any other group." In 1992, just two years before his death, May said, "We have discovered that we also tend to lose our sensitivity and that we also face dangers similar to those faced by the AMA before us." He did not question the intelligence or experience of his students at the California School of Professional Psychology, but he asked, "Are we training technicians or professionals?"[19]

Many of the graduates with whom May had worked spoke to him unhappily about serving as the "McDonald's of therapy" or how "some of the fire that used to make therapy creative and fun seems to have diminished." In these disillusioned psychologists, May saw the profession falling victim to the same mindset of medicine and psychiatry in the 1950s. "We take refuge in definitions, putting aside our awareness that every moment in psychotherapy is distinctive and needs to be seen new," he said. This was what Rogers had meant, May believed, with his emphasis on empathy: "the need to experience each client as unique" and not "just like the others." This was also why May called the standardization of the teaching of psychotherapy "a great mistake." He said, "The content of the standardizations are generally the technique things by which you learn to not understand other people but rather to say what should be said." That, in May's view, was what "the real war against the medics" boiled down to, and he was not pessimistic about the future. "Now we read all kinds of different trainings, and we won our battle against the whole AMA, brought all these big guns into this battle. We won it because people underneath realized that we had something to give that wasn't the customary, technical prescribing but rather it was hearing human beings and this turned out to be more important than the standardized training. I think the problem is much more difficult."[20]

* * *

To Grob, psychiatry's shift from psychodynamic to biological orientations represented "a cyclical pattern that has alternated between enthusiastic optimism and fatalistic pessimism, between an emphasis on environment and one on heredity, and between a somatic and a psychogenic interpretation." Although May saw signs of "revolt" against standardization in psychology in the 1980s, much as there had been in the 1950s, he did not portray this trend as being "cyclical." His 1953 description of the profession as enduring its "frontier struggles" was as true then as it was four decades later, when May died in 1994. Throughout much of his career, but especially in his later years, the frontier would stand for him as a powerful symbol or myth. The frontier stood for how "America was to become for the West a myth of the rebirth of humanity, without the sin or evil or poverty or injustice or prosecution which had characterized the Old World"; the frontiersman symbolized American individualism, self-reliance, and puritanism. However, when May referred to psychology's frontier in the 1950s, he used the term as his mentor, Paul Tillich, did.[21]

Shortly after fleeing Germany and coming to New York, Tillich in 1936 published his autobiography, which covered his first fifty years. The book, *On the Boundary*, was what Tillich described as a "self-characterization with which I introduced myself to America." Tillich described the book as reporting "on many frontiers which are universally human and at the same time matters of personal destiny: the boundary between country and city, between feudalism and civil service, between bourgeoise society and Bohemianism, between theology and philosophy—and finally, on the personal side, between two continents." The journey from one extreme to the other was the "dialectic of experience," Tillich said, in which "each of life's possibilities drives of its own accord to a boundary and beyond the boundary where it meets that which limits it. The man who stands on many boundaries experiences the unrest, insecurity, and inner limitation of existence in many forms. He knows the impossibility of attaining serenity, security, and perfection."[22]

In the early 1950s, May and his fellow New York psychologists on the Joint Council stood on the boundaries between science and humanism, between legal recognition of psychology's independence as a profession and its subordination to medicine. In the years that followed, especially after the 1958 publication of *Existence*, May remained on the boundary, even as his friends in academia decried existentialism as "Horrible!" and implored him to "drop this quickly." Proudly, late in life, May said, "But I didn't drop it." When critics blasted him for his "moralizing and exhortatory form of psychotherapy" that was "notoriously transitory and superficial in its effects," the New York Times in 1971 noted May had accepted such criticism "as the price of operating 'on the frontier,' as he puts it." In fact, he embraced it, and People later noted how, in the wake of the fight against the AMA, "May prefers to call himself a 'frontiersman.'"[23]

To Tillich, existence on the frontier was "full of tension and movement." There was no idleness; instead there was "a crossing and return, a repetition of return and crossing, a back-and-forth—the aim of which is to create a third area beyond the bounded territories, an area where one can stand for a while without being enclosed in something tightly bound."[24]

In the late 1940s and early 1950s, New York was that frontier; it was where May and his little band of psychologists created this "third area beyond the bounded area" during their years of warring with the AMA and APA. They gave psychology's third force a place to "stand for a while without being enclosed in something tightly bound."

List of Psychology Laws, 1945–77[1]

T = Nonrestrictive by Title
T and F = Nonrestrictive by Title and Function
T and/or F = Nonrestrictive by Title and/or Function

State	Year	Chapter	Type of Nonrestrictive Legislation
CT	1945	257	T
VA	1946	280	T
KY	1948	169	T and F
GA	1951	276	T and F
MN	1951	672	T
TN	1953	169	T and F
ME	1953	243	T
WA	1955	305	T
AR	1955	129	T and F
NY	1956	737	T and F
CA	1957	2320	T and F
MD	1957	748	T and F
NH	1957	121	T and F
MI	1959	257	T and F
UT	1959	100	T and F
CO	1961	192	T and F
FL	1961	490	T and F
DE	1962	415	T and F

OR	1963	675	T and F
ID	1963	186	T and/or F
NV	1963	641	T and F
NM	1963	92	T and F
IL	1963	2912	T and F
AL	1963	535	T and F
LA	1964	347	T and F
AZ	1965	102	T and F
WY	1965	102	T and/or F
OK	1965	347	T and/or F
NJ	1966	282	T and/or F
MS	1966	510	T and F
ND	1967	357	T and F
KS	1967	432	T and F
AK	1967	136	T and/or F
NE	1967	429	T and/or F
ID	1967	23	T and/or F
HI	1967	290	T and F
NC	1967	910	T and/or F
ME	1967	54 & 58	T and F
SC	1968	1006	T and F
RI	1969	233	T and F
TX	1969	713	T and F
WI	1969	455	T and F
WV	1970	30	T and/or F
MT	1971	73	T and/or F
OH	1971	276	T and/or F
MA	1971	1021	T and/or F
PA	1972	52	T and/or F
IA	1974	1086	T and/or F
SD	1976	235	T and/or F
VT	1976	228	T and/or F
MO	1977	H.B. 255	T and/or F

Original Manuscripts Key

CSS	Community Service Society, Rare Book and Manuscript Library, Columbia University, New York
DMP	Don May Papers, Newberry Library, Chicago
EFA	Erich Fromm Archive, Tübingen, Germany
EFP	Erich Fromm Papers, New York Public Library, New York
LKFP	Lawrence K. Frank Papers, Archives and Modern Manuscripts Program, National Library of Medicine, Bethesda, MD
LMP	Lewis Mumford Papers, Kislak Center for Special Collections, Rare Books and Manuscripts, University of Pennsylvania, Philadelphia
MHP	Molly Harrower Papers, Archives of the History of American Psychology, University of Akron, Akron, OH
NYSL	New York State Library, Albany, NY
NYSVJ1951	New York Veto Jackets 1951, New York State Library, Albany, NY
PELB	Papers of Edward L. Bernays, Manuscript Division, Library of Congress, Washington, DC
PTD	Public Papers of Thomas E. Dewey, New York State Library, Albany, NY
RKP	Raymond Katzell Papers, Archives of the History of American Psychology, University of Akron, Akron, OH
RMP	Rollo May Papers, Department of Special Research Collections, University of Santa Barbara, Santa Barbara, CA
WAWIRR	William Alanson White Institute, Registrar Records, New York
1956BJ	1956 Bill Jackets, Chapters 706–50, New York State Library, Albany, NY

Notes

Preface

[1] May, *Man's Search for Himself*, 192, 194, 197.

[2] May, *Paulus*, 83–84; May, *Man's Search for Himself*, 203. May borrowed the phrase the "courage of one's acceptance" from Paul Tillich, whose *The Courage to Be* was published a year before *Man's Search for Himself*. However, Tillich considered his book as a response to May's *The Meaning of Anxiety*. May, *Paulus*, 23.

[3] May, *Psychology and the Human Dilemma*, x–xi. May's comments about the "war" were not included in the 1967 edition of *Psychology and the Human Dilemma* but were added in the 1979 edition.

[4] Buchanan, "Legislative Warriors," 239–41; Grob, *From Asylum to Community*, 109–11; Hogan, "A History of the New York State Psychological Association," 21–32.

[5] May, *Man's Search for Himself*, 90–91.

[6] Abzug, *Psyche and Soul in America*, xiii; May, *Man's Search for Himself*, 203.

[7] Nietzsche, *Philosophy in the Tragic Age of the Greeks*, 43; Pickersgill, "From Psyche to Soma?," 301; Grob, review of *The Emperor's New Drugs*, 34; May, *The Discovery of Being*, 87.

Introduction

[1] May, "Foreword," in Freedheim et al., *History of Psychotherapy*, xxiii. In the *History of Psychotherapy*, May identified his office as being at the Master Hotel, but his correspondence from the early 1950s placed his office at 411 West 114th Street. He appears to have moved to the Master Hotel in the mid-1950s. May to Joint Council Members, [New York], March 11, 1953, M3242.2, folder 1953, MHP.

[2] May to Joint Council Members, New York, October 31, 1952, M3242.2, folder 1952, MHP; G. R. Wendt to M.z Harrower, Rochester, NY, December 3, 1948, M3242.2, folder 1948, MHP; May, "Foreword," in Freedheim et al., *History of Psychotherapy*, xxiii.

[3] May, "Foreword," in Freedheim et al., *History of Psychotherapy*, xxiii; "Meeting of the Joint Council of Psychologists on Legislation," March 16, 1953, HPA mass 46, box 46, folder 10, RMP; "Psychologists Charge Doctors Attempt to Subordinate Them," *New York Herald-Tribune*, March 4, 1953.

[4] May, "Foreword," in Freedheim et al., *History of Psychotherapy*, xxiii; New York State Senate, S. 2659, print number 2805; People v Mulford (1910) 140 App. Div. 716, 125 NYS 680; Bennett, *Informal opinions of the Attorney-General*, 116; "Legislature Votes Psychologist Bill," *New York Times*, March 17, 1951; Wolfle, "Methods of Controlling Psychological Frauds," 171.

[5] Whitaker, *Anatomy of an Epidemic*, 58–59.

[6] May, *Psychology and the Human Dilemma*, xi.

[7] Sanford, "Across the Secretary's Desk," 172.

[8] "State Bill Fought by Psychologists," *New York Times*, March 4, 1953.

[9] May, "Foreword," in Freedheim et al., *History of Psychotherapy*, xxiii; May, *Psychology and the Human Dilemma*, xi, author's analysis, see "List of Psychology Laws, 1945–1977."

[10] R. May, "The Problems of Evil: An Open Letter to Carl Rogers," in Greening, *American Politics and Humanistic Psychology*, 17-18. Emphasis original. A few years after the battle of the professions ended in New York, May joined eleven other practicing therapists in assessing the effectiveness of Rogers's client-centered therapy on schizophrenics at a VA hospital in Madison, Wisconsin. May and several of the other judges observed "the therapy was good as a whole, [but] there was one glaring omission": the client-centered therapist "did not (or could not) deal with the angry, hostile, negative…feelings of the clients" When listening to audio tapes of client-centered sessions, May got the impression "there were not two people in the room"; the reflecting techniques resulted in "an amorphous kind of identity rather than two subjects interacting in a world in which both participate, and in which love and hate, trust and doubt, conflicts and dependence, come out and can be understood and assimilated." After receiving this feedback, Rogers even admitted the client-entered therapist "for some reason seems less open to receiving negative, hostile, or aggressive feelings." He posited that client-centered therapists may "have little respect for, or understandings of their own negative, hostile, or aggressive feelings, and are thus unable to receive these feelings from the patient. Do they simply 'not believe in' the importance of negative feelings?"

[11] May, *Psychology and the Human Dilemma*, x–xi; May, *The Meaning of Anxiety*, 229.

[12] May to Joint Council Members, [New York], March 11, 1953, M3242.2, folder 1953, MHP.

[13] Sherman, "Theodor Reik and Lay Analysis," 380–81; Freud, *The Question of Lay Analysis*, xxvii.

[14] Freud, "The Origin and Development of Psychoanalysis," 182; Wallerstein, *Lay Analysis*, 7–10.

[15] Freud, *The Question of Lay Analysis*, 66, 81. Emphasis original.

[16] Freud, "Concluding Remarks on the Question of Lay Analysis," 392, 398.

[17] Jones, "Discussion on Lay Analysis," 221, 224, 246-47, 259.

Notes

[18] Freud, *The Question of Lay Analysis*, 85–86.

[19] Howard, "The Geography of APA Membership," 622; May, *Psychology and the Human Dilemma*, xi.

Chapter 1

[1] May, "The Present Function of Counseling," 9–10; "U.S. on the Offensive in France," *Brooklyn Daily Eagle*, July 3, 1944; "Japan Bombed Again by U.S.," *Brooklyn Daily Eagle*, July 7, 1944; Virgil Pinkley, "Allies Pierce Enemy Lines—All Out Caen Offensive," *Brooklyn Daily Eagle*, July 8, 1944; Lyle C. Wilson, "F.D.R. Will Run Again," *Brooklyn Daily Eagle*, July 11, 1944; Lansing Warren, "U.S. Health Dangers Pictured; One Third of Draftees Held Unfit," *New York Times*, July 11, 1944.

[2] Lansing Warren, "U.S. Health Dangers Pictured; One Third of Draftees Held Unfit," *New York Times*, July 11, 1944.

[3] B. Rowes, "'Love and Will'—You Need Them Both in This Age of Anxiety, Says Pioneering Psychoanalyst Rollo May," *People*, December 20, 1976; David Dempsey, "Love and Will and Rollo May," *New York Times*, March 28, 1971; R. May, "Yes Begins with a No," *Time*, June 22, 1970; R. May to L. Mumford, Trudeau, NY, November 14, [1942], folder 3195, LMP.

[4] F. H. Heise, "The Treatment of Tuberculosis," in Gardner, *Tuberculosis in Industry*, 14–23; Sandra Afflick (assistant registrar of operations and records at the Teachers College) to Schlett, correspondence with author, August 10, 2017; T. G. Harris, "The Devil and Rollo May," *Psychology Today*, August 1969; May, "Yes Begins with a No"; Rowes, "'Love and Will'"; May, *Power and Innocence*, 13; Rowes, "'Love and Will'"; R. May to E. Fromm, Naperville, IL, September 8, [1943], 97M28, EFP.

[5] Warren, "U.S. Health Dangers Pictured."

[6] Tillich, "Existential Philosophy," 68; Fromm, *Escape from Freedom*, 134, 141; Frank, "Society as the Patient," 335.

[7] Freud, *Civilization and Its Discontents*, 80–82; Kubie, *Practical and Theoretical Aspects of Psychoanalysis*, 11; Riggs, *Just Nerves*, 19, 39–44; Galdston, "The Relation of Physical and Mental Health," 213.

[8] Schlett to Afflick; Dempsey, "Love and Will and Rollo May"; Harris, "The Devil and Rollo May"; May, *Paulus*, 3; Eric Pace, "Rollo May Dead at 85; Was Innovator in Psychology," *New York Times*, October 24, 1994.

[9] May, "The Present Function of Counseling," 10; "New Miracle Drug Cures Shell-Shock in Two Hours," *Eugene Guard*, June 23, 1944.

[10] Rowes, "'Love and Will'"; May, "The Present Function of Counseling," 9–11; Harris, "The Devil and Rollo May"; Dempsey, "Love and Will and Rollo May."

[11] May, *The Discovery of Being*, 14; May, *Paulus*, 21; R. May to L. Frank, New York, [1965], M3207, folder 28, MHP. In this undated letter marking Frank's seventy-fifth birthday, which was December 6, 1965, May recounted this "old memory" of visiting Frank's Waverly Place home on "an afternoon twenty-one years ago." That places the time of this meeting in 1944.

[12] Dempsey, "Love and Will and Rollo May"; Rowes, "'Love and Will.'"

[13] Senn et al., "Lawrence K. Frank," 347; Bryson, "Lawrence K. Frank, Knowledge, and the Production of the 'Social,'" 403–4.

[14] Mead, "Lawrence Keslo Frank 1890–1968," 57; Senn et al., "Lawrence K. Frank," 349. R. May to L. Frank, New York, [1965], M3207, folder 28, MHP.

[15] May to L. Frank, New York, [1965], M3207, folder 28, MHP; May, "The Present Function of Counseling," 14. In this 1944 essay, May reports interviewing, on behalf of the Court of Family Relations, a pregnant girl whose Rorschach test indicated a fear of imminent birth. But she denied being fearful, saying, "Oh, no, I have no fear at all. But I'm willing to suffer the tortures of the damned to get it over with. All the girls around here tell of hearing women scream in the hospital. They talk of Caesarian births and they come around to me and say, 'You're just the kind to have one!'" This is almost verbatim the response of "Helen," the fourth case study reviewed in May's dissertation. May, *The Meaning of Anxiety*, 269–72.

[16] R. May to L. Frank, New York, [no date], M3207m, folder 28, MHP. May's letter states Frank discussed a study by "Alexander." *The Meaning of Anxiety* cites only one paper by an Alexander: Franz Alexander's "The Influence of Psychologic Factors upon Gastro-intestinal Disturbances. May, *The Meaning of Anxiety*, 72, 361; May, *The Meaning of Anxiety*, v.

[17] Jacobs, "Introduction," in Auden, *The Age of Anxiety*, xii, xv; Auden lived at James Stern's apartment at 207 East Fifty-Seventh Street (Auden, *In Solitude for Company*, 88); May, *The Meaning of Anxiety*, 4–5, 173–74; Auden, "A Preface to Kierkegaard," 214; Dewey, *Public Papers of Thomas E. Dewey, 1944*, 725.

[18] Emphasis original. May, *The Meaning of Anxiety*, 32n45, 140–42; May, *The Discovery of Being*, 14, 15; May, *The Meaning of Anxiety*, 115–19; Kierkegaard, *The Concept of Dread*, 38–39, 45, 55, 69, 107. When quoting from *The Concept of Dread*, the author has continued May's practice of replacing, in most instances, Lowrie's translation of *angst* as "dread" with "anxiety."

[19] May, *The Meaning of Anxiety*, 3–4; Lynd and Lynd, *Middletown*, 9; Lawrence Frank is believed to have influenced Robert Lynd's decision to take an anthropological or "cultural approach" toward Muncie as opposed to the "fact-finding mission" endorsed by other research staff or the moral-reform initiative pushed by the study's sponsor, the Rockefeller-backed Institute of Social and Religious Research. Gilkeson, *Anthropologists and the Rediscovery of America, 1886–1965*, 75–76.

[20] Lynd and Lynd, *Middletown in Transition*, 3, 426–27; Lynd and Lynd, *Middletown*, 12–15, 87, 222, 495.

[21] Lynd and Lynd, *Middletown in Transition*, 177, 422n25.

[22] Tillich, "Existential Philosophy," 48, 66–67; Rollo May, "The Origin and Significance of the Existential Movement in Psychology," in May et al., *Existence*, 4–5.

[23] Spiegelberg, *Phenomenology in Psychology and Psychiatry*, xxxii, 146; Henri F. Ellenberger, "A Clinical Introduction to Psychiatric Phenomenology and Existential Analysis," in May et al., *Existence*, 94–97, 117–21.

[24] Magnuson, "Arthur Wright Combs," 38–39; "Guide to the Arthur W. Combs Papers," Online Archive of California, accessed November 18, 2017, www.oac.cdlib.org.

[25] Combs, "Phenomenological Concepts in Nondirective Therapy," 198–99.

[26] Spiegelberg, *Phenomenology in Psychology and Psychiatry*, 156; Rogers, "Some Observations on the Organization of Personality," 366.

[27] Magnuson, "Arthur Wright Combs," 37–38; Richards and Gonzalez, "Arthur Wright Combs (1912–1999)," 1150; Laura N. Rice and Leslie S. Greenberg, "Humanistic Approaches to Psychotherapy," in Freedheim et al., *History of Psychotherapy*, 199–200.

[28] Magnuson, "Arthur Wright Combs," 38.

[29] Dewey, "Transmitting Conclusions and Recommendations of the New York State Temporary Veterans' Commission," January 29, 1945, in *Public Papers of Thomas E. Dewey*, 1945, 34–39.

[30] Binger, *The Doctor's Job*, 232–33; Cobb, *Borderlands of Psychiatry*, ix–xiii.

[31] Cobb, *Borderlands of Psychiatry*, 19–20, 136.

[32] Allport, "The Psychologist's Frame of Reference," 2–3, 12, 27n11.

[33] Ibid., 14, 22, 26–27. Emphasis original.

Chapter 2

[1] Steiner, *Where Do People Take Their Troubles?*, x–xi.

[2] Ibid., ix–x; author's correspondence with Nanci Young (Smith College archivist), December 21, 2017.

[3] Steiner, *Where Do People Take Their Troubles?*, 1–4.

[4] Yates, *Psychological Racketeers*, 202–3; Fernberger, "The American Psychological Association," 47–49.

[5] Fernberger, "The American Psychological Association," 51–54.

[6] Fishbein, *Morris Fishbein, M. D.*, 43–47; "A Book a Day," *Newark Advocate* (Newark, Ohio), November 3, 1932; Fishbein, *The New Medical Follies*, 200–204.

[7] "Governor Signs Medical Practice Measure," *Ithaca Journal*, May 17, 1926; Freud, *The Question of Lay Analysis*, 87, 95.

[8] Fishbein, *The New Medical Follies*, 359; "Senator Love Asks Inquiry," *Brooklyn Daily Eagle*, June 20, 1931; "Bootlegging Psychology," *Brooklyn Daily Eagle*, December 13, 1931; "Senator Love's Views on the Psychiatrists," *Brooklyn Daily Eagle*, December 17, 1931.

[9] "Seek Two as Tests Reveal Faithfull Girl Was Drugged," *Brooklyn Daily Eagle*, June 16, 1931; "Starr Faithfull Death before Grand Jury Again," *St. Louis Post-Dispatch*, July 25, 1931; "Scotland Yard Seeks Clues in Starr Faithfull Murder," *Salt Lake Telegram*, June 13, 1931.

[10] *Muncie Evening Press*, "Faithfull Girl's Mind Warped by Her Friend," June 20, 1931; *New York Times*, "Hits Quack Psychologists," November 29, 1931; New York State Senate, S. 1601, print number 1880, 1932.

[11] New York State Senate, S. 1601 (1932); "Bootlegging Psychologists"; "Mcooey Hints

Way to Ditch Senator Love," *Brooklyn Daily Eagle*, February 22, 1932; "See Love as Primary Winner Despite His Defeat in Primary," *Brooklyn Daily Enterprise*, September 21, 1932; "Eagle's Poll Forecast Winners in 3 Races," *Brooklyn Daily Eagle*, November 9, 1932.

[12] "Woman Accused as Fake Healer," *New York Times*, December 19, 1933; "Woman 'Healer' Pays $500 Fine," *New York Daily News*, June 20, 1934.

[13] People v. Cole, 219 NY 98 (1916).

[14] "Psychologists Ask Law to Ban Quacks," *New York Times*, January 4, 1937.

[15] Symonds, "The Province of Psychological Counseling," 323, 325, 326; Hildreth, "Psychology as a Career," 26.

[16] Britt, "Pending Developments in the Legal Status of Psychologists," 55; New York State Senate, S. 1809, print number 1225 (1937); New York Academy of Medicine, "Committee on Public Health Relations Report of Activities for the Year 1936," 219; New York State Senate, S. 1534, print number 1840 (1936); Laws of the State of New York, Chapter 459 (1936).

[17] Britt, "Model 'Certified Psychologists' Act," 123; Lucas, "Steuart-Henderson Britt," 67.

[18] "Psychologists Continue Fight on Clinic Plan," *Brooklyn Daily Eagle*, October, 31, 1930; Saffir, "Practical Issues in the Enactment of Legislation for the Certification of Psychologists," 71; Luckey, "Résumé of Pennsylvania Round Table on Licensing Psychologists," 79.

[19] Britt, "Pending Developments in the Legal Status of Psychologists," 54-55; Fryer, "Introduction: Contribution of Certification to Unified Professional Status in Psychology," 49-51; New York State Senate, S. 1534, print number 1840 (1936).

[20] Fryer, "Introduction: Contribution of Certification to Unified Professional Status in Psychology," 50; Landis, "Certification of Psychologists by the State as Contrasted to Certification by Psychological Organizations," 58.

[21] Fryer, "Introduction: Contribution of Certification to Unified Professional Status in Psychology," 49; Britt, "Pending Developments in the Legal Status of Psychologists," 55.

[22] Capshew, *Psychologists on the March*, 55, 67.

[23] Heiser, "Certification of Psychologists in Connecticut," 624-26.

[24] Ibid., 624, 627-29.

[25] Connecticut General Assembly Committee on Licensed Occupations Committee, "Joint Standing Committee Hearings," March 14, 1945; Bennett and Engle, "Faulty Management of Psychiatric Syndromes Simulating Organic Disease," 1203-7.

Chapter 3

[1] Harrower, "Till now I have lived in the suburbs of myself," in *Time to Squander, Time to Reap*, 72; Molly Harrower, unpublished autobiography, M3216, folder 17, MHP, [238]; Harrower, "Incredible Crags of Manhattan," in *Time to Squander, Time to Reap*, 78; "Decrees Granted," *Nevada State Journal* (Reno), July 7, 1945; Heims, *The Cybernetics Group*, 235; Harrower, "Life, you will lose a lover when I die," in *Time to Squander, Time to Reap*, 70; New York Telephone Company, *Manhattan, New York City Telephone Directory* (Fall–Winter 1946), 532; Harrower,

unpublished autobiography, [242].

[2] Harrower, unpublished autobiography, [241–47]; Harrower, "Molly R. Harrower," in O'Connell and Russo, *Models of Achievement*, 166.

[3] Harrower, unpublished autobiography, [238, 243].

[4] Harrower, "Molly R. Harrower," 160; "Elected by Mental Hygiene Group," *New York Times*, December 27, 1945; Bonita Weddle, "Mental Health in New York State 1945–1998: A Historical Overview," p. [3]n3, Publication no. 70 1998, New York State Archives; "Mental Hygiene for Reconstruction," *Hartford Courant*, February 5, 1919; Harrower, "Inkblots and Poems," in The History of Clinical Psychology in Autobiography, ed. Walker, 166; Albert Deutsch, "To Tackle Causes of War and Peace," *Gazette and Daily* (York, PA), November 8, 1947.

[5] Harrower, "Inkblots and Poems," 149.

[6] Wanke, "American Military Psychiatry and Its Role among Ground Forces in World War II," 143; National Mental Health Act, 60 Stat. 421 (1946), P.L. 79–487; *National Neuropsychiatric Institute Act: Hearings on H.R. 2550, Day 1, Before the Subcommittee of the Committee on Interstate and Foreign Commerce*, 79th Cong. (1946) (statements of T. Parran and W. B. Miller).

[7] National Mental Health Act, 60 Stat. 421 (1946), P.L. 79–487.

[8] *National Neuropsychiatric Institute Act: Hearings on H.R. 2550, Days 1 and 3, Before the Subcommittee of the Committee on Interstate and Foreign Commerce*, 79th Cong. (1946) (statements of T. Parran, D. A. Marquis, R. A. Levine, and F. Braeland).

[9] "GI Mental Illnesses Increasing Steadily," *New York Times*, July 27, 1947; Blain, "Some Essentials in National Mental Health Planning," 374; "Veterans' Chief Praises Fort Harrison Activities," *Great Falls Tribune* (Great Falls, MT), June 14, 1948; Frank Carey, "'Chaotic' Conditions of US Turning Vets into Neurotics," *Paris News* (Paris, TX), June 2, 1946; Virginia Irwin, "Many a Veteran, in Need of Psychiatric Care, Is in Prison Today Because of a Crime Brought on by a Mind Bruised and Battered by War," *St. Louis Post-Dispatch*, May 26, 1946.

[10] "Dr. Blain Gets Veterans Post," *New York Times*, October 26, 1945; Betty MacDonald, "Rest Homes Help Bring Victims Back to Health," *Battle Creek Enquirer* (Battle Creek, MI), July 25, 1943; Appel, "Daniel Blain, M.D.," 100, 102.

[11] Appel, "Psychiatric Therapy," in Hunt, *Personality and Behavior Disorders*, 1127–28; Riggs, *Just Nerves*, 79–84.

[12] Kubie, *The Riggs Story*, 141; Association for the Advancement of Psychotherapy, "Notes and Comments," (October 1947): 503–4; Millet, "Tratelja Farms," 34–36; Mosse, "A Vacation Experiment with a Group of Psychoanalytic Patients," 219; Kubie, *The Riggs Story*, 30–31; Millet, "Tratelja Farms," 38.

[13] Association for the Advancement of Psychotherapy, "Notes and Comments," (October 1947): 504

[14] Campbell, "The Role of the Clinical Psychologist in a Veterans Administration Mental Hygiene Clinic," 15; Blain, "Some Essentials in National Mental Health Planning," 377, 383.

[15] Blain, "Some Essentials in National Mental Health Planning," 374–75, 379, 383.

[16] bid., 374

[17] Reeves, *The Psychology of Rollo May*, 256; Rogers and Wallen, *Counseling with Returned Servicemen*, 17, 90.

[18] Combs, "Basic Aspects of Non-directive Therapy," 603; "The Church Steeple," *Fitchburg Sentinel* (Fitchburg, MA), August 12, 1944; Richard Shaner, "Churches Draft Aid to Services," *Marion Star* (Marion, OH), June 29, 1944; Reeves, *The Psychology of Rollo May*, 256.

[19] "Psychology Course Starts at Y.M.C.A.," *Brooklyn Daily Eagle*, October 15, 1935; Tyron, *Alumni Catalogue 1836–1947*, xxxvi; Lieberman, *Acts of Will*, 396–97; Nin, *The Diary of Anaïs Nin*, 1:325, 350.

[20] May, *Paulus*, 6; May, "Portrait of Men Students," 318; May, *The Art of Counseling*, [unnumbered page in foreword]; "Don't Delay Marriage," *Philadelphia Enquirer*, November 10, 1937.

[21] May, *The Art of Counseling*, [unnumbered page in foreword]; May, *Paulus*, 20–21; May, *The Art of Counseling*, [unnumbered page in foreword], 49; May, *The Springs of Creative Living*, 251.

[22] Cooper, *Paul Tillich and Psychology*, 99–100, 147, 172, 178.

[23] Blain, "The Psychiatrist and the Psychologist," 4–5.

[24] Ibid., 4, 6, 9–10.

[25] Grob, "Psychiatric and Social Activism," 483–85.

[26] Ibid., 481–82, 488, 490–91.

[27] American Psychiatric Association, "Comment: Appointment of Dr. Blain," 581.

Chapter 4

[1] New York State Senate, S. 1609, print number 1111 (1948); "Desmond Bill Would Affect Psychologists," *Journal News* (White Plains, NY), February 3, 1948; "New Desmond Bill Would Bar Quack Doctors," *Dunkirk Evening Observer* (Dunkirk, NY), February 2, 1948; "Society Urges State Certify Psychologists," *Democrat and Chronicle* (Rochester, NY), February 12, 1948.

[2] New York State Senate, S. 1488, print number 1621 (1947); Long, "Professional Status and Training of Psychologists," 104–5, 108.

[3] Long, "Professional Status and Training of Psychologists," 104; Hogan, "A History of the New York State Psychological Association," 22; Combs, "A Report of the 1951 Licensing Effort in New York State," 541; McCollom, "Licensing Psychologists in San Diego," 553; Committee on Training and Standards, "The Certification of Clinical Psychologists in Virginia," 395–96.

[4] Harrower, "The Evolution of a Clinical Psychologist," 24, 27; Heims, *The Cybernetics Group*, 25–26, 234–35.

[5] "Qualified Psychiatrists Are Scarce," *News-Journal* (Mansfield, OH), August 1, 1948; "Psychology for Children Urged," *The Times* (San Mateo, CA), September 13, 1948.

[6] Roe et al., "Training Needs of Clinical Psychologists in Practice," 407–9; M. Harrower to Lenore Seltzer, New York, December 2, 1948, M3212, folder 19, MHP; A. Stern to M. Harrower, New York, August 11, 1947, M3212, folder 19, MHP; M. Edelstein to M. H. Whitney, New York, October 30, 1947, M3212, folder 19, MHP.

[7] Edelstein to Whitney.

[8] "Desmond Bill Would Affect Psychologists"; "Society Urges State Certify Psychologists". H. L. Corwin, Subcommittee on Certification of Psychologists, minutes, May 26, 1948, M3242.2, folder 1948, MHP; T. Juzak to M. Herman, New York, February 17, 1948, M3242.2, folder 1948, MHP.

[9] Francis B. Carroll to Mental Hygiene Clinic Chiefs, Boston, January 16, 1948, M3242.2, folder 1948, MHP; H. I. Harris to M. Harrower, Boston, January, 21, 1948, M3242.2, folder 1948, MHP.

[10] Association for the Advancement of Psychotherapy, "Notes and Comments," (April 1948): 301–2; M. Harrower, unpublished autobiography, [p. 241], M3216, folder 17, MHP; Wolfle, "Across the Secretary's Desk," 210; Corwin, Subcommittee on Certification of Psychologists, May 26, 1948.

[11] Juzak to Herman.

[12] T. S. Weiss and F. Halpern to E. H. L. Corwin, New York, February 19, 1948, M3242.2, folder 1948, MHP; Lucy Freeman, "Psychiatric Plan Offered for City," *New York Times*, October 29, 1948.

[13] Weiss and Halpern to Corwin; Freeman, "Psychiatric Plan Offered for City."

[14] Weiss and Halpern to Corwin.

[15] The May 26, 1948, minutes for the Subcommittee on Certification of Psychologists' do not specify the location of this meeting, though correspondence from Corwin to subcommittee members frequently identified room 558 of the academy as its meeting location. E. H. L. Corwin to S. Bayne-Jones, C. Binger, M. R. Harrower, and S. B. Wortis, New York, February 25, 1948, M3242.2, folder 1948, MHP; E. H. L. Corwin to S. Bayne-Jones, C. Binger, M. R. Harrower, and S. B. Wortis, New York, April 28, 1948, M3242.2, folder 1948, MHP; Association for the Advancement of Psychotherapy, "Notes and Comments," (April 1948): 301–2; Ochroch and Kalinkowitz, "Florence Halpern (1900–1982)," 1396; Halpern, "Rorschach Interpretation of the Personality Structure of Schizophrenics Who Benefit from Insulin Therapy," 826; Lawrence Van Gelder, "Dr. Joseph Wortis, an Editor and a Psychiatrist, 88, Dies," *New York Times*, February 28, 1995; Searls, *The Inkblots*, 205; Shorter and Healy, *Shock Therapy*, 54–55; Harrower-Erickson, review, 313–15.

[16] T. C. Desmond to E. H. L. Corwin, Albany, NY, March 10, 1948, M3242.2, folder 1948, MHP; E. H. L. Corwin to M. Harrower, New York, April 8, 1948, M3242.2, folder 1948, MHP.

[17] K. F. Heiser to M. Harrower, [Ann Arbor, MI], May 31, 1948, M3242.2, folder 1948, MHP; Graydon DeCamp, "Karl Heiser Discovered World at Close Hand," *Cincinnati Enquirer*, June 24, 1974; Corwin, Subcommittee on Certification of Psychologists.

[18] Heiser to Harrower; DeCamp, "Karl Heiser Discovered World at Close Hand"; Corwin, Subcommittee on Certification of Psychologists, May 26, 1948.

[19] Corwin, Subcommittee on Certification of Psychologists, May 26, 1948.

[20] Ibid.; S. Bayne-Jones, chair's notes to the Subcommittee on Certification of Psychologists, October 1, 1948, M3242.2, folder 1948, MHP; Heiser to Harrower.

[21] Heiser to Harrower.

[22] M. Harrower to K. F. Heiser, New York, June 5, 1948, M3242.2, folder 1948, MHP.

[23] Ibid.; M. Harrower to E. H. L. Corwin, New York, June 5, 1948, M3242.2, folder 1948, MHP.

[24] E. H. L. Corwin, Subcommittee on Certification of Psychologists, minutes, June 9, 1948 meeting, M3242.2, folder 1948, MHP; Bennett, "A New Era in Business and Industrial Psychology," 473.

[25] "Bill Seeks to Prohibit Withholding of School Aid Due to Poor Ratings," *Courier-Journal* (Louisville, KY), February 5, 1948; Acts of the Commonwealth of Kentucky, Chapter 169 (1948); "Kentucky Has 176 New Laws on Books Effective Today," *Owensboro Messenger* (Owensboro, KY), June 18, 1948; Corwin, Subcommittee on Certification of Psychologists, June 9, 1948; Frank et al. vs. South et al., State Board of Health (KY), 194 S. W. R. 375.

[26] "Act to Halt Fake Psychologists," *Los Angeles Times*, August 23, 1948.

Chapter 5

[1] G. R. Wendt to M. Harrower, Rochester, NY, December 3, 1948, M3242.2, folder 1948, MHP; "U. of R. Post Resigned by Dr. Wendt," *Democrat and Chronicle* (Rochester, NY), May 3, 1960; J. M. Hunt to [G. K.] Bennett, [A.] Combs, [M.] Harrower, [J. G.] Peatman, [G. R.] Wendt, and [W. H.] Wulleck, New York, December 7, 1948, M3242.2, folder 1948, MHP; "Officers Elected by Psychologists," *Ithaca Journal* (Ithaca, NY), February 2, 1948.

[2] Hunt to Bennett et al.; Wendt to Harrower; J. M. Hunt to M. Harrower, New York, June 30, 1948, M3190, folder 7, MHP; M. Harrower to J. M. Hunt, New York, July 13, 1948, M3190, folder 7, MHP.

[3] S. Bayne-Jones to Subcommittee on Certification of Psychologists, [New York], November 24, 1948, M3242.2, folder 1948, MHP; G. R. Wendt to M. Harrower, Rochester, NY, January 10, 1949, M3242.2, folder 1949, MHP.

[4] M. Harrower to G. R. Wendt, [New York], December 15, 1948, M3242.2, folder 1948, MHP; Hunt to Bennett et al.

[5] S. Bayne-Jones to G. R. Wendt, New York, December 21, 1948, M3242.2, folder 1948, MHP; T. C. Desmond to S. Bayne-Jones, Newburgh, NY, December 29, 1948, M3242.2, folder 1948, MHP.

[6] Wendt to Harrower.

[7] Ibid.; G. R. Wendt to M. Harrower, Rochester, NY, January 18, 1949, M3242.2, folder 1949, MHP; S. Bayne-Jones to M. Harrower, New York, January 18, 1949, M3242.2, folder 1949, MHP; M. Harrower to G. R. Wendt, New York, January 20, 1949, M3242.2, folder 1949, MHP.

[8] Wendt to Harrower; J. W. Kosseff, unpublished *New York Times* letter to the editor, February 4, 1949, M3242.2, folder 1949, MHP.

Notes

[9] Fishbein, "Beware the Mind Meddler," 33.

[10] Ibid., 35–36.

[11] Richard B. Shields, "Clinical Psychologists," letter to the editor, *Courier-Journal* (Louisville, KY), November 28, 1948; Fishbein, "Beware the Mind Meddler," 36; S. Parker, "The Practice of Psychiatry," letter to the editor, *New York Times*, January 21, 1949.

[12] Beutel and Rice, "Regulation of Psychological Counseling and Psychotherapy," 475; The nineteen states, districts, and territories with basic science laws were Alaska (1946), Arizona (1936), Arkansas (1929), Colorado (1937), Connecticut (1925), District of Columbia (1929), Florida (1939), Iowa (1935), Michigan (1937), Minnesota (1927), Nebraska (1927), New Mexico (1941), Oklahoma (1937), Oregon (1933), Rhode Island (1940), South Dakota (1939), Tennessee (1943), Washington (1927), and Wisconsin (1925). "Basic Science Question Remains a Hot Issue," *Des Moines Tribune* (Des Moines, IA), February 17, 1949; "521st Session Record Proves Salons Very Health-Minded," *Austin American* (Austin, TX), July 6, 1949.

[13] Fishbein, "Beware the Mind Meddler," 34; Parker, "The Practice of Psychiatry"; S. Parker, "Reflections on Paul Schilder," in Shaskan and Roller, *Paul Schilder*, 21–24.

[14] W. Roller, "Introductory Note on Phenomenological Method," in Shaskan and Roller, *Paul Schilder*, 55, 57; S. Parker, "The Character of Modern Psychiatry," in Shaskan and Roller, *Paul Schilder*, 60, 61, 63, 65; I. Galdston, "Paul Schilder and Integrative Psychiatry," in Shaskan and Roller, *Paul Schilder*, 39.

[15] *New York University Bulletin* 30 (March 15, 1930): 27, 74; Bender, "Paul Schilder's Work on the Body Image," in *Paul Schilder: Mind Explorer*, Shaskan and Roller, eds., 192, 199; Parker, "Reflections on Paul Schilder," 25; Galdston, "Paul Schilder and Integrative Psychiatry," 41.

[16] G. Rubin-Rabson, "Licenses for Psychologists," letter to the editor, *New York Times*, February 4, 1949; Kosseff, unpublished *New York Times* letter.

[17] Mearns, *The New York Red Book* (1949), 93; New York State Senate, S. 1836, print number 1989 (1949); "Albany Gets Bill to Outlaw 'Quack' Psychiatrists," *Brooklyn Daily Eagle*, February 18, 1949; "Legislators Will Help Cities with Parking Problem," *Times Record* (Troy, NY), February 18, 1949; [Sanford], "Legislation in Various States," 577.

[18] Association for the Advancement of Psychotherapy, "Editorial," 209; Goodman, Siller, and Andronico, "Arthur Teicher (1914–2003)," 813; Teicher, "Psychology and Clinical Psychology: A Reply," 450–51.

[19] "Boro's First Psychiatric Society Wins Praise at Inaugural Rites," *Brooklyn Daily Eagle*, April 22, 1949.

[20] American Psychiatric Association, "News and Notes," 76; Knapp, Levin, and French, *A History of the Pennsylvania Psychological Association*, 116–17; Pennsylvania Senate, S. 848, print number 609 (1949); Laws of the Commonwealth of Pennsylvania, Pamphlet Laws 639 (1911).

[21] Grob, "Psychiatric and Social Activism," 491–92; American Psychiatric Association, "Summary of Meetings of Council and Executive Committee," 784.

[22] Group for the Advancement of Psychiatry Committee on Clinical Psychology, "The Relation of Clinical Psychology to Psychiatry," 351; Schilder, *Psychotherapy*, 255.

[23] Lucy Freeman, "Legal Basis Urged on Psychologists," *New York Times*, September 11, 1949; Peatman, "The Problem of Protecting the Public by Appropriate Legislation for the Practice of Psychology," 102–3; Combs, "A Report of the 1951 Licensing Effort in New York State," 542.

[24] Capshew, *Psychologists on the March*, 173–74; Jacobsen, "Clinical Psychology as Related to Legislative Problems," 110–11.

Chapter 6

[1] R. May, application to William Alanson White Institute, May 27, 1948, WAWIRR; R. May to Clara Thompson, New York, September 14, 1949, WAWIRR; Sandra Afflick (assistant registrar of operations and records at the Teachers College), email correspondence with author, July 31, 2017; E. Fromm to R. May, [New York], November 6, 1943, EFA; D. May to R. May, Anaheim, CA, August 26, 1948, DMP; R. May to E. Fromm, New York, October 16, [1949], EFA.

[2] B. Rowes, "'Love and Will'—You Need Them Both in This Age of Anxiety, Says Pioneering Psychoanalyst Rollo May," *People*, December 20, 1976; R. May to E. Fromm, New York, November 19, [1949], EFA.

[3] "Psychologist Urges Licenses," *Democrat and Chronicle* (Rochester, NY), January 11, 1950; "State Licensing of Psychologists Discussed at Meet," *Democrat and Chronicle*, January 18, 1950.

[4] "Psychologist Bill Draws Criticism," *New York Times*, January 22, 1950; New York State Senate, S. 2697, print number 2849 (1950).

[5] Sherman, "Theodor Reik and Lay Analysis," 384–87.

[6] "Psychologist Bill Draws Criticism," *New York Times*, January 22, 1950.

[7] D. Blain to M. Herman, [Washington, DC], January 3, 1950, M3242.2, folder 1950, MHP.

[8] "Curbing Assailed in Psychotherapy," *New York Times*, January 28, 1950; Jones et al., "Discussion on Lay Analysis," 201, 207.

[9] New York State Assembly, A. 2697, print number 2849 (1950); Mearns, *The New York Red Book* (1950), 179–80.

[10] Combs, "A Report of the 1951 Licensing Effort in New York State," 542.

[11] Ibid., 542–43; Joint Council of Psychologists on Legislation, financial report, April 2, 1951, HPA Mss46, folder 10, RMP.

[12] May, "Religion, Psychotherapy, and the Achievement of Selfhood, Part III," 26; May, *Man's Search for Himself*, 90–91.

[13] May, "Religion, Psychotherapy, and the Achievement of Selfhood, Part II," 16.

[14] May, "Religion, Psychotherapy, and the Achievement of Selfhood, Part III," 27.

[15] Snygg and Combs, *Individual Behavior*, 313.

[16] Combs, "A Report of the 1951 Licensing Effort in New York State," 542.

[17] "Jersey Pact of Defense Included," *Press and Sun-Bulletin* (Binghamton, NY), Decem-

ber 12, 1950; Combs, "A Report of the 1951 Licensing Effort in New York State," 542; "Legislature Votes Psychologist Bill," *New York Times*, March 17, 1951; F. S. Freeman to M. Harrower, Ithaca, NY, January 3, 1951, M3242.2, folder 1951, MHP; New York State Senate, S. 2366, print numbers 2523, 3038 (1951).

[18] Henry K. Kaessler to A. W. Combs, Bronxville, NY, February 14, 1951, M3212, folder 4, MHP; New York State Senate, S. 2366, print numbers 2523, 3038 (1951); "Brees Asks Psychology Exam Unit," *Press and Sun-Bulletin* (Binghamton, NY), February 13, 1951.

[19] New York State Senate, S. 2366, print numbers 2523, 3038 (1951).

[20] Joint Council of Psychologists on Legislation, financial report; "Legislature Votes Psychologist Bill," *New York Times*, March 17, 1951; Joseph D. Sullivan to T. E. Dewey, New York, March 21, 1951, NYSVJ1951, Senate Int. 2366 to 2864 Assembly Int. 43 to 838, Reel 3, NYSL.

[21] "Thomas E. Dewey Is Dead at 68," *New York Times*, March 17, 1971; "Notable Names: Thomas E. Dewey," The Mob Museum, accessed January 6, 2019, https://themobmuseum.org/notable_names/thomas-dewey/; Malcolm Wilson, "Governor Thomas E. Dewey as an Innovator," in Benjamin, *Memories of Thomas E. Dewey*, 9–12.

[22] S. C. Clark to T. E. Dewey, Alfred, NY, March 21, 1951, NYSVJ1951, Senate Int. 2366 to 2864 Assembly Int. 43 to 838, Reel 3, NYSL; A. W. Combs to L. E. Walsh, Syracuse, NY, March 23, 1951, NYSVJ1951, Senate Int. 2366 to 2864 Assembly Int. 43 to 838, Reel 3, NYSL; H. Bone, E. Fromm, R. May, D. Slesinger, and H. J. Zucker to T. E. Dewey, New York, March 22, 1951, NYSVJ1951, Senate Int. 2366 to 2864 Assembly Int. 43 to 838, Reel 3, NYSL; O. M. Brees to L. E. Walsh, [Albany, NY], March 16, 1951, NYSVJ1951, Senate Int. 2366 to 2864 Assembly Int. 43 to 838, Reel 3, NYSL.

[23] Joint Council of Psychologists on Legislation, minutes from the twenty-fourth meeting, April 2, 1951, HPA MSS 46, folder 10, RMP.

[24] Ibid.

[25] Ibid.

[26] Ibid.

Chapter 7

[1] A. W. Combs to T. E. Dewey, Syracuse, NY, April 9, 1951, NYSVJ1951, Senate Int. 2366 to 2864 Assembly Int. 43 to 838, Reel 3, NYSL.

[2] Ibid.

[3] Sidney S. Leshine to T. E. Dewey, Flushing, NY, March 20, 1951, NYSVJ1951, Senate Int. 2366 to 2864 Assembly Int. 43 to 838, Reel 3, NYSL; H. Bruner Sutton to T. E. Dewey, Ithaca, NY, March 20, 1951, NYSVJ1951, Senate Int. 2366 to 2864 Assembly Int. 43 to 838, Reel 3, NYSL; Eugene Davidoff to Laurence E. Walsh, Schenectady, March 21, 1951, NYSVJ1951, Senate Int. 2366 to 2864 Assembly Int. 43 to 838, Reel 3, NYSL.

[4] D. Blain to T. E. Dewey, Washington, DC, March 21, 1951, NYSVJ1951, Senate Int. 2366 to 2864 Assembly Int. 43 to 838, Reel 3, NYSL.

[5] D. Blain to T. E. Dewey, [Washington, DC], March 31, 1951, M3242.2, folder 51, MHP.

[6] Ibid.; Grob, "Origins of DSM-I," 424, 428–30; G. N. Raines, "Foreword," in American Psychiatric Association, *Diagnostic and Statistical Manual*, vii–ix.

[7] T. E. Dewey, veto message for senate bill 2366, April 10, 1951, pp. 240–41, PTD.

[8] T. E. Dewey, veto message for senate bill 2366, April 10, 951, pp. 240-41, PTD.

[9] "Creedmoor under Inquiry," *Poughkeepsie Journal* (Poughkeepsie, NY), March 12, 1943; T. R. Dewey, annual message to the legislature, January 5, 1944, p. 11, PTD.

[10] T. E. Dewey, annual message to the legislature, January 4, 1950, pp. 12, 14–16, PTD ; T. E. Dewey, "Proclamations: Mental Health Week," p. 473, 1944, PTD.

[11] H. Bone to A. W. Combs, New York, July 15, 1951, M3242.2, folder 1951, MHP; L. Long to Members of the New York State Psychological Association, December 10, 1951, M3242.2, folder 1951, MHP.

[12] F. J. Gerty to Paul Huston, [Chicago], May 21, 1951, M3242.2, folder 1951, MHP; F. J. Gerty to D. Blain, [Chicago], May 22, 1951, M3242.2, folder 1951, MHP.

[13] B. Locke to A. W. Combs, [New York], June 21, 1951, M3242.2, folder 1951, MHP.

[14] H. Bone to M. Harrower, New York, July 15, 1951, M3242.2, folder 1951, MHP; Bone to Combs.

[15] Locke to Combs.

[16] Joint Council of Psychologists on Legislation, minutes of the twenty-ninth meeting, June 26, 1951, July 10, 1951, M3242.1, folder 8, MHP.

[17] M. Harrower to B. S. Wortis, [New York], June 22, 1951, M3242.2, folder 1951, MHP; Bone to Harrower.

[18] Bone to Harrower; [A. S. Thompson], "Notes on Discussion Held on July 17, 1951 at Dr. Harrower's Apartment," [July 1951], HPA Mass 46, box 46, folder 10, RMP.

[19] [Thompson], "Notes on Discussion."

[20] L. S. Kubie to Leo Bartemeier, [New York], April 26, 1951, M3242.2, folder 1951, MHP; L. S. Kubie to M. Harrower, New York, June 8, 1951, M3242.2, folder 1951, MHP; Frank S. Freeman to Arthur W. Combs, Ithaca, NY, July 9, 1951, M3242.2, folder 1951, MHP.

[21] M. Harrower to A. W. Combs, [New York], July 20, 1951, M3242.2, folder 1951, MHP; M. Harrower to Lucy Freeman, [New York], September 13, 1951, M3242.2, folder 1951, MHP; A. S. Thompson, "Minutes of the Thirty-First Meeting of the Joint Council of Psychologists on Legislation," September 10, 1951, HPA Mass 46, box 46, folder 10, RMP; A. S. Thompson, "Minutes of the Thirty-Second Meeting of the Joint Council of Psychologists on Legislation," October 15, 1951, HPA Mass 46, box 46, folder 10, RMP.

[22] Thompson, "Minutes of the Thirty-Second Meeting"; Gerty, Holloway, and Mackay, "Licensure or Certification of Clinical Psychologists," 273; M. Harrower to Members of the Joint Council, [New York], [November 1951], M3242.2, folder 1951, MHP; American Psychiatric Association, "Joint Report of the Committee on Clinical Psychology and Legal Aspects of Psychiatry," New York, November 3, 1951, M3242.2, folder 1951, MHP.

[23] M. Harrower to M. Herman, official correspondence, [New York], November 13, 1951,

M3242.2, folder 1951, MHP; M. Harrower to M. Herman, personal correspondence, [New York], November 13, 1951, M3242.2, folder 1951, MHP.

[24] C. Thompson to R. May, [New York], May 22, 1951, WAWIRR; R. May to C. Thompson, May 25, 1951, WAWIRR; C. Thompson to R. May, December 31, 1951, WAWIRR.

[25] May, *Man's Search for Himself*, 8; "Alumnus of Mills College to Hold Annual Council," *Petaluma Argus-Courier* (Petaluma, CA), October 27, 1951; "Mills College Expects 700 to Enroll in Its 100th Year," *Oakland Tribune*, September 21, 1951; Jack Ryan, "Common Man Suffers from 20th 'Centuritis,' Consulting Psychologist Tells Mills Parley," *Oakland Tribune*, November 2, 1951; May, *Man's Search for Himself*, 110–11.

Chapter 8

[1] M. Harrower to Members of the Joint Council, [New York], January 3, 1952, HPA Mass 46, box 46, folder 10, RMP; A. S. Thompson, "Notes on Joint Conference, December 21, 1951, December 27, 1951," HPA Mass 46, box 46, folder 10, RMP.

[2] Harrower to Members of the Joint Council; Thompson, "Notes on Joint Conference."

[3] Harrower to Members of the Joint Council; Thompson, "Notes on Joint Conference."

[4] Harrower to Members of the Joint Council; Thompson, "Notes on Joint Conference."

[5] Harrower to Members of the Joint Council; A. W. Combs to M. Harrower, Syracuse, NY, December 18, 1951, M3242.2, folder 1951, MHP.

[6] Harrower to Members of the Joint Council; A. S. Thompson, "Minutes of the Thirty-Second Meeting of the Joint Council of Psychologists on Legislation," October 15, 1951, HPA Mass 46, box 46, folder 10, RMP.

[7] M. Harrower, "Information in Regard to the Proposed Amendment to the Medical Practice Act," January 30, 1952, M3242.2, folder 1952, MHP; People v. Maybrook, 89 N.Y.S.2d 275 (1949).

[8] Harrower, "Information in Regard"; Grob, "Psychiatric and Social Activism," 498.

[9] A. S. Thompson, "Minutes of the Thirty-Fourth Meeting of the Joint Council of Psychologists on Legislation," January 14, 1952, M3242.1, folder 8, MHP; Miller, *Instructor's Manual for Albert Ellis on REBT*, 20.

[10] A. S. Thompson, "Minutes of the Thirty-Eighth Meeting of the Joint Council of Psychologists on Legislation," May 19, 1952, M3242.1, folder 8, MHP; Georges Schopp, "Clark Williams, Margaret (1910–1975)," in de Mijolla, *International Dictionary of Psychoanalysis*, 303–4.

[11] A. S. Thompson, "Minutes of the Thirty-Fifth Meeting of the Joint Council of Psychologists on Legislation," January 28, 1952, HPA Mass 46, Box 46, folder 10, RMP.

[12] Ibid.; M. Harrower to C. Scofield, [New York], January 29, 1952, M3242.2, folder 8, MHP; C. Scofield to M. Harrower, Buffalo, NY, January 30, 1952, M3242.2, folder 8, MHP.

[13] C. Scofield to M. Harrower, Buffalo, NY, February 11, 1952, M3242.2, folder 1952, MHP; Thompson, "Minutes of the Thirty-Fifth Meeting."

[14] New York State Senate, S. 2052, print number 3853 (1952); A. S. Thompson, "Minutes

of the Thirty-Sixth Meeting of the Joint Council of Psychologists on Legislation," March 3, 1952, HPA Mass 46, box 46, folder 10, RMP; Mearns, *The New York Red Book* (1953), 125–26; A. S. Thompson, "Minutes of the Thirty-Seventh Meeting of the Joint Council of Psychologists on Legislation," April 21, 1952, HPA Mass 46, box 46, folder 10, RMP.

[15] Thompson, "Minutes of the Thirty-Seventh Meeting."

[16] A. S. Thompson, "Minutes of the Thirty-Eighth Meeting of the Joint Council of Psychologists on Legislation," May 19, 1952, M3242.1, folder 8, MHP; A. S. Thompson, "Minutes of the 41st Meeting of the Joint Council of Psychologists on Legislation," [October 22], 1952, HPA Mass 46, Box 46, folder 10, RMP.

[17] "Installed as Chair of Psychologists Council," *New York Times*, May 20, 1952.

[18] Hyde and Wolff, "The American Medical Association," 955, 1012–15; Gerty, Holloway, and Mackay, "Licensure or Certification of Clinical Psychologists," 271.

[19] Thompson, "Minutes of the Thirty-Seventh Meeting"; Sanford, "Summary Report of the 1952 Annual Meeting," 638–39.

[20] R. May, "Foreword," in Freedheim et al., *History of Psychotherapy*, xxiv.

[21] R. May to Joint Council Members, New York, October 31, 1952, M3242.2, folder 1952, MHP; "Steps Asked to Bar Quack Psychologists," *Los Angeles Times*, May 19, 1953; A. S. Thompson, "Minutes of the 42nd Meeting of the Joint Council of Psychologists on Legislation," November 17, 1952, HPA Mass 46, box 46, folder 10, RMP.

[22] May to Joint Council Members.

[23] Ibid.

[24] Thompson, "Minutes of the 42nd Meeting"; A. S. Thompson, "Minutes of the 41st Meeting of the Joint Council of Psychologists on Legislation," October 20, 1952, M3242.1, folder 8, MHP; R. May to Fellow psychologist, New York, November 10, 1952, M3242.2, folder 1952, MHP.

Chapter 9

[1] A. S. Thompson, "Minutes of the 44th Meeting of the Joint Council of Psychologists on Legislation," February 9, 1953, HPA Mass 46, box 46, folder 10, RMP; Sanford, "Across the Secretary's Desk," 170.

[2] Wiener, "Some Legislative and Legal Problems of Psychologists," 566.

[3] R. May, "Psychologists and Legislation in New York State," January 31, 1953, HPA Mass 46, box 149, folder 14, RMP.

[4] Ibid.

[5] Thompson, "Minutes of the 44th Meeting"; "Legislature Asked to Probe State's Healing Art Licenses," *Star-Gazette* (Elmira, NY), February 11, 1953.

[6] Mearns, *The New York Red Book* (1953), 125–26; "Psychologists Charge Doctors Attempt to Subordinate Them," *New York Herald-Tribune*, March 4, 1953; New York State Senate, S. 2659, print number 2805, 1953. Emphasis mine.

Notes

[7] Mearns, *The New York Red Book* (1953), 259–60.

[8] New York State Senate, S. 2659, print number 2805, 1959; Sanford, "Across the Secretary's Desk," 171; Thompson, "Minutes of the 44th Meeting."

[9] R. May to Joint Council Members, [New York], March 11, 1953, M3242.2, folder 1953, MHP.

[10] Thompson, "Minutes of the 45th Meeting"; "Psychologists Charge Doctors Attempt to Subordinate Them"; R. May to Fellow Psychologists, New York, May 19, 1953, M3242.2, folder 1953, MHP.

[11] Sanford, "Across the Secretary's Desk," 169–70, 172; "Psychologists Charge Doctors Attempt to Subordinate Them."

[12] "State Bill Fought by Psychologists"; R. May to Joint Council Members, [New York], March 11, 1953, M3242.2, folder 1953, MHP.

[13] May to Fellow Psychologists; M. Harrower to R. May, [New York], June 18, 1952, M3213, folder 9, MHP; M. Harrower to W. Milmoe, [New York], February 25, 1953, M3242.2, folder 1953, MHP.

[14] Thompson, "Minutes of the 44th Meeting"; A. S. Thompson, "Minutes of the 45th Meeting of the Joint Council of Psychologists on Legislation," March 16, 1953, HPA Mass 46, box 46, folder 10, RMP; "Medicine and the Law," *New York Herald-Tribune*, March 7, 1953.

[15] "Medicine and the Law"; May to Joint Council Members; May to Fellow Psychologists.

[16] Thompson, "Minutes of the 45th Meeting"; May to Joint Council Members; T. Robie, "Psychologists and M.D.s," *New York Herald-Tribune*, March 16, 1953; "Theodore R. Robie, 76, Dies; Backed Electro-Shock Therapy," *New York Times*, May 23, 1976.

[17] "Curbs on Treating Mental Ills Urged," *New York Times*, March 17, 1953; Blain, "Private Practice of Psychiatry," 138.

[18] May to Joint Council Members.

[19] Thompson, "Minutes of the 45th Meeting"; M. M. Kassell to Robert S. Holzman, Albany, NY, March 9, 1953, HPA Mass 46, box 46, folder 10, RMP; May to Fellow Psychologists.

[20] Thompson, "Minutes of the 45th Meeting"; May to Joint Council Members.

[21] A. S. Thompson, "Minutes of the 46th Meeting of the Joint Council of Psychologists on Legislation," April 20, 1953, HPA Mass 46, box 46, folder 10, RMP; May to Fellow Psychologists; Sanford, "Across the Secretary's Desk," 173.

[22] May to Joint Council Members; Wolfgang Saxon, "Jean Stralem, 86, Philanthropist Known for Work With the Blind," *New York Times*, December 22, 1994; M. Harrower to J. Stalem, [New York], May 8, 1953, M3242.2, folder 1953, MHP; G. Shapiro to J. Stralem, [Albany, NY], [May 1953], M3242.2, folder 1953, MHP; M. Harrower to J. Stalem, [New York], May 27, 1953, M3242.2, folder 1953, MHP; Alan Greg, "Minutes of the 49th Meeting of the Joint Council," September 21, 1953, M3242.1, folder 8, MHP.

[23] C. Binger to R. May, New York, May 19, 1953, HPA Mss 46, box 42, folder 8, RMP; May, *Man's Search for Himself*, [unmarked page].

[24] J. A. P. Millet to R. May, New York, May 21, 1953, HPA Mss 46, box 42, folder 8, RMP; L. Kubie to R. May, New York, May 20, 1953, HPA Mss 46, Box 42, folder 8, RMP.

[25] Thompson, "Minutes of the 46th Meeting"; May to Fellow Psychologists.

Chapter 10

[1] A. S. Thompson, "Minutes of the 47th Meeting of the Joint Council," May 25, 1953, HPA Mass 46, box 46, folder 10, RMP; R. May to [F. H.] Sanford, [L.] Shaffer, and [O. H.] Mowrer, [New York], [June 1953], HPA Mass 46, Box 46, folder 13, RMP; D. Blain, "Illinois Psychiatrists and Psychologists Work on Legislation Acceptable to Both," *A.P.A. Newsletter*, May 1953, HPA Mass 46, box 46, folder 13, RMP; "Steps Asked to Bar Quack Psychologists," *New York Times*, May 19, 1953.

[2] May to Sanford, Shaffer, and Mowrer.

[3] Page, "Preserving Guilt in the 'Age of Psychology,'" 11–15.

[4] A. Grey, "Minutes of the 49th Meeting of the Joint Council," September 21, 1953, M32421.1, folder 8, MHP; Smith, "Stuart Cook (1913–1993): Obituary," 521.

[5] Smith, "Stuart Cook (1913–1993): Obituary," 521; "Segregation Held Breeder of Evils," *New York Times*, February 19, 1949; Speer, *The Case of the Century*, 1, 222.

[6] Grey, "Minutes of the 49th Meeting."

[7] Ibid.; A. Grey, "Minutes of the 50th Meeting of the Joint Council," October 12, 1953, M32421.1, folder 8, MHP; "Max Siegel, Ex Leader of Psychologists' Group," *Sun Sentinel* (Deerfield Beach, FL), January 6, 1988; Mark Zaloudek, "Psychologist Had a 50-Year Career in New York City," *Herald-Tribune* (Sarasota, FL), October 3, 2008.

[8] Sanford, "Legislation for Psychologists," 545.

[9] [Sanford], "Legislation in Various States," 577–78, 580–81; Laws of the State of Tennessee, chapter 169 (1953).

[10] Bobbitt et al., "Implications for Legislation in the Report of the Ad Hoc Committee on Relations between Psychology and Other Professions," 550; Sanford, "Legislation for Psychologists," 545.

[11] May, "Psychology and Legislation," 585–86.

[12] Combs, "Problems and Definitions in Legislation," 554–63; R. May, "Understanding Therapy, in Psychotherapy," in Mowrer, *Psychotherapy*, 34–35. Emphasis original.

[13] [Sanford], "Legislation in Various States," 579; A. Grey, "Minutes of the 54th Meeting of the Joint Council," January 18, 1954, M3212, folder 4, MHP; S. Cook to Psychologist, New York, November 19, 1953, M3242.2, folder 1953, MHP; A. Grey, "Minutes of the 51st Meeting of the Joint Council," November 2, 1953, M3242.1, folder 8, MHP; A. Grey, "Minutes of the 53rd Meeting of the Joint Council," December 21, 1953, M3212, folder 4, MHP.

[14] [Joint Council], "Suggested Considerations in Regard to Visiting Legislators," November 7, 1953, 3212, folder 4, MHP; H. J. Zucker to M. Harrower, [New York], November 10, 1953, M3212, folder 4, MHP; Grey, "Minutes of the 54th Meeting."

[15] Grey, "Minutes of the 51st Meeting"; [Sanford], "Legislation in Various States," 578–79, 582–84; H. Seashore to Charles N. Cofer, New York, October 2, 1953, M2990.1, folder 1, RKP; A. S. Thompson, "Minutes of the Thirty-Eighth Meeting.".

[16] Grey, "Minutes of the 53rd Meeting"; Grey, "Minutes of the 54th Meeting."

[17] Grey, "Minutes of the 54th Meeting."

[18] Bernays, *Public Relations*, 7–8, 72–73, 78–79; Tye, *The Father of Spin*, 50–51, 56, 77–81.

[19] Tye, *The Father of Spin*, 175–76, 185–89; Grey, "Minutes of the 54th Meeting"; Bernays, *Public Relations*, 73.

[20] "Test Board Set Up by Psychologists," *New York Times*, January 31, 1954; Board of Directors to Members of the New York State Psychological Corporation, December 29, 1953, M3212, folder 4, MHP.

[21] "Test Board Set Up by Psychologists"; Nietzsche, *Philosophy in the Tragic Age of the Greeks*, 43–44.

Chapter 11

[1] Joint Council of New York State Psychologists on Legislation, "Emergency Mass Meeting of New York State Psychologists," February 11, 1954, M3212, folder 4, MHP; David W. Dunlap, "Tammany Hall's Auditorium, Where Politics Once Took Center Stage, Will Be Demolished," *New York Times*, July 4, 2006; [S. Cook], "Campaign to Defeat the Greenberg Amendment," memorandum, February 18, 1954, M3212, folder 4, MHP.

[2] New York State Senate, S.1789, print number 1917 (1954); NYSCP, "A Call to Arms," flier for emergency meeting, [February 1954], M3212, folder 4, MHP; Joint Council of New York State Psychologists on Legislation, "Emergency Mass Meeting of New York State Psychologists"; H. McNeil to Colleague, [New York], February 19, 1954, M3212 folder 4, MHP; M. Siegel to Colleague, Brooklyn, NY, February 12, 1954, M3212, folder 4, MHP.

[3] A. Grey, "Minutes of the 55th Meeting of the Joint Council," February 8, 1954, M3212, folder 4, MHP; A. Grey, "Minutes of the 54th Meeting of the Joint Council," January 18, 1954, M3212, folder 4, MHP.

[4] Joint Council of New York State Psychologists, "Psychologists and Co-workers Protest State Medical Bill Which Would Control Treatment of Mentally Ill Persons," press release, February 15, 1954, HPA Mss 46, box 46, folder 15, RMP; Associated Press, "5 Clergymen Balk at State Mental Bill," *Poughkeepsie Journal* (Poughkeepsie, NY), February 16, 1954; L. Kubie to M. Harrower, New York, January 5, 1954, M3212, folder 4, MHP.

[5] [R. May], "Talk at Psych Mass Meeting," February 15, [1954], HPA Mss 46, box 46, folder 15, RMP.

[6] Ibid.

[7] Ibid.

[8] Joint Council of New York State Psychologists, "Psychologists and Co-workers Protest"; Edith [Achilles?] to Dr. May, [New York], February 17, 1954, HPA Mss 46, box 46, folder 15, RMP.

[9] S. Cook to Joint Council Members, [New York], February 8, 1954, M3212, folder 4, MHP; S. Cook to E. L. Bernays, New York, March 31, 1954, MSS12534, Part I, BOX I:202, Correspondence 1954, PELB.

[10] R. May, "Restricting Psychologists," *New York Times*, February 18, 1954; Grey, "Minutes of the 55th Meeting."

[11] S. Parker, "Treating Mental Disorders," *New York Times*, February 23, 1954. The five other letters in the debate were J. Cotton et al., "Defining Medical Practice," *New York Times*, March 1, 1954; R. L. Frank, "Practice of Psychoanalysis," *New York Times*, March 11, 1954; L. J. Stone, "Function of Psychologist," *New York Times*, March 9, 1954; F. S. Freeman, Gordon Hamilton, Laurin E. Hyde, Laurence F. Shaffer, Donald E. Super, "Greenberg Bill Opposed," *New York Times*, March 15, 1954; and T. R. Robie and M. Pellens, "Treating Mental Disorders," *New York Times*, March 17, 1954.

[12] [Cook], "Campaign to Defeat the Greenberg Amendment"; Cook and Zucker, "The Demise of the Greenberg Amendment," 549–50; S. Cook to Fellow Psychologists, New York, February 19, 1954; L. Egan, "Medical Plan Stirs State Controversy," *New York Times*, February 21, 1954.

[13] Joel E. Rothenberg to S. Greenberg, Brooklyn, NY, March 4, 1954, box 348, CSS; H. J. Zucker to Ted Landsman, [New York], June 21, 1954, M29901.1, folder 1, RKP; S. L. Green to R. Finley Gayle, [Brooklyn, NY], April 22, 1954, box 348, CSS; D. Blain to S. L. Green, Washington, DC, May 17, 1954, box 348, CSS; K. E. Appel to S. L. Green, Washington, DC, April 26, 1954, box 348, CSS.

[14] Executive Committee of the [American Psychiatric] Association, "A Statement of the America Psychiatric Association's Position on Amending State Medical Practice Acts and Related Matters," March 7, 1954, box 348, CSS.

[15] Cook and Zucker, "The Demise of the Greenberg Amendment," 550; "8 Social Agencies Oppose Curb on Mental Ills," *New York Herald-Tribune*, March 18, 1954.

[16] Hyde and Wolff, "The American Medical Association," 944, 947–48.

[17] Ibid., 945n48, 946–51.

[18] Cook and Zucker, "The Demise of the Greenberg Amendment," 549; E. L. Bernays to S. W. Cook, [New York], April 2, 1954, MSS12534, Part I, BOX I:202, Correspondence 1954, PELB.

[19] Cook and Zucker, "The Demise of the Greenberg Amendment," 549.

[20] "Thomas E. Dewey Is Dead at 68," *New York Times*, March 17, 1971; "Charges 'Mail Order' Psychologists Bilk Public of Millions," *Chicago Tribune*, September 9, 1954; Zucker to Landsman.

Chapter 12

[1] Joint Council of New York Psychologists on Legislation, "News Flash," [fall 1954], MSS12534, Part I, Box I:202, Correspondence 1954, PELB.

Notes

[2] Joint Council of New York Psychologists on Legislation, "Organization of the Joint Council of New York Psychologists on Legislation: 1954–1955," [1954], MSS12534, Part I, BOX I:202, Correspondence 1954, PELB; S. Cook to R. A. Katzell, New York, November 24, 1954, MSS12534, Part I, Box I:202, Correspondence 1954, PELB.

[3] E. L. Bernays to Raymond A. Katzell, [New York], October 20, 1954, MSS12534, Part I, Box I:202, Correspondence 1954, PELB; J. K. Javits to E. L. Bernays, Albany, NY, February 3, 1955, MSS12534, Part I, Box I:202, Correspondence 1955, PELB; R. A. Katzell, "News Letter," November 12, 1954, MSS12534, Part I, Box I:202, Correspondence 1954, PELB.

[4] R. May to L. Frank, New York, [1965], M3207, folder 28, MHP.

[5] Frank, "The Promotion of Mental Health," 174; Mead, "Lawrence Keslo Frank 1890–1968," 57.

[6] R. May, "Foreword," in Miner and May, "Psychotherapy and Counseling," 321–23; R. May, "Foreword," in Freedheim et al., *History of Psychotherapy*, xxiii–xiv; Frank, "The Promotion of Mental Health," 168–70.

[7] May to Frank; Martin, Noyes, and Hendrick, "Psychotherapy—The Need for Definition," 79–80.

[8] May, *Psychology and the Human Dilemma*, xi; "Dr. Carl Binger, 86, Pioneer in Psychosomatic Medicine, Dies," *New York Times*, March 24, 1976; "Events Today," *New York Times*, December 3, 1954; May, "Foreword," in Miner and May, "Psychotherapy and Counseling," 321.

[9] N. Sanford, "The Findings of the Commission in Psychology," in Miner and May, "Psychotherapy and Counseling," 341–49.

[10] R. May to L. K. Frank, New York, September 19, 1955, box 15, LKFP; R. May to Eunice Thomas Miner, [New York], September 17, 1955, box 15, LKFP; May, *Psychology and the Human Dilemma*, ix

[11] T. M. Kavanagh, Opinion 2359, January 20, 1956, in *Biennial Report of the Attorney General of the State of Michigan*, vol. 2 (Lansing, Michigan: Speaker-Hines and Thomas,1956), 24–25. Emphasis original. Kavanagh misidentifies Mowrer's *Psychotherapy* as *Psychotherapeutics*.; May, "Foreword," in Freedheim et al., *History of Psychotherapy*, xxiv; May to Frank, [1965].

[12] R. May, "New York State Psychological Association: Report of the President," January 1955, HPA Mss. 46, box 47, folder 4, RMP; Ruth P. Richardson, "New York State Psychological Association: Minutes of the 18th Annual Meeting," January 29, 1955, HPA Mss. 46, box 47, folder 4, RMP.

[13] United Press Association, special news service for Edward L. Bernays, February 1, 1955, MSS12534, Part I, Box I:202, Correspondence 1955, PELB; Laws of the State of Arkansas, chapter 129 (1955); Laws of the State of Washington, chapter 305 (1955).

[14] R. A. Katzell, "Newsletter of the Joint Council of New York State Psychologists on Legislation," October 24, 1955, M2990.1, folder 1, RKP; S. W. Cook and W. M. Hales, "Joint Report of the APA and CSPA Committees on Legislation," 727–28, 736.

[15] Cook and Hales, "Joint Report of the APA and CSPA Committees on Legislation," 737–38, 752–54.

[16] Ibid., 727, 754–56.

[17] Katzell, "Newsletter of the Joint Council"; A. Grey et al., "1955 Report of the Finance Committee," October 15, 1955, M2990.1, folder 1, RKP; R. A. Katzell to E. Nyquist, [New York], February 6, 1956, M2990.1, folder 1, RKP.

[18] [R. A. Katzell], "Significant Features of the Bill for Licensing Psychologists," [October 1955], M2990.1, folder 1, RKP.

[19] Katzell, "Newsletter of the Joint Council"; R. A. Katzell and A. S. Thompson, "News Flash from the Joint Council of New York State Psychologists on Legislation," March 1, 1956, M2990.1, folder 1, RKP.

[20] Katzell and Thompson, "News Flash"; [R. A. Katzell], "Annotated Summary of New York Bill Re Psychology," January 11, 1956, M2990.1, folder 1, RKP; New York State Senate, S. 3239, print number 3508 (1956).

[21] "Summary of State Legislature's Actions on Major Bills," New York Times, March 25, 1956; David Gerst to R. A. Katzell, New York, March 17, 1957, New York (State) 1956BJ; A. Harriman, approval message for senate bill 3239, April 17, 1956, New York (State) 1956BJ.

[22] A. Harriman, [Approval message for Senate bill 3239], April 17, 1956, New York (State) 1956BJ; H. B. Smith to D. Gutman, Albany, New York, March 29, 1956, New York (State) 1956BJ; D. Blain to D. Gutman, Washington, D.C., March 30, 1956, New York (State) 1956BJ.

[23] Laws of the State of New York, chapter 459 (1936); "Psychologists Listed," *New York Times*, April 1, 1958.

[24] "3 Leaders Favor Psychological Code," *New York Times*, March 29, 1959; National Psychological Ass'n for Psychoanalysis, Inc. v. University of New York 18 Misc. 2d 722 (N.Y. Misc. 1959).

[25] "3 Leaders Favor Psychological Code"; National Psychological Ass'n v. University of New York.

[26] National Psychological Ass'n v. University of New York.

Conclusion

[1] Grob, *From Asylum to Community*, 110; McKeachie and Hoch, "Psychology in the States," 589.

[2] Laws of the State of Maryland, chapter 748 (1957); Laws of the State of New Hampshire, chapter 121 (1957); Laws of the State of California, chapter 2320 (1957); Deutsch, "After Legislation—What Price Psychology," 647.

[3] States with nonrestrictive legislation by title (author's analysis, see "List of Psychology Laws, 1945–1977"): CT, VA, MN, ME (1953), WA.

[4] States with nonrestrictive legislation by title and function (author's analysis, see "List of Psychology Laws, 1945–1977"): KY, GA, TN, AR, NY, CA, MD, NH, MI, UT, CO, FL, DE, OR, NV, NM, IL, AL, LA, AZ, MS, ND, KS, HI, ME (1967), SC, RI, TX, WI.

[5] States with nonrestrictive legislation by title and/or function (author's analysis, see "List of Psychology Laws, 1945–1977"): ID (1963), WY, OK, NJ, AK, NE, ID (1967), NC,

Notes

WV, MT, OH, MA, PA, IA, SD, VT, MO. Listed are only the laws that explicitly prohibited the practice of psychology regardless of what the practitioners called themselves.

[6] States with New York "psychologist" definitions (author's analysis, see "List of Psychology Laws, 1945–1977"): NH, FL, NV, IL, OK, KS, ID (1967).

[7] States with restrictions on the terms "psychology," "psychological," and "psychologist" (author's analysis, see "List of Psychology Laws, 1945–1977"): CA, MD, NH, UT, CO, FL, DE, ID (1963), NV, NM, IL, AL, LA, AZ, WY, OK, NJ, MS, ND, KS, NE, ID (1967), NC, ME (1967), SC, TX, WI, WV, MT, OH, PA, IA, VT, MO.

[8] States with restrictions on the terms "psychologic," "psychology," "psychological," and "psychologist" (author's analysis, see "List of Psychology Laws, 1945–1977"): WY, KS, NE, NC, MT, OH.

[9] States with laws requiring communication channels with medicine (author's analysis, see "List of Psychology Laws, 1945–1977"): TN, AR, CA, UT, CO, DE, OR, IL, AL, LA, NE, NC.

[10] Laws of the State of Louisiana, act 347 (1964).

[11] Giorgi, "The Crisis of Humanistic Psychology," 8–9; Grob, "Psychiatry's Holy Grail," 214.

[12] Giorgi, "The Crisis of Humanistic Psychology," 5–8; Taylor, "Existential-Humanistic Psychology," 6–7; May, "The Emergence of Existential Psychology," in *Existential Psychology*, 16, 18.

[13] Giorgi, "The Crisis of Humanistic Psychology," 5

[14] Sanford, "The Findings of the Commission in Psychology," 346–59; May, "Existential Psychiatry an Evaluation," 36; Giorgi, "The Crisis of Humanistic Psychology," 8.

[15] Giorgi, "The Crisis of Humanistic Psychology," 6–12; May, "Existential Psychiatry an Evaluation," 34–35.

[16] Grob, "Psychiatry's Holy Grail," 214–15.

[17] Whitaker, *Anatomy of an Epidemic*, 48–57.

[18] Grob, "Psychiatry's Holy Grail," 215–16; May, *Psychology and the Human Dilemma*, xix.

[19] Giorgi, "The Crisis of Humanistic Psychology," 18–19; May, "Foreword," in Freedheim et al., *History of Psychotherapy*, xxiv–xv.

[20] May, "Foreword," in Freedheim et al., *History of Psychotherapy*, xxvi–xxvii; Schneider, Galvin, and Serlin, "Rollo May on Existential Psychotherapy," 426–27.

[21] Grob, "Psychiatry's Holy Grail," 216–17; Schneider, Galvin, and Serlin, "Rollo May on Existential Psychotherapy," 427; May, *Innocence and Power*, 93–94.

[22] Tillich, *On the Boundary*, 97; Tillich, "Frontiers," 17.

[23] K. J. Schneider, Galvin, and Serlin, "Rollo May on Existential Psychotherapy," 424; David Dempsey, "Love and Will and Rollo May," *New York Times*, March 28, 1971; Barbara Rowes, "'Love and Will'—You Need Them Both in This Age of Anxiety, Says Pioneering Psychoanalyst Rollo May," *People*, December 20, 1976.

[24] Tillich, "Frontiers," 17–18.

List of Psychology Laws, 1945–77

[1] States and years based on list from Eshleman, "A Mini-Review of 'A Chronology of Noteworthy Events in American Psychology,'" 266. Laws identified as nonrestrictive by title and/or function are those that explicitly prohibited the practice of psychology regardless of what the practitioners called themselves. Definitions for the types of nonrestrictive legislations are based on those presented in "Joint Report of the APA and CSPA Committees on Legislation" in the November 1955 edition of the *American Psychologist*.

Bibliography

Abzug, Robert H. *Psyche and Soul in America: The Spiritual Odyssey of Rollo May.* New York: Oxford University Press, 2021.
Allport, Gordon W. "The Psychologist's Frame of Reference." *Psychological Bulletin* 37 (January 1940): 1–28.
American Psychiatric Association. "Comment: Appointment of Dr. Blain." *American Journal of Psychiatry* 104 (March 1948): 581.
———. "Committee on Nomenclature and Statistics." *Diagnostic and Statistical Manual of Mental Disorders* [Vol. 1], Washington, DC: American Psychiatric Association Mental Hospital Service, 1952.
———. "News and Notes." *American Journal of Psychiatry* 106 (July 1949): 75–77.
———. "Summary of Meetings of Council and Executive Committee: June 26, 1949 to May 5, 1950." *American Journal of Psychiatry* 107 (October 1950): 291–99.
Appel, Kenneth E. "Daniel Blain, M.D.: A Biographical Sketch." *Transactions and Studies of the College of Physicians of Philadelphia* 38 (October 1970): 99–111.
Association for the Advancement of Psychotherapy. "Editorial." *American Journal of Psychotherapy* 3 (April 1949): 207–12.
———. "Notes and Comments." *American Journal of Psychotherapy* 1 (October 1947): 500–505.
———. "Notes and Comments." *American Journal of Psychotherapy* 2 (April 1948): 295–304.
Auden, Wystan H. *The Age of Anxiety: A Baroque Eclogue.* 1946. Reprint, edited and introduction by Alan Jacobs. Princeton, NJ: Princeton University Press, 2011.
———. "A Preface to Kierkegaard." *New Republic* 21 (August 1944), cited in W. H. Auden, *The Complete Works of W. H. Auden: Prose, 1939–1948*, edited by Edward Mendelson. Princeton, NJ: Princeton University Press, 2002.
———. *In Solitude for Company: W. H. Auden after 1940*, edited by Katherine Bucknell and Nicholas Jenkins. Auden Studies 3. Oxford: Clarendon Press, 1995.
Benjamin, Gerald, ed. *Memories of Thomas E. Dewey.* Albany, NY: Nelson A. Rockefeller Institute of Government, 1991.
Bennett, Abram E., and Beatrice Engle. "Faulty Management of Psychiatric Syndromes Simulating Organic Disease." *Journal of the American Medical Association* 130 (April 17, 1946): 1203–8.

Bennett, George K. "A New Era in Business and Industrial Psychology." *Personnel Psychology* 1 (Winter 1948): 473–77.
Bennett, John J. Jr. *Informal Opinions of the Attorney-General* for the Year Ending December 31, 1934. Albany: J. B. Lyons Company, 1935.
Bernays, Edward L. *Public Relations*. Norman: University of Oklahoma Press, 1952.
Beutel, Frederick K. and Ralph S. Rice, "Beutel, "Regulation of Psychological Counseling and Psychotherapy." *Columbia Law Review*, 15 (April 1951): 474-495.
Binger, Carl A. L. *The Doctor's Job*. New York: W. W. Norton, 1945.
Blain, Daniel. "Private Practice of Psychiatry." *Annals of the American Academy of Political and Social Science* 28 (March 1953): 136–49.
———. "The Psychiatrist and the Psychologist." *Journal of Clinical Psychology* 1 (January 1947): 4–10.
———. "Some Essentials in National Mental Health Planning." *Social Service Review* 20 (September 1946): 374–84.
Bobbitt, Joseph, Arthur W. Combs, Meredith Crawford, J. McV. Hunt, Carlyle Jacobsen, Rensis Likert, Rollo May, Fillmore H. Sanford, David Shakow, and E. Lowell Kelly. "Implications for Legislation in the Report of the Ad Hoc Committee on Relations between Psychology and Other Professions." *American Psychologist* 8 (October 1953): 346–550.
Boothe, Helvi. Review of "Psychotherapy and Counseling." By Roy W. Miner and Rollo May, eds. *Social Service Review* 30 (January 1956): 201–3.
Britt, Steuart Henderson. "Model 'Certified Psychologist' Act." *Journal of Consulting Psychology* 3 (July–August 1939): 123–27.
———. "Pending Developments in the Legal Status of Psychologists." *Journal of Consulting Psychology* 5 (March–April 1941): 52–56.
Bryon, Dennis. "Lawrence K. Frank, Knowledge, and the Production of the 'Social.'" *Poetics Today* 19 (Autumn 1998): 401–21.
Buchanan, Roderick D. "Legislative Warriors: American Psychiatrists, Psychologists, and Competing Claims over Psychotherapy in the 1950s." *Journal of the History of Behavioral Sciences* 39 (Summer 2003): 225–49.
Campbell, Helen M. "The Role of the Clinical Psychologist in a Veterans Administration Mental Hygiene Clinic." *Journal of Clinical Psychology* 1 (January 1947): 15–21.
Capshew, James H. *Psychologists on the March: Science, Practice, and Professional Identity in America, 1929–1969*. New York: Cambridge University Press, 1999.
Cobb, Stanley. *Borderlands of Psychiatry*. Cambridge, MA: Harvard University Press, 1943.
Combs, Arthur W. "Basic Aspects of Non-directive Therapy." *American Journal of Orthopsychiatry* 16 (1946): 589–605.
———. "Phenomenological Concepts in Nondirective Therapy." *Journal of Consulting Psychology* 12 (July–August 1948): 107–208.
———. "Problems and Definitions in Legislation." *American Psychologist* 8 (October 1953): 554–63.
———. "A Report of the 1951 Licensing Effort in New York State." *American Psychologist* 6 (October 1951): 541–48.
Committee on Training and Standards, Psychology Section, Virginia Academy of Science. "The Certification of Clinical Psychologists in Virginia." *American Psychologist* 1 (September 1946): 395–98.

Cook, Stuart W., and Herbert Zucker. "The Demise of the Greenberg Amendment." *American Psychologist* 9 (September 1954): 549–52.
Cook, Stuart W., and William M. Hales. "Joint Report of the APA and CSPA Committees on Legislation." *American Psychologist* 10 (November 1955): 727–56.
Cooper, Terry D. *Paul Tillich and Psychology*. Mercer, GA: Mercer University Press, 2005.
de Mijolla, Alain, ed. *International Dictionary of Psychoanalysis*. Vol. 1. Farmington Hills, MI: Thomas Gale, 2005.
Deutsch, Cynthia P. "After Legislation—What Price Psychology." *American Psychologist* 13 (November 1958): 645–52.
Dewey, Thomas E. *Public Papers of Thomas E. Dewey*. Vols. 1944–1954. Albany, NY: Williams Press, 1946.
Dewsbury, Donald A. "Molly R. Harrower (1906–1999)." *American Psychologist* 55 (September 2000): 1058.
Ellis, Albert. "Pros and Cons of Legislation for Psychologists." *American Psychologist* 8 (October 1953): 551–53.
Eshleman, John. "A Mini-Review of 'A Chronology of Noteworthy Events in American Psychology.'" *Behavior Analyst Today* 4 (2003): 265–68.
Fennell, Phil. *Treatment Without Consent: Law, Psychiatry and the Treatment of Mentally Disordered People Since 1845*. London: Routledge, 1996.
Fernberger, Samuel W. "The American Psychological Association: A Historical Summary, 1892–1930." *Psychological Bulletin* 29 (January 1932): 1–89.
Fishbein, Morris. "Beware the Mind Meddler." *Reader's Digest* 54 (February 1949): 33–36. Reprint from *Women's Home Companion* (December 1948).
———. *The Medical Follies: An Analysis of the Foibles of Some Healing Cults, Including Osteopathy, Homeopathy, Chiropractic, and the Electronic Reactions of Abrams, with Essays on the Antivivisectionists, Health Legislation, Physical Culture, Birth Control, and Rejuvenation*. New York: Boni and Liveright, 1925.
———. *Morris Fishbein, M.D.; An Autobiography*. New York: Doubleday, 1969.
———. *The New Medical Follies; An Encyclopedia of Cultism and Quackery in These United States, with Essays on the Cult of Beauty, the Craze for Reduction, Rejuvenation, Eclecticism, Bread and Dietary Fads, Physical Therapy, and a Forecast as to the Physician of the Future*. New York: Boni and Liveright, 1927.
Fowerbaugh, Clarence C. "Legal Status of Psychologists in Ohio." *Journal of Consulting Psychology* 9 (July–August 1945): 196–200.
Frank, Lawrence K. "The Promotion of Mental Health." *Annals of the American Academy of Political and Social Science* 286 (March 1953): 167–74
———. "Society as the Patient." *American Journal of Sociology* 42 (November 1946): 335–44.
Freedheim, Donald K., Herbert J. Freudenberger, Donald R. Peterson, Jane W. Kessler, Hans H. Strupp, Stanley B. Messer, and Paul L. Wachtel, eds. *History of Psychotherapy: A Century of Change*. Washington, DC: American Psychological Association, 1992.
Freud, Sigmund. *Civilization and its Discontents*. 1930. Reprint, translated and edited by James Strachey. New York: W. W. Norton, 1961.
———. "Concluding Remarks on the Question of Lay Analysis." *International Journal of Psycho-Analysis* 8 (1927): 392–98.

———. "The Origin and Development of Psychoanalysis." *American Journal of Psychology* 21 (April 1910): 181–218.

———. *The Question of Lay Analysis: An Introduction to Psycho-analysis*. Translated by James Strachey. New York: W. W. Norton, 1978. Reprint of 1959 translation. First published in German in 1926.

Fromm, Erich. *Escape from Freedom*. New York: Farrar and Rinehart, 1941.

Fryer, Douglas. "Introduction: Contribution of Certification to Unified Professional Status in Psychology." *Journal of Consulting Psychology* 5 (March–April): 49–52.

Galdston, Iago. "The Relation of Physical and Mental Health." *Journal of Educational Sociology* 5 (December 1931): 207–14.

Gardner, Leroy U., ed. *Tuberculosis in Industry*. New York: National Tuberculosis Association, 1942.

Gerty, Francis J., J. W. Holloway Jr., and R. P. Mackay, "Licensure or Certification of Clinical Psychologists." *JAMA* 148 (January 26, 1952): 271–73.

Gilkeson, John S. *Anthropologists and the Rediscovery of America, 1886–1965*. New York: Cambridge University Press, 2010.

Giorgi, Amedeo. "The Crisis of Humanistic Psychology." *Humanistic Psychologist* 15 (Spring 1987): 5–20.

Goodman, Morris, Jerome Siller, and Michael Andronico. "Arthur Teicher (1914–2003)." *American Psychologist* 58 (October 2003): 813.

Greening, Tom, ed. *American Politics and Humanistic Psychology*. San Francisco: Saybrook Institute Press, 1984.

Grob, Gerald N. *From Asylum to Community: Mental Health Policy in Modern America*. Princeton, NJ: Princeton University Press, 1991.

———. "Origins of DSM-I: A Study in Appearance and Reality." *American Journal of Psychiatry* 148 (April 1991): 421–31.

———. "Psychiatric and Social Activism: The Politics of a Specialty in Postwar America." *Bulletin of the History of Medicine* 60 (Winter 1986): 477–501.

———. "Psychiatry's Holy Grail: The Search for the Mechanisms of Mental Diseases." *Bulletin of the History of Medicine* 72 (Summer 1998): 189–219.

———. Review of *The Emperor's New Drugs: Exploding the Antidepressant Myth*, by Irving Kirsch. *Pharmacy in History* 35 (2013): 34–35.

Group for the Advancement of Psychiatry Committee on Clinical Psychology. "The Relation of Clinical Psychology to Psychiatry." *American Journal of Orthopsychiatry* 20 (April 1950): 346–55.

Halpern, Florence. "Rorschach Interpretation of the Personality Structure of Schizophrenics Who Benefit from Insulin Therapy." *Psychiatric Quarterly* 14 (December 1940): 826–33.

Harrower, Molly R. "The Evolution of a Clinical Psychologist." *Canadian Journal of Psychology* 2 (March 1948): 23–27.

———. *Genetic Psychology* 62 (January 1943): 119–33. Originally published in *Rorschach Research Exchange*, (May 1941): 130–44.

———. *Time to Squander, Time to Reap*. New Bedford, MA: Reynolds Publishing, 1946.

Harrower-Erickson, Molly. Review of *The Clinical Application of the Rorschach Test*, by Ruth Bochner and Florence Halpern. *American Journal of Psychology* 56 (April 1943): 313–15.

Heims, Steve J. *The Cybernetics Group*. Cambridge, MA: MIT Press, 1991.

Heiser, Karl F. "Certification of Psychologists in Connecticut." *Psychological Bulletin* 42 (November 1945): 624–30.
Hildreth, Gertrude. "Psychology as a Career." *Journal of Consulting Psychology* 1 (March–April 1937): 25–28.
Hogan, John D. "A History of the New York State Psychological Association: The Early Years." Working paper, St. John's University, New York, March 1, 1994.
Howard, Alvin R. "The Geography of APA Membership." *American Psychologist* 13 (November 1958): 621-26.
Hunt, Joseph McVicker, ed. *Personality and Behavior Disorders: A Handbook Based on Experimental and Clinical Research*. Vol. 2. New York: Ronald Press, 1944.
Hyde, David R., and Payson Wolff. "The American Medical Association: Power, Purpose, and Politics in Organized Medicine." *Yale Law Journal* 63 (May 1954): 937–1022.
Jacobsen, Carlyle F. "Clinical Psychology as Related to Legislative Problems." *American Psychologist* 5 (April 1950): 110–11.
Jones, Ernst, ed. "Discussion on Lay Analysis." *International Journal of Psycho-Analysis* 8 (1927): 174–283.
Katzell, Raymond A., and Albert S. Thompson. "After Legislation—What Price Psychology." *American Psychologist* 13 (November 1958): 652–54.
Kierkegaard, Søren. *The Concept of Dread*. Translated by Walter Lowrie. Princeton, NJ: Princeton University Press, 1944.
Knapp, Samuel, Zito O. Levin, and Joseph L. French. *A History of the Pennsylvania Psychological Association*. Harrisburg: Pennsylvania Psychological Association, 1993.
Kubie, Lawrence S. *Practical and Theoretical Aspects of Psychoanalysis*. 2nd ed. New York: International Universities Press, 1950.
——— . *The Riggs Story: The Development of the Austen Riggs Center for the Study and Treatment of the Neuroses*. New York: Paul B. Hoeber, 1960.
Landis, Carney. "Certification of Psychologists by the State as Contrasted to Certification by Psychological Organizations." *Journal of Consulting Psychology* 5 (March–April 1941): 56–58.
Lieberman, E. James. *Acts of Will: The Life and Work of Otto Rank*. New York: Free Press, 1985.
Long, Louis. "Professional Status and Training of Psychologists: Report on Annual Meeting of NYSAAP." *American Psychologist* 1 (February 1946): 104–8.
Lucas, Darrell B. "Steuart-Henderson Britt." *Journal of Marketing* 38 (January 1974): 67–69.
Luckey, Bertha M. "Résumé of Pennsylvania Round Table on Licensing Psychologists." *Journal of Consulting Psychology* 5 (March–April 1941): 78–79.
Lynd, Robert S., and Helen M. Lynd. *Middletown*. New York: Harcourt, Brace, 1929.
——— . *Middletown in Transition: A Study in Cultural Conflicts*. New York: Harcourt, Brace, 1937.
Magnuson, Sandy. "Arthur Wright Combs." *Journal of Humanistic Counseling* 51 (April 2012): 33–50.
Martin, William B., Arthur P. Noyes, and Ives Hendrick. "Psychotherapy—The Need for Definition." *Social Service Review* 29 (March 1955): 79–80.
May, Rollo. *The Art of Counseling: How to Gain and Give Mental Health*. New York: Abingdon-Cokesbury, 1939.

———. *The Discovery of Being: Writings in Existential Psychology*. 1983. Reprint, New York: W. W. Norton, 1994.
———. "Existential Psychiatry an Evaluation." *Journal of Religion and Health* 1 (October 1961): 31–40.
———, ed. *Existential Psychology*. New York: Random House, 1961.
———. *Innocence and Power*. New York: W. W. Norton, 1991.
———. *Man's Search for Himself*. New York: W. W. Norton, 1953.
———. *The Meaning of Anxiety*. New York: Ronald Press, 1950.
———. *Paulus: Reminiscences of a Friendship*. New York: Harper and Row, 1973.
———. "Portrait of Men Students." *Christian Education* 19 (April 1936): 318–25.
———. *Power and Innocence: A Search for the Sources of Violence*. 1972. Reprint, New York: W. W. Norton, 1998.
———. "The Present Function of Counseling." *Teachers College Record* 46 (October 1944): 9–16.
———. "Psychology and Legislation." *American Psychologist* 9 (September 1954): 585–86.
———. *Psychology and the Human Dilemma*. 1979. Reprint, New York: W. W. Norton, 1996.
———. "Religion, Psychotherapy, and the Achievement of Selfhood." *Pastoral Psychology* 2 (October 1951): 29–33.
———. "Religion, Psychotherapy, and the Achievement of Selfhood, Part II." *Pastoral Psychology* 2 (November 1951): 15–20.
———. "Religion, Psychotherapy, and the Achievement of Selfhood, Part III." *Pastoral Psychology* 2 (January 1952): 26–33.
———. *The Springs of Creative Living: A Study of Human Nature and God*. New York: Abingdon-Cokesbury, 1940.
May, Rollo, Ernest Angel, and Henri F. Ellenerger, eds. *Existence*. 1958. Reprint, Northvale, NJ: Jason Aronson, 1994.
McCollom, Ivan N. "Licensing Psychologists in San Diego." *American Psychologist* 6 (October 1951): 553–54.
McKeachie, W. J., and E. L. Hoch. "Psychology in the States: AMA and Legislation." *American Psychologist* 12 (September 1957): 589.
Mead, Margaret. "Lawrence Keslo Frank 1890–1968." *American Sociologist* 4 (February 1969): 57–58.
Mearns, John, ed. *The New York Red Book*. 57th ed. Albany, NY: Williams Press, 1948.
———, ed. *The New York Red Book*. 58th ed. Albany, NY: Williams Press, 1949.
———, ed. *The New York Red Book*. 59th ed. Albany, NY: Williams Press, 1950.
———, ed. *The New York Red Book*. 62nd ed. Albany, NY: Williams Press, 1953.
Mendelson, Edward. *Later Auden*. New York: Farrar, Strauss and Giroux, 1999.
Menninger, Karl A. "Psychology and Psychiatry." *American Psychologist* 2 (April 1947): 139–40.
Miller, Ali. *Instructor's Manual for Albert Ellis on REBT*. Mill Valley: CaliforniaPsychotherapy.net, 2012.
Millet, John A. P. "Tratelja Farms." *Harvard Medical Alumni Bulletin* 15 (January 1941): 34–38.
Miner, Roy W., and Rollo May, eds. "Psychotherapy and Counseling." Special issue, *Annals of the New York Academy of Sciences* 63 (November 7, 1955): 319–42.

Morgan, Jane D. "Training Clinical Psychologists in the Veterans Administration." *Journal of Clinical Psychology* 3 (January 1947): 28–38.
Mosse, Eric P. "A Vacation Experiment with a Group of Psychoanalytic Patients." *Psychoanalytic Review* 32 (April 1945): 219–24.
Mowrer, O. Herbert, ed. *Psychotherapy: Theory and Research*. New York: Ronald Press, 1953.
New York Academy of Medicine. "Committee on Public Health Relations Report of Activities for the Year 1936." *Bulletin of the New York Academy of Medicine* 13 (March 1937): 201–19.
Nietzsche, Friedrich. *Philosophy in the Tragic Age of the Greeks*. Translated and introduction by Marianne Cowan. Gateway ed. Washington, DC: Regnery Publishing, 1962.
Nin, Anaïs. *The Diary of Anaïs Nin*. Vol. 1. Athens, OH: Swallow Press, 1966.
Ochroch, Ruth, and Bernard N. Kalinkowitz. "Florence Halpern (1900–1982)." *American Psychologist* 37 (December 1982): 1396.
O'Connell, Agnes N., and Nancy Felipe Russo. *Models of Achievement: Reflections of Eminent Women in Psychology*. New York: Columbia University Press, 1983.
Page, Corbin. "Preserving Guilt in the 'Age of Psychology': The Curious Career of O. Hobart Mowrer." *History of Psychology* 20 (February 2017): 1–27.
Peatman, John G. "The Problem of Protecting the Public by Appropriate Legislation for the Practice of Psychology." *American Psychologist* 5 (April 1950): 102–3.
Perry, Jr, W. G. "The Findings of the Commission in Counseling and Guidance: On the Relation of Psychotherapy to Counseling." *Annual New York Academy of Sciences* 63, vol. 3 (1955): 396–407.
Pickersgill, Martyn. "From Psyche to Soma? Changing Accounts of Antisocial Personality Disorders in the *American Journal of Psychiatry*." *History of Psychiatry* 21 (September 2010): 294–311.
Pols, Hans. "War Neurosis, Adjustment Problems in Veterans, and an Ill Nation: The Disciplinary Project of American Psychology during and after World War II." *Osiris* 22 (2017): 72–92.
Reeves, Clement. *The Psychology of Rollo May*. San Francisco: Jossey-Bass, 1977.
Richards, Anne C., and David M. Gonzalez. "Arthur Wright Combs (1912–1999)." *American Psychologist* 55 (October 2000): 1150.
Riggs, Austen F. *Just Nerves*. Boston: Houghton Mifflin, 1922.
Roe, Anne, Fred Gaudet, Quinter Holsopple, Zena O'Connor, and Seymour Sarason. "Training Needs of Clinical Psychologists in Practice." *American Psychologist* 4 (October 1949): 407–9.
Roger, Karen B. "The Lifelong Productivity of Terman's Original Women Researchers." Paper presented at the Annual Meeting of the American Educational Research Association, Chicago, March 24–28, 1997.
Rogers, Carl R. *Carl Rogers on Personal Power*. New York: Delacorte Press, 1977.
———. "Some Observations on the Organization of Personality." *American Psychologist* 2 (September 1947): 358–68.
———. "War Challenges Family Relationships." *Marriage and Family Living* 5 (November 1943): 86–87.
Rogers, Carl R., and John L. Wallen. *Counseling with Returned Servicemen*. New York: McGraw-Hill Book Company, 1946.
Saffir, Milton A. "Practical Issues in the Enactment of Legislation for the Certification of Psychologists." *Journal of Consulting Psychology* 5 (March–April 1941): 70–73.

Sanford, Fillmore H. "Across the Secretary's Desk: Relations with Psychiatry." *American Psychiatrist* 8 (April 1953): 169–73.
———. "Legislation for Psychologists." *American Psychologist* 8 (October 1953): 545.
[———]. "Legislation in Various States." *American Psychologist* 8 (October 1953): 572–84.
———. "Summary Report of the 1952 Annual Meeting." *American Psychologist* 7 (November 1952): 634–44.
Schilder, Paul. *Psychotherapy*. New York: W. W. Norton, 1938.
Schneider, Kirk J., John Galvin, and Ilene Serlin. "Rollo May on Existential Psychotherapy." *Journal of Humanistic Psychology* 49 (October 2009): 419–34.
Searls, Damion. *The Inkblots: Hermann Rorschach, His Iconic Test, and the Power of Seeing*. New York: Crown, 2017.
Senn, Milton J. E., Lois Barclay Murphy, J. Roswell Gallagher, Lois Meek Stolz and Herbert R. Stolz. "Lawrence K. Frank." *Child Development* 40 (June 1969): 447–53.
Shaskan, Donald A., and William L. Roller, eds. *Paul Schilder: Mind Explorer*. New York: Human Sciences, 1985.
Sherman, Murray H. "Theodor Reik and Lay Analysis." *Psychoanalytic Review* 75 (Fall 1988): 380–92.
Shorter, Edward, and David Healy. *Shock Therapy: A History of Electroconvulsive Treatment in Mental Illness*. New Brunswick, NJ: Rutgers University Press, 2007.
Smith, M. Brewster. "Stuart Cook (1913–1993): Obituary." *American Psychologist* 6 (June 1994): 521–22.
Snygg, Donald, and Arthur W. Combs. *Individual Behavior: A New Frame of Reference for Psychology*. New York: Harper and Brothers, 1949.
Speer, Hugh W. *The Case of the Century: A Historical and Social Perspective on Brown v. Board of Education of Topeka with Present and Future Implications*. Kansas City: University of Missouri 1968.
Spiegelberg, Herbert. *Phenomenology in Psychology and Psychiatry: A Historical Introduction*. Evanston, IL: Northwestern University Press, 1972.
Steiner, Lee R. *Where Do People Take Their Troubles?* Boston: Houghton Mifflin, 1945.
Symonds, Percival M. "The Province of Psychological Counseling." *Teachers College Record* 37 (January 1936): 313–27.
Taylor, Eugene I. "Existential-Humanistic Psychology." In *The Mystery of Personality: A History of Psychodynamic Theories*, 261–308. New York: Springer, 2009.
Teicher, Arthur. "Psychology and Clinical Psychology: A Reply." *American Psychologist* 3 (October 1948): 450–51.
Tillich, Paul. *The Courage to Be*. 1952. Reprint, New York: Yale Nota Bene, 2000.
———. "Existential Philosophy." *Journal of the History of Ideas* 5 (January 1944): 44–70.
———. "Frontiers." *Journal of Bible and Religion* 33 (January 1965): 17–23.
———. *On the Boundary*. Revision and new translation of 1936 version. New York: Charles Scribner's Sons, 1964.
Tye, Larry. *The Father of Spin: Edward L. Bernays and the Birth of Public Relations*. Owl Books ed. New York: Henry Holt, 2002.
Tyron, Harold H. *Alumni Catalogue 1836–1947*. New York: Union Theological Seminary, 1948.
Walker, C. Eugene, ed. *The History of Clinical Psychology in Autobiography*. Vol. 1. Pacific Grove, CA: Brooks/Cole Publishing, 1990.

Wallerstein, Robert S. *Lay Analysis: Life inside the Controversy*. Hillsdale, NJ: Analytic Press, 1998.

Wanke, Paul. "American Military Psychiatry and Its Role among Ground Forces in World War II." *Journal of Military History* 63 (January 1999): 127–46.

Whitaker, Robert. *Anatomy of an Epidemic*. New York: Crown Publishers, 2010.

Wiener, Daniel N. "Some Legislative and Legal Problems of Psychologists." *American Psychologist* 8 (October 1953): 564–69.

Wilder, Amos N., ed. *Liberal Learning and Religion*. New York: Harpers and Brothers Publishers, 1951.

Wolfle, Dael. "Across the Secretary's Desk: Psychology and Clinical Psychology." *American Psychologist* 3 (June 1948): 209–12.

———. "Methods of Controlling Psychological Frauds." *Transactions of the New York Academy of Sciences* 10 (March 1948): 169–79.

Yates, Dorothy H. *Psychological Racketeers*. Boston: Gorham Press, 1923.

Index

Abramson, Joseph, 154
Ackerly, Spafford, 102
Adler, Alfred, 11, 17, 18
Age of Anxiety, 2, 21, 22, 192n17
Alexander, Francis, 110, 112, 121
Alexander, Franz, 21, 124, 192n16
Allen, Frederick, 163
Allport, Gordon W., 29, 177
American Association of Applied Psychology, 36, 37
American Association of Social Workers, 142
American Medical Association, 3, 6, 10, 32, 33, 74, 102–3, 104, 107–8, 114, 118, 123, 127, 134, 136–37, 141, 143, 149, 150–51, 154–56, 162–63, 174, 176, 178–81, 183
  anti-quackery campaigns. *See* Fishbein, Morris
  congressional lobbying efforts, 118–19
  House of Delegates, 118, 136, 139, 142, 156, 169
  Legal Bureau, 102
  Legislative Committee, 103
  organizational dynamics, 155–56
American Mental Health Foundation, 171
American Psychiatric Association, 3, 4, 6, 10, 11, 46, 52, 53, 74, 80, 84, 86, 92, 93, 98, 100–101, 106–8, 114, 124, 126–27, 131–34, 137, 142–43, 151, 153–54, 159, 162–64, 166, 168, 171, 174, 176, 178–80, 183

Committee for the Preservation of Medical Standards in Psychiatry, 79, 130
Committee on Clinical Psychology ("Gerty committee"), 61, 80, 102, 108, 126
Committee on Legal Aspects of Psychiatry, 108
Committee on the Relationship between Psychiatry and Psychology, 106
Group for the Advancement of Psychiatry, 52, 61, 67, 79, 80, 86, 114
American Psychoanalytic Association, 9, 162
American Psychological Association, 3, 6, 10, 32, 33, 74, 102–4, 107–8, 114, 118–19, 123, 134, 136–37, 141, 143, 150–51, 154–56, 174, 176, 178–81, 183
American Board for Psychological Service, 157
certification efforts, 32, 157
Committee on Legislation, 37, 38, 39, 166, 167, 169
Committee on Relations with Other Professions, 107
Conference of State Psychological Associations, 72, 80, 166
Anderton, Walter P., 113
Angell, Ernest, 177
anxiety, ix, 2, 6, 16, 19–22, 25, 27, 43, 82, 83, 87, 100, 109, 111, 120, 124, 130, 161, 191n18
Association of Analytic Psychologists, 92

Association of Consulting Psychologists, 36–38, 58, 68
Association of School Psychologists for New York City Public Schools, 94
Auden, W. H., 2, 21, 22, 192n17
Austen Riggs Center. *See* Riggs, Austin F.

Bartemeier, Leo, 92, 93
Bayne-Jones, Stanhope, 64, 65, 71–73, 197n15
Bellevue Hospital, 61, 62, 63, 64, 76, 77, 105, 106, 113
Bennett, Abram E., 41
Bennett, George, 68–69, 70
Benzenberg Mayer, May, 35, 36, 60
Bernays, Edward L., 11, 144–46, 151, 156–57, 160, 165, 169
Binger, Carl, 64, 68, 71, 73, 133–34, 163
biology, x, 7, 8, 52, 76, 79, 142, 149, 176, 180, 182
Blain, Daniel
  as APA medical director, 6, 53, 79, 84, 98, 100, 102, 114, 131, 132, 171
  medical training, 46–47
  as Public Health Service officer, 47
  as VA Neuropsychiatric Services director, 46–48, 51, 52
  as War Shipping Administration medical director, 18, 46, 47
Blythewood Sanitarium, 46
Bone, Harry
  as Joint Council member, 11, 86, 92, 94, 102–6, 109, 114–15, 118, 120, 130, 139, 161
  psychological training, 49–50
  relationship with May, 50, 51, 92, 109
"Boulder Conference" (Conference on Clinical Training in Psychology), 81
Brees, Orlo M., 89, 92, 121
Brill, Abraham A., 10
Britt, Steuart Henderson, 38–41, 68
Brooklyn Association for Mental Health, 153
Brooklyn Psychiatric Society, 79, 153
Brown v. Board of Education, 6, 138
Buchanan, Roderick, x
Burlingame, C. C., 80

Cameron, D. Edwin, 130, 132
Cartesian dichotomy. *See* mind-body dichotomy
Chein, Isodor, 138

Clark, Kenneth B., 138
Clark, Stephen C, 92
Clark-Williams, Margaret, 115
client-centered therapy, 5, 25, 119, 190n10
Cobb, Stanley, 3, 6, 26–29, 45, 46, 48, 100
cognitive psychology, 178
Combs, Arthur W.
  graduate studies, 24, 25, 49
  as Joint Council lobbyist/member, 2, 3, 4, 111–12, 118, 120–21, 128, 139–39, 141
  as Joint Council/NYSA president, 3, 5, 70
  on phenomenology, 5, 24, 25, 76, 85, 86, 88–90, 92–94, 97, 99, 103, 104, 108
Committee on Certification of Consulting Psychologists, 32
Community Service Society of New York, 153
Concept of Dread, 22, 192n18
Conference on Psychotherapy and Counseling, 5, 161–65, 174
Cook, Stuart W., 5, 6, 137–40, 142–44, 148, 150–53, 156–57, 159–60, 165–66, 169
Corwin, Edward H. L., 63–64, 67, 68, 75, 197n15
Court of Appeals, New York, 36, 69, 113–14
courage, ix, xi–xii, 125, 133, 189n2

dehumanization, x, xii, 4, 51, 52, 128, 176–80
Desmond, Thomas C., 57, 58, 60–64, 66, 67, 72, 73
Deutsch, Cynthia P., 175
Dewey, Thomas E.
  early political career, 90
  as governor, 26, 91, 92, 117, 133, 134, 138, 157, 160
  as presidential candidate, 15, 22, 25, 90, 92
  veto of Desmond bill, 3, 6, 11, 93, 97–102, 104, 120, 128, 141, 168, 171
Diagnostic and Statistical Manual
  first edition, 27, 100, 102, 155, 164
  third edition, xii, 180

eclecticism, 7, 76, 178
Ellenberger, Henri, 177
Ellis, Albert, 114, 139
existentialism, x, 6, 24, 177, 178

Faithfull, Starr, 34
Federal Bar Association, 142, 148
Fernberger, Samuel W., 32
Fishbein, Morris, 33, 74, 75

Index 225

Fodor, Nandor, 172
Frank, Lawrence K., xii, 5, 17, 20–21, 82, 161–65, 192n15, 192n16, 192n19
Frankel, Edward, 172
frontier, ix, xi, 134, 176, 177, 182, 183
Freeman, Frank S., 89, 107, 138, 171
Freud, Sigmund, 7–11, 17, 18, 22, 33, 47, 48, 50, 77, 83, 85, 87, 135, 144, 145–46, 150
Fromm, Erich, 11, 17, 51, 82, 92
Fryer, Douglas H., 38, 39, 68

Galdston, Iago, 6, 17, 77, 84
Gerty, Francis J., 102
Gestalt, 24, 76, 178
Giorgi, Amedeo, 177, 178, 180
Goldstein, Kurt, 22
Green, Sidney L., 153–54
Greenberg, Samuel L., 73–74, 78, 111, 147, 152–53
Grob, Gerald N., x, 52, 80, 100, 114, 179, 180, 182
Group for Applied Freudian Psychology, 94
Gurevitz, Saul, 172

Halpern, Florence, 63–66, 70, 86, 102, 111, 114, 127, 171
Harriman, W. Averill, 102, 160, 170–71
Harris, Herbert I., 61
Harrower, Molly
  as Joint Council consultant/member, 103, 116–18, 129, 133, 139, 142
  as Joint Council president, 6, 104–10, 112–14
  as NYSCP member/president, 57, 59, 129
  private practice, 42–44
  on psychology-psychiatry relations, 42–44, 59–61, 64–68, 71, 73, 101, 142, 149, 156
Heiser, Karl, 40, 41, 65–69, 71
Herman, Morris, 6, 62, 77, 84, 106–8, 110–11, 113–14, 177
Hershey, Lewis B., 15
Heuyer, Georges, 116
Hiltner, Seward, 49, 51
Hogan, John D., x
Holsopple, James Q., 38
Horney, Karen, 10
Hunt, Joseph McVicker, 70–71, 85, 93, 141
Husserl, Edward G. A., 24, 76
Hyde, David R., 155
Illinois Psychiatric Society, 136

Illinois Psychological Association, 136
Indiana Psychological Association, 78
Individual Behavior: A New Frame of Reference for Psychology, 24

Jacobsen, Carlyle F., 81
Javits, Jacob K., 160
Jelliffe, Smith E., 10
Joint Council for New York State Psychologists on Legislation
  formation, 1, 85, 86
  legislative campaigns
    1951, 3, 88–94, 97–102, 104
    1956, 169–72
  Legislative Policy Committee, 169
  non-legislative initiatives, 119, 131
  public relations, 73, 115, 118, 127–30, 132, 141, 144, 147–52, 156, 160, 169–70
Josiah Macy, Jr. Foundation, 20, 59
Jung, Karl, 17
Juzak, Tatiana, 62

Karnosh, Louis J., 103
Katzell, Raymond A., xi, 159–60, 168–72
Kavanagh, Thomas M., 165, 209n11
Keegan, Joseph G., 127
Kelly, Lowell, 142
Kierkegaard, Søren, 22, 23
Kings County Psychiatric Hospital, 62
Kosseff, Jerome W., 74, 77
Kubie, Lawrence, 17, 59, 106–7, 114, 134, 149, 153, 163
lay analysis, 8–11, 33, 59–60, 76–78, 84–85, 115, 124, 127, 145, 172–73
laws
  certification, psychology
    Connecticut (1945), 3, 41, 46, 47, 62, 65, 74, 75, 140, 175, 185
    Maine (1953), 140
    Virginia (1946), 58, 62, 74, 185
  licensure, psychology
    California (1957), 174–75
    Kentucky (1948), 68, 69, 71, 79, 166, 185
    Louisiana (1964), 176
    Maryland (1958), 174, 185
    Michigan (1959), 176, 185
    Missouri (186), xii, 175, 180, 186
    Nevada (1963), 176, 186
    New Hampshire (1957), 174–75, 185
    New York (1956). *See* legislation, Van Wiggeren-Savarese bill

laws, licensure, psychology (*continued*)
   San Diego (1946), 58
   Tennessee (1951), 140–41, 166, 175, 185
legislation, New York
   AAAP Model 'Certified Psychologist'
      Act (1939), 37, 38
   ACP draft bill (1937), 36–38, 58
   Desmond bill (1947), 57
   Desmond II bill (1948), 57, 58, 60, 61–64, 67, 68, 74, 106
   Greenberg bill (1949), 77–79, 81, 107, 111, 113, 126, 147
   Greenberg II bill (1954), 147, 148, 150–59
   Love bill (1931), 34–36
   Metcalf-Brees bill (1951), 89, 90, 93, 94, 97–102, 121, 125
   Milmoe-Waters bill (1953), 104, 126–32, 147
   Noonan bill (1950), 85, 89, 90, 143
   Van Wiggeren-Savarese bill (1956), 4, 11, 169–73, 185
Lennon, Roger T., 121, 148
Love, William L., 34–35

machine. *See* dehumanization
Mahoney, Walter J., 93, 152
Marquis, Donald G., 45
Maslow, Abraham, 177, 179
May, Rollo
   books
      Art of Counseling, The, 50
      Existence: A New Dimension in Psychology and Psychiatry, 177, 182
      Liberal Learning and Religion (chapter), 86
      Man's Search for Himself, 9, 11, 109, 120, 128, 133, 162, 189n2
      Meaning of Anxiety, The, 6, 83, 109, 161, 189n2
      Psychotherapy (chapter), 142, 165, 209n11
      Springs of Creative Living, The, 51
   as Conference on Psychotherapy and Counseling organizer, 5, 161–65
   graduate studies, 15–22, 82, 84
   as Joint Council chairman, 115–24, 126–37, 139–43
   as minister, 18, 50, 83, 139
   as NYSPA president, 146–52, 154, 159
   tuberculosis, ix, 16, 22, 51

mechanization. *See* dehumanization
Menninger, Karl, 52, 79
Menninger, William, 52
Mental Hygiene Law (New York), 34, 62, 63
Medical Practice Act (Michigan), 142, 165
Medical Practice Act (New York). *See* legislation
Medical Practice Act (Pennsylvania), 79
Medical Society for the State of New York, 2–4, 6, 89, 98, 101–2, 106–7, 113, 116, 123, 126, 127, 139, 142, 166, 169, 171
Metcalf, George R., 89, 121, 125, 128, 129
Metropolitan New York Association for Applied Psychology, 60–61, 94
Middletown studies, 22, 23
Millet, John A. P., 47, 134
Milmoe, Wheeler, 116–17, 125–26, 128–31
mind-body dichotomy, 3, 27–29, 76, 100, 131
Montefiore Hospital, 106
Mowrer, Orval H., 137, 141, 165, 209n11

Nathan, Edgar J., 172–73
National Committee for Mental Hygiene, 44, 79
National Mental Health Act, 44, 45, 52
National Psychological Association for Psychoanalysis, 84, 94, 145, 172
New Jersey Psychological Association, 142
New York Academy of Medicine, 57–58, 64, 65, 67, 71, 73, 77, 84, 108
   Committee on Public Health Relations, 37, 62, 64, 71, 72, 74
   Medical Information Bureau, 6, 17
   Subcommittee on Certification of Psychologists, 64, 65, 71, 133
New York Association for Individual Psychologists, 94
New York Psychiatric Advancement Committee, 60, 63
New York Psychoanalytical Society, 9
New York Society of Clinical Psychiatry, 106, 110, 134, 154
New York Society for Clinical Psychologists, 61–63, 65–67, 70, 72–74, 77–78, 117, 129, 147–48
New York Society of Clinical Psychologists in Private Practice, 94
New York State Association of Applied Psychologists, 39, 58, 60
New York State Bar Association, 148

Index 227

New York State Psychological Association, 1, 5, 6, 58, 68–72, 83, 85, 86, 93, 94, 102–3, 106, 111, 118, 120, 123, 126, 134, 141, 143, 146, 148, 150, 157, 159, 161, 165, 169–70, 172, 176, 179
New Yorker Hotel, 5, 127, 147
Nietzsche, Fredrich, v, xi, 146
Nin, Anaïs, 50
nondirective therapy, 5, 19, 24–25, 49, 63, 88, 174
Nydes, Jule, 145

Oberndorf, Clarence P., 85

Paris Psychoanalytic Society, 116
Parker, Samuel, 6, 75–80, 107, 113, 152
Peatman, John G., 70, 81
Pennsylvania Medical Society, 79
Pennsylvania Psychological Association, 79
Pfeiffer, William L., 93
Pfister, Oscar, 8
practice of medicine, 2, 36, 60, 69, 75, 78, 98, 113, 123, 125–26, 140, 147, 152, 165, 170, 172
practice of psychology, 33, 37, 38, 60, 61, 64, 65, 68, 78, 79, 83, 85, 89, 100–101, 106, 108, 111–12, 167–69, 170, 175–77
psychoanalysis, 8, 10, 33–36, 42, 47, 60, 64, 76, 79, 83, 84, 94, 115, 124, 145–46, 172, 179
Psychological Corporation, 32, 68, 86, 93, 116, 128, 146
psychology
  definition, 37, 38, 41, 60, 64, 66, 68–69, 71, 72, 79, 83, 85, 89, 98, 100–101, 108, 111–12, 129, 140–41, 162, 165–70, 174–76, 181, 212n1
  fields
    behaviorism, 25, 176, 179
    child, 20, 115
    consulting, 4, 11, 27, 32, 36, 38, 43, 48, 50, 53, 82, 168
    humanistic, x, xii, 4, 5, 7, 86, 134, 176–80, 182
    industrial, 4, 41, 62, 68, 140, 159
    marriage, 30, 124
    pastoral, 11, 48–50, 83, 127, 139
    phenomenology, 5, 23–25, 70, 76, 88
    vocational, 2, 11, 31, 62, 68, 72, 74, 111, 124, 139, 155, 162
Public Health Service, US, 44–47, 52, 81

Question of Lay Analysis, The, 8–10, 33, 77, 83, 124, 127, 145, 172

Raines, George, 102
Rank, Otto, 11, 49
Reese, Hans, 136–37
Reik, Theodore, 7–9, 33, 77, 83–85, 115, 172
Reiss, Bernard F., 94
Research Center for Human Relations, New York University, 138, 143
Riggs, Austin F., 17, 46, 47, 61
Robie, Theodore R., 130–31
Robinson, Robert L., 154
Rochester Psychology Society, 60
Rogers, Carl, 5, 6, 19, 24, 25, 49, 51, 70, 88, 119, 177–78, 181, 190n10
Roosevelt, Franklin D., 15, 25, 90
Rorschach test, 6, 42, 43, 64, 192n15
Rowntree, Leonard, 15–19, 45
Rubin-Rabson, Grace, 77

Sanders, Joseph R., 172
Sanford, Fillmore, 4, 119, 126, 128, 132, 137, 139, 141, 150–51
Sanford, Nevitt, 161, 164, 178
Savarese, Anthony P., 169
Shaffer, Laurence, 119, 127, 137, 150
Schilder, Paul F., 7, 10, 76, 77, 80, 84, 100
Schwartz, Emanuel, 110, 112
Scofield, Carleton, 104, 112, 115–18
Sears, Robert R., 92, 93
self, ix, xi, 86, 87, 109, 120, 141, 177, 182
Shakow, David, 61
Shapiro, George, 134, 138
Siegel, Max, 139, 147
Skinner, B. F., 137
Slesinger, Donald, 92
Snygg, Donald, 24, 70, 76
Southern California Society for Mental Hygiene, 136
Staff, Clement, 112, 116
Stanton, Frank, 92
Steiner, Lee R., 30, 31, 40, 58
Stevenson, George S., 79
Stralem, Joan, 133
symposiums, psychological
  on certification and licensing (1941), 39
  on certification and licensing (1949), 80
  on lay analysis (1927), 9–11, 33, 85
  on legislation (1953), 139, 141
  on existentialism (1959), 177

Teicher, Arthur, 78, 117
Thompson, Albert S., 11–12, 170, 172
Thompson, Clara, 109
Tillich, Paul, 16, 20, 24, 50, 51, 87, 182–83, 189n2
Tratelja Farms Sanitarium, 47, 134

Ullman, Sol, 35, 36
Union Theological Seminary, 16–18, 49, 50
Upper New York State Psychological Association, 94
Upstate Psychological Association, 60

Van Wiggeren, Walter, 169
Vassar College, 102, 103, 161
Veterans Administration, US, 45–48, 51, 53, 61–63, 81, 103–04, 190n10
Vienna Psychoanalytic Society, 8
von Jauregg, Wagner, 8
Von Storch, Theodore J. C., 105–07

Walsh, Lawrence E., 92
War Shipping Administration, US, 18, 46, 47

Washington Psychological Association, 84
Waters, Alonzo L., 126
Wechsler-Bellevue, 42
Weiss, Theodore S., 63
Wendt, George R., 70–74, 81, 83–86, 88
Where Do People Take Their Troubles?, 31, 58
William Alanston White Institute, 10, 82, 84, 109, 115, 161
Wolff, Payson, 155
World War II, 2, 10, 11, 15, 17, 18, 20, 25, 40, 43, 44, 49, 51, 58, 70, 78, 101, 137, 139, 159
Wortis, S. Bernard, 64, 65, 68, 73, 105, 107, 197n15
Wulfleck, Wallace H., 70, 118

Young Men's Christian Association, 49, 50

Zucker, Herbert J., 92, 111, 112, 114, 118, 143–45, 148, 156–58, 166

Printed in the United States
by Baker & Taylor Publisher Services